Music Theory
VOLUME II

Earl Henry

Department of Music
Webster University

PRENTICE-HALL, INC., Englewood Cliffs, New Jersey 07632

Library of Congress Cataloging in Publication Data

HENRY, EARL.
    Music theory.

    Includes index.
    1. Music—Theory.   I. Title.
    MT6.H525M9   1984   781   83-21140
    ISBN   0-13-607870-2 (v. 1)
    ISBN   0-13-607961-X (v. 2)

Editorial/production supervision and
    interior design: Fred Bernardi
Cover design: Jeannette Jacobs
Manufacturing buyer: Ray Keating
Page layouts: Diane Koromhas

Printed in the United States of America

10   9   8   7   6   5   4   3   2   1

ISBN   0-13-607961-X   01

PRENTICE-HALL INTERNATIONAL, INC., *London*
PRENTICE-HALL OF AUSTRALIA PTY. LIMITED, *Sydney*
EDITORA PRENTICE-HALL DO BRASIL, LTDA., *Rio de Janeiro*
PRENTICE-HALL CANADA INC., *Toronto*
PRENTICE-HALL OF INDIA PRIVATE LIMITED, *New Delhi*
PRENTICE-HALL OF JAPAN, INC., *Tokyo*
PRENTICE-HALL OF SOUTHEAST ASIA PTE. LTD., *Singapore*
WHITEHALL BOOKS LIMITED, *Wellington, New Zealand*

For my mother and father

Contents

Chapter 8 The Sonata Principle 179

Key Relationships. Thematic Relationships. THE "CLASSICAL" SONATA.
The Binary Structure. The Themes and Their Roles. Formal Analysis.
The Exposition. *W.A. Mozart*, Sonata in D Major, K. 576: *Exposition.*
The Development. *Mozart*, K. 576: *Development.* The Recapitulation.
Mozart, K. 576: *Recapitulation.* Later Developments.

Chapter 9 The Rondo Principle 205

The Classical Rondo. *The Rondo Theme. The Transition. The First Episode.*
The Return of the Rondo Theme. The Second Episode. The Third Episode.
Final Statement and Coda. The Sonata-Rondo. Summary.

Chapter 10 The Dissolution of the Common Practice Style 233

Melody: A Renaissance. *Nonharmonic Tones. Multiple Tonal Axes.*
Extended Tertian Harmony: Ninth Chords. *Construction and Resolution.*
Use of Ninth Chords. Altered Chords of Dominant Function.
The Altered Dominant. "First Class" Augmented Sixth Chords. *Third Relation.*
Nonfunctional Harmony. *The Augmented Triad. Diminished Seventh Chords.*
Parenthetical Harmony. Nonharmonic Tones. Chordal Mutation. Summary.

PART III THE TWENTIETH CENTURY

Chapter 11 Impressionism 261

IMPRESSIONISM IN MUSIC. MELODY. *The Whole Tone Scale.*
The Pentatonic Scale. The Church Modes. Synthetic Scales.
HARMONY: NEW CONCEPTS. Planing. *Chord-Type Planing.*
Diatonic Planing. Mixed Planing. Pandiatonicism.
Other New Harmonic Resources. *Whole Tone Harmony. Quartal Harmony.*
Traditional Harmonic Materials. *Seventh and Ninth Chords.*
Third and Tritone Relations. Added Tone Harmony.
FORM, RHYTHM, AND ORCHESTRATION. *Phrase Structure.* Rhythm.
Orchestration. The Analysis of Contemporary Music: Chord Chemistry.
Summary. Suggestions for Additional Projects. Suggested Listening.

Chapter 12 New Concepts and Materials 299

NEW CONCEPTS IN MELODY. *Melodic Style. The Melodic Cell.*
NEW CONCEPTS IN HARMONY. Dissonance. Tonality. *The Ostinato.*
Modulation. Bimodality. Polychords. Polytonality. *Simultaneity.*
NONTERTIAN HARMONY. Quartal Harmony.
Secundal Harmony. *Clusters. Secundal Harmony.*
The Analysis of Contemporary Music: Harmonic Fluctuation.
Determination of Chord Root. Harmonic Fluctuation.
NEW CONCEPTS IN RHYTHM. NEW CONCEPTS IN FORM.
Neoclassicism. Arch Form. INNOVATIONS IN TIMBRE. Sprechstimme.
Klangfarbenmelodie. Summary. Suggested Composition Projects.
Suggested Listening.

Preface

This text has been written to provide a historical–analytical approach to the study of theory and harmony, and accomplish this in an informal and practical style. The philosophy underlying all facets of the book is simply stated: although theory in the abstract is important, it is the practical application of theoretical principles that is the day-to-day business of most professional musicians. The word *professional* is important, because it implies much more than a superficial understanding of rules and formulas. Whatever one's area of specialization, a *comprehensive* knowledge of the field and how it has evolved from one era to the next is crucial in understanding both the materials and the role of music in today's society.

Analysis and Composition

ANALYSIS is the first step in understanding the use of tonal materials and style differences. Throughout the text, the four basic parameters of music (melody, harmony, rhythm, and form) are emphasized; analysis in one or more parameters affords students an opportunity to develop their perception about the abstract materials they study and the way composers have used these same materials to produce quite different results.

Another area of emphasis in this text is STYLISTIC COMPOSITION. An important (perhaps *the* most important) measure of one's understanding of theoretical materials is the ability to use those materials in recreating a given style. Accordingly, composition projects of various types are presented throughout the two volumes of the text. Although certain restrictions must always be imposed, stylistic composition offers students a chance to explore their creative potential as they reinforce basic theoretical concepts.

Common Practice Music

Although some disdain the term *common practice*, there can be little doubt that between about 1600 and 1900 (spanning the Baroque, Classical, and Romantic Eras), composers approached tonal composition in pretty much the same way. Despite significant style differences between nationalities, generations, and individual composers, the *concepts* of tonality and functional harmony remained essentially unchanged. In this respect, many elements of composition were indeed "common."

Lamentable as many think it, most music heard on concert and recital programs today is from the Common Practice Period. Whatever style of music one might prefer, for the professional musician a thorough knowledge of common practice music is crucial. Even popular and commercial music, modern in the sense that it happens "today," is deeply rooted in the melodic, rhythmic, and harmonic practices of the eighteenth century. Aside from the chapters that deal with twentieth-century trends (chapters 11 to 15 of volume II), common practice music is the focus of this text; unless otherwise specified, all examples and explanations must be taken within this context.

With only a few exceptions, the musical examples used to illustrate the materials and procedures discussed in this book are drawn from the literature. They have been chosen with care, and although one may be obscured occasionally by rhythmic or melodic complexities, the use of actual *music* seems infinitely preferable to newly-composed "textbook" examples that reflect the theoretical, but none of the creative processes inherent in music.

To the Student

The theory of music is not a subject especially suited to independent study. Classroom experiences are essential not only for drill and amplification, but also for the opportunity to share with one's colleagues and instructors the joys and frustrations of studying music and being a musician.

This text has been designed to serve the college music major in three ways. First, it is a *preparation* for the intense study of theoretical materials by placing them historically, by presenting the essential concepts in straightforward language, and by providing appropriate examples. The text has been developed to provide background that will *precede* a classroom discussion; in no way does the book pretend to include any but the most "typical" materials used in the most "typical" fashion. The fascinating study of the way composers adapted these materials to their unique creative instincts is a subject better suited to the classroom.

Second, *Music Theory* is intended to serve as a *reference* for the materials of music from the late sixteenth century to the present day—their origin, structure, and transformation. The book should be used outside the classroom for review, for an appropriate approach to the various phases of analysis and composition, and for independent study. The process of analysis is covered in detail—often with step-by-step procedures, sample analyses, and suggestions for examining the various parameters of music. The fundamentals of music are discussed thoroughly with step-by-step procedures designed to minimize errors and reinforce basic concepts. Appendices covering topics such as calligraphy and instrumentation are available for reference at any time.

Finally, the book is intended to act as a *supplement* to classroom instruction by providing under one cover not only text and examples, but drill exercises, suggested composition projects (often with score paper provided), excerpts, and complete movements for analysis. Self-tests are included with the chapters on fundamentals (chapters 1 to 5 of volume I), as are Projects for Individual Research for the more experienced student. Many subjects are included that are often treated in separate courses. The chapters on twentieth-century trends, those on large forms, and the appendices on acoustics, temperament and tuning, and instrumentation provide reference material as well as areas for independent study.

Acknowledgments

I am indebted to several of my colleagues at Webster University for their help during the writing of this text. Professor Robert Chamberlin helped me class-test the manuscript, provided insight and encouragement, and guided me through the chapter on music after 1945. Professor Steven Schenkel wrote the appendix on the materials of jazz that appears in the second volume. I thank Professor Kendall Stallings not only for his valuable advice on virtually every phase of the project, but also for his help with the chapters on atonality and serial technique as well as the appendices on acoustics and temperament and tuning.

Among others I wish to thank is Dr. Michael Hunt who permitted me to use some of the exercises from his *Figured Bass Primer*. Dr. Scott Huston, Professor of Theory and Composition at the University of Cincinnati's College-Conservatory of Music studied the manuscript, corrected a number of my analyses, and was able to point out many important details that I had overlooked. I thank also Dr. Roger Hannay, Composer-in-Residence at the University of North Carolina at Chapel Hill who read the book in its early stages and provided encouragement and helpful suggestions.

Although every effort has been made to make the book accurate, I thank in advance those students and instructors who will use the text, find a misprint here, a misstatement there and call it to my attention or that of Prentice-Hall. In this way we can improve subsequent printings and editions.

Finally, and perhaps most important, I thank my students who suffered through numerous early versions of the two volumes and who generally accepted misleading statements, typographical errors, and unsolvable exercise problems with resignation if not humor. Without the inspiration of my students, I would have never begun this text; without their help, I would never have completed it.

Earl Henry

Chapter 1
The Fugue

Introduction to Chapters 1 to 5: The Eighteenth-Century Style
The predominant texture of eighteenth-century music is COUNTERPOINT—
polyphony based on the combination of two or more equal voices. Imitative
counterpoint reached its full potential in the eighteenth-century FUGUE. Also
during this time, the ancient principle of VARIATION was refined and
adapted to Baroque tastes. Like the fugue, however, the variation principle
has remained important in music right up to the present day.

Chapters 2, 3, and 4 deal with the contrapuntal vocal style—the essence
of common practice music. No other form has been employed so universally
in the study of this style as the CHORALE—a composition which sounds
homophonic, but is actually comprised of four independent voices. Through
the four-part vocal format, concepts of melody and harmony, balance and
control, phrase construction, chord connection, and voice leading are
learned and reinforced.

Students should view the study of chorale harmony not as an imitation
of some past and forgotten style, but as an immersion in traditional practices
which embody not only the theoretical basis of jazz and commercial music,
but the underlying structure of almost all music performed in concerts and
recitals today.

Since the time of Bach, the fugue has had a special attraction for composers
both as a discipline and as an art form. The fugue is based on IMITATIVE
COUNTERPOINT—the combination of several equal voices through successive statements of a single motive. As a technique of composition, imitative
counterpoint developed during the sixteenth century—principally through the
works of Josquin des Prez (1450–1521). Josquin's masses and motets are sectional works in which a melodic fragment called a SUBJECT is stated, then
imitated successively. After stating the subject, each voice continues in free
counterpoint; when the subject has been imitated in several voices, a cadence
brings the section to a close. A typical Josquin work features several sections
(or "Points") of imitation—each based on a different subject. In Example 1–1
below, notice that the third statement of the subject is transposed to the
dominant.

EXAMPLE 1–1

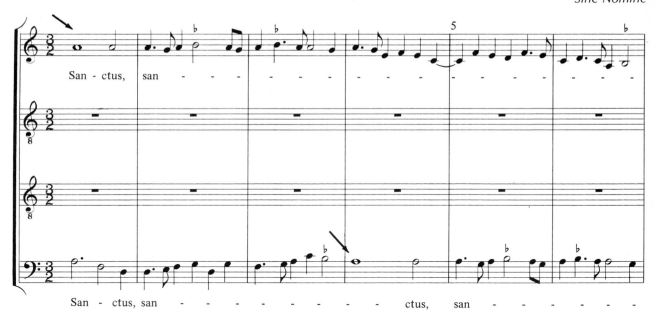

While Palestrina and his contemporaries refined the principles of imitative counterpoint in their own sacred vocal polyphony, the adaptation of the technique to an instrumental medium offered new possibilities. The *canzona* and *ricercar*, early Baroque keyboard forms, both involve the imitation of a subject at various tonal levels. In the *Canzon* below (Example 1–2), the second and fourth entries are different from the first and third; they are slightly altered in rhythm, they begin with the dominant rather than the tonic pitch, and they have as their initial interval a perfect fourth rather than a perfect fifth. As will be discussed presently, such alteration in some statements of the subject is typical of imitative writing.

EXAMPLE 1–2   Claudio Merulo, *Canzon*

The final step in the evolution of the fugue occurred as the sectional nature of the canzona and ricercar was gradually replaced by the use of the *same* subject throughout the work. The monothematic ricercar is the most direct predecessor of the fugue.

The fugue is not a form, but a *procedure* of composition. While a "student's fugue" may conform to a "classical" model, in the hands of a skilled composer, each fugue is itself a unique form.

A FUGUE is a work for two or more independent voices based on the systematic imitation of a subject at various tonal levels. Sections of imitative counterpoint alternate with sections of free counterpoint called *episodes*.

THE SUBJECT AND ANSWER

A fugue begins with a statement of the subject successively in each voice. Typically, these statements occur in pairs. The subject appears in one voice and is followed by an ANSWER—a transposition of the subject to the dominant.

The Subject

In character and length, fugue subjects vary considerably. Some, associated with the ricercar, are slow moving and lack rhythmic identity; others, more like the canzona, are freer and more lively. Both types of subject are clearly defined in terms of tonal scheme; more than anything else, harmonic implications determine whether the answer to the subject is *real* or *tonal*.[1]

The Real Answer

In the "classical" fugue, the answer is a transposition of the subject to the dominant. When the answer is an exact intervallic transposition, it is known as a REAL ANSWER. The subject of Bach's *Fugue in G♯ Minor (WTC II)* is given a real answer (Example 1–3).

EXAMPLE 1–3   J.S. Bach, *Fugue in G♯ Minor (WTC II)*

The Tonal Answer

When a modulation to the dominant occurs near the beginning of the subject (or even a strong implication of the dominant), the answer is adjusted intervallically so that instead of modulating to (or implying) the dominant of the dominant, the tonic key is strengthened.

The *G Minor Fugue* from Volume I of Bach's *Well-Tempered Clavier* illustrates the tonal answer. The subject opens with the dominant pitch and moves quickly to the tonic. The answer begins not with the pitch A (which would imply the dominant of the dominant), but with G—the tonic pitch. The first interval in the subject, therefore, is a third instead of a second (Example 1–4).

---

[1]The discussion of subject and answer here concerns only the *first* entries which are typically in tonic–dominant key relationships. Subsequent entries are often less clearly defined in subject–answer roles; the term *subject entry* can be used in such instances.

EXAMPLE 1–4   J.S. Bach, *Fugue in G Minor (WTC I)*

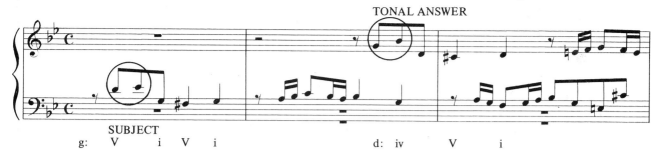

In the example above, the tonic–dominant tonal scheme is typical of subject and answer. To strengthen the tonic, however, Bach answers the original progression in G minor:

(g:) V i V i

with a different progression in the dominant:

(d:) iv̲ V i

The adjustment is nearly imperceptible, but permits an emphasis on G minor within the dominant key.

Another tonal answer is shown in Example 1–5. As is customary, Bach answers the perfect fifth of the subject (D♯–A♯) with a perfect fourth (A♯–D♯).

EXAMPLE 1–5   J.S. Bach, *Fugue in D♯ Minor (WTC I)*

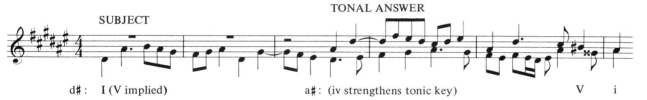

Although melodic and harmonic factors primarily control the use of a real or tonal answer, composers sometimes alter a subject or answer simply to permit smoother modulation (often called real *adjusted* and tonal *adjusted* answers respectively).

Because each subject is different in terms of melodic and harmonic construction, and because composers have rarely limited themselves to any model of form or procedure, clear guidelines for the composition of appropriate answers are difficult to formulate. The purpose of the present unit, however, is analysis—not composition. To this end, a number of subjects and answers from Bach's *Well-Tempered Clavier* (Volume I) are given in Example 1–6. Study the subjects and answers and be prepared to comment on their character, principal motives and implied harmonic scheme. Note as well the characteristics of each subject which led to the use of either a real or a tonal answer.

EXAMPLE 1–6   Subjects and Answers from Bach's
                                                                     Well-Tempered Clavier, Volume I

Fugue in C Major

Fugue in C minor

Fugue in C♯ Major

Fugue in C♯ Minor

The Countersubject

In some fugues, a recurring counterpoint is heard along with each subject or answer entry. Known as a COUNTERSUBJECT, this material is generally more figural in character and somewhat more freely treated than the subject.

The *Fugue in F Major* from Volume I of Bach's *Well-Tempered Clavier* is for three voices; it begins in the alto and is answered tonally in the soprano. The counterpoint which occurs with the answer is a countersubject (Example 1–7).

EXAMPLE 1–7   J.S. Bach, *Fugue in F Major (WTC I)*

Each time the subject or answer is heard, the countersubject is present also. Notice that in measures 18–20, the countersubject is divided between alto and tenor voices.

THE STATEMENT SECTION

The opening section of a fugue, in which each voice enters with the subject or its answer is known as the STATEMENT SECTION.[2] The Statement establishes both the fugue subject and the tonic key. These first entries generally have clear tonic-dominant key relationships and can be discussed in terms of

---

[2]Many authorities refer to the initial section of a fugue as the *Exposition;* the term is equally valid, but in this text, "Exposition" is used solely with sonata-form (Chapter 8).

subject and answer. In a four-voice fugue, for example, the following schemes are common:

SUBJECT	ANSWER	SUBJECT	ANSWER
Tonic	Dominant	Tonic	Dominant

SUBJECT	ANSWER	SUBJECT	ANSWER
Tonic	Dominant	Dominant	Tonic

Depending on the overall proportions of the fugue, the first entries may be separated by several beats (or even several measures) of free counterpoint. The number of voices and the order of their entries vary; typical arrangements for four, three, and five voice fugues are shown in Example 1–8.

EXAMPLE 1–8   Typical Subject Entry Patterns

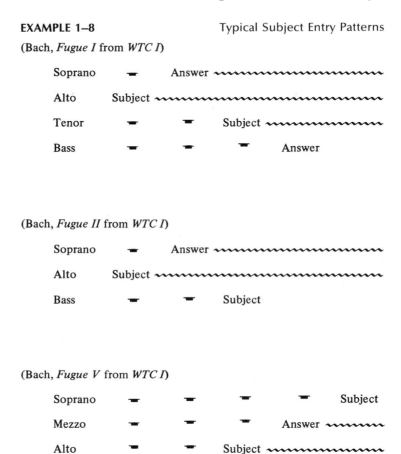

(Bach, *Fugue I* from *WTC I*)

(Bach, *Fugue II* from *WTC I*)

(Bach, *Fugue V* from *WTC I*)

Although the first is the more formal, some fugues have two statement sections. A second series of subject–answer entries immediately following the first comprises a DOUBLE STATEMENT. More often, however, subsequent subject entries are developmental and are included in the middle section.

Study the statement section of the four voice fugue from Handel's *Second Clavier Suite* (Example 1–9). The two measure subject is given a tonal answer. After a measure and a half of free counterpoint, the second pair of entries occurs. The statement section ends in measure 11 with a modulation to the dominant.

EXAMPLE 1–9

THE MIDDLE SECTION ("WORKING OUT")

The middle section of a fugue alternates between episodes and subject entries. These sections may or may not be connected by brief transitions.[3] An EPISODE is a passage of free counterpoint in which the subject does not appear; it is usually based on material derived from the subject or countersubject, however, and may include the use of one or more of the traditional *Contrapuntal Devices.*

---

[3]Transitions are distinguished from episodes by the former's relatively lesser length. Some prefer the term "Episode" to designate any passage of free counterpoint which does not include a subject entry. In this text, however, *transition* refers to material with a clear connecting role; *episode*, on the other hand, designates material of substantial formal importance.

Contrapuntal Devices

Originating in the *cantus firmus* masses of the fifteenth century, a number of standard techniques of motivic variation—CONTRAPUNTAL DEVICES—found their way into the common practice vocabulary.

Inversion (Contrary Motion).   When interval direction is reversed, the result is new material with clear ties to the original subject. As shown in Example 1–10, a subject may appear in a MIRROR INVERSION using either the original or transposed pitches.

EXAMPLE 1–10   Inversion (Contrary Motion)

Retrograde.   A Renaissance canonic technique *not* often found in common practice fugues but which reappears in imitative counterpoint of the twentieth century is the reverse or retrograde form. A RETROGRADE FORM is the statement of the subject backwards. A RETROGRADE INVERSION (also rare in common practice fugues) is a reverse statement of an inverted subject (Example 1–11).

EXAMPLE 1–11   Retrograde and Retrograde Inversion

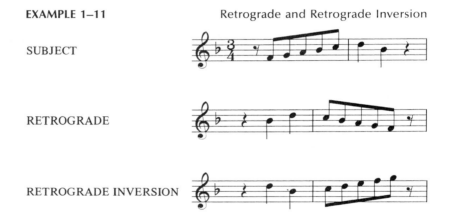

Augmentation and Diminution.   Any form of a subject may be stated with increased rhythmic values. This device is known as AUGMENTATION. A decrease in rhythmic values is termed DIMINUTION. Both techniques provide new material from the subject or one of its forms (Example 1–12).

EXAMPLE 1–12   Augmentation and Diminution

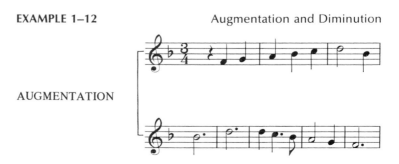

DIMINUTION

Stretto

Most fugues include a passage in which several voices state the subject in over-lapping entries. This section, known as STRETTO, represents a high degree of tension and usually occurs toward the end of the fugue. The distance between subject entries varies, but in the stretto, they occur more rapidly than in the statement section.

In the statement section of Bach's *Bb Minor Fugue* from the *Well-Tempered Clavier* (Volume I), the subject and answer are separated by two measures. In the stretto, however, the entries are much more closely spaced (Example 1–13 A and B).

EXAMPLE 1–13   J.S. Bach, *Fugue in Bb Minor (WTC I)*

The stretto is an important technique because it creates tension to be relaxed in the final cadence. In some fugues the use of stretto is minimal; in others, there are two or more stretto sections.

THE RESTATEMENT

The final section of a fugue, called the RESTATEMENT, begins with (or at least includes) an entry of the subject in the tonic key. This restatement may be in the form of a stretto (as in Example 1–13) or it may come after a stretto with the subject–answer entries more clearly defined. The final statement(s) often occur over a pedal and lead to a strong cadence in the tonic key.

In short, the fugue is a procedure, not a form. Entries of the subject alternate with episodes of free counterpoint. Near the end of the work, there is usually a stretto to create a sense of expectation. The work concludes with an entry in the tonic key. The formation of more specific notions about fugal structure is invariably contradicted by the literature.

ANALYSIS: J.S. BACH, *FUGUE IN G MINOR (WTC I)*

The *G Minor Fugue* is for four voices. The subject begins with the fifth scale degree and is, therefore, answered tonally. A countersubject (based on a rhythmic motive from the subject) occurs in measure 3. After a transition of one measure, the third and fourth voices enter in the traditional tonic–dominant key relationship. The seven measure statement section introduces the subject, the countersubject, the key, and each of the four voices (Example 1–14).

EXAMPLE 1–14   J.S. Bach, *Fugue in G Minor (WTC I)*

The middle section of the fugue begins in measure 8 with an episode which leads to a cadence in the relative major. The melodic material, freely treated, is from the second half of the subject (Example 1–15).

EXAMPLE 1–15

MIDDLE SECTION

The middle section continues with subject–answer pairs in B♭ major (tonic–dominant, then dominant–tonic). Additional subject entries occur in C minor (measures 20–22) and G minor (measure 23) (Example 1–16).

EXAMPLE 1–16

A second episode begins in measure 24 and is based on the same material as the first (Example 1–17).

EXAMPLE 1–17

EPISODE II

The restatement section begins with a stretto in measure 28. Three subject entries are spaced two beats apart. Following a one measure transition, a final pair of entries concludes the fugue (Example 1–18).

EXAMPLE 1–18

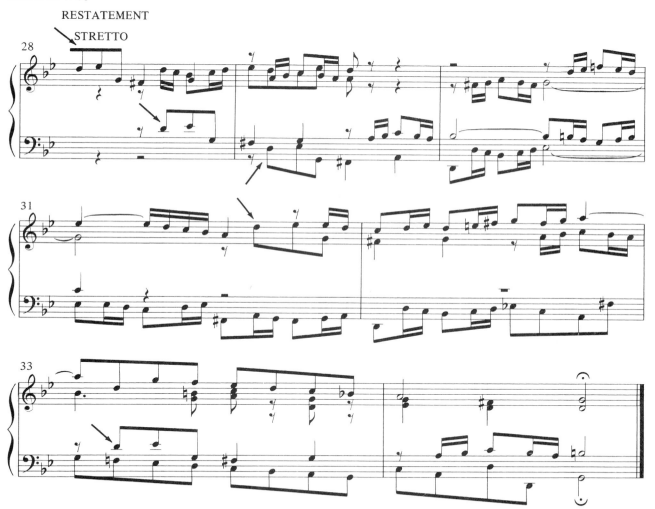

An additional point about the *G Minor Fugue* is that it is SUBJECT-STRUCTURED—the subject appears many times throughout the work and is prominent in all three sections. An EPISODE-STRUCTURED fugue is one in which free counterpoint dominates; episodes tend to be longer and the subject entries relatively less important.

The formal structure of Bach's *G Minor Fugue* includes the three basic fugal elements: statement, "working out" (middle section), and restatement. All three sections of the fugue are joined by brief transitions of free counterpoint.

SUMMARY

While the fugues of Bach are generally thought to represent the full fruition of the art, few composers have not written either formal fugues or fugal sections (called *fugatos*) in works such as symphonies or sonatas. The combination of genius and craftsmanship required to produce a work such as Beethoven's *Grosse Fugue* (Op. 133) or Stravinsky's *Symphony of Psalms* (second movement), however, is a rare phenomenon. Nevertheless, the fugue represents one of the most important and consistently practiced procedures of composition since the eighteenth century.

J.K.F. Fischer, *Fugue in E Major* from
Ariadne Musica (1702)

J.S. Bach, *Fugue in E Major (WTC II)*

J.S. Bach, *Fugue in C Major (WTC I)*

Chapter 2
Introduction to Counterpoint

The word "counterpoint" (abbreviated Cpt.) originates from the Latin phrase *punctus contra punctus,* usually translated "note against note." Perhaps a more descriptive translation would be "melody against melody," for COUNTERPOINT is the combination of two or more independent melodic lines with conscious regard for the resulting harmony. In the present chapter, the study of counterpoint is limited largely to eighteenth-century vocal polyphony and is intended to serve as a prelude to the process of harmonizing a melody. In the four-part chorale, the contrapuntal movement between soprano and bass embodies the principles of melodic combination without involving the complexities of imitative writing. In its traditional forms (invention, fugue, chorale prelude, and so on), imitative counterpoint is a complex subject usually reserved for a separate course in counterpoint.

THE DEVELOPMENT OF COUNTERPOINT

Before the ninth century, Western music was monophonic. Scholars disagree as to how and even why polyphony began, but the significance of its emergence is universally recognized. Found in a ninth-century manuscript, the *Musica Enchiriadis,* the earliest known polyphony consists mostly of parallel perfect fourths and fifths (Example 2–1).

EXAMPLE 2–1   Free Organum (ninth century)

The music of the *Musica Enchiriadis* is discussed in a companion volume, the *Scholia Enchiriadis.* Although the goal of counterpoint has always been the creation of a work of art through a blending of independent melodies into a unified and aesthetically pleasing whole, the *Scholia Enchiriadis* is the first known in a long series of counterpoint texts to approach the subject through rules. In the *Scholia,* an unknown theorist discusses various types of organum, defines terms, and comments on problems associated with the tritone.

Later Medieval theorists wrote about contrapuntal motion, cadence formulas, and the mathematical relationships governing consonance and dissonance. In the thirteenth century, Franco of Cologne stipulated that perfect consonances were to be employed on accented beats. This rule, which eventually became known as the "Franconian Law," coincided with the development of meter; for the first time, consonance and dissonance were assigned to strong and weak metric positions respectively.

As counterpoint developed to incorporate three and four voices as well as new harmonic and melodic materials, theorists were even more explicit in describing the possibilities for combining melodies. Johannes Tinctoris (1436–1511) and Gioseffe Zarlino (1517–1590) wrote influential counterpoint texts in their respective centuries.

SPECIES COUNTERPOINT

Today, the study of counterpoint is divided into two distinct categories. MODAL COUNTERPOINT is based on the sixteenth-century *a cappella* style of Palestrina; TONAL COUNTERPOINT involves the study and recreation of the eighteenth-century style of J.S. Bach.

Modal counterpoint is commonly approached through SPECIES—progressive exercises in five distinct patterns. The use of species counterpoint as a pedagogical tool was popularized by the phenomenal success of Johannes Fux's early eighteenth-century treatise *Gradus ad Parnassum*. Based not on the style of his own era but on that of Palestrina, Fux's book remained for over one hundred years the most influential counterpoint text. Thus while composers like Mozart, Beethoven, and Brahms wrote in the styles of their respective eras, they had learned counterpoint in the same style and in much the same way.

The five species adopted by Fux have been perpetuated virtually unchanged in many modern counterpoint texts. To a given melody—the CANTUS FIRMUS—the student is asked to supply a counterpoint either above or below. Before beginning the study of canon or fugue, the student first progresses through the five species in two, three, and finally in four voices. Examples of the various species (taken from Fux's text) are shown below (Example 2–2). Remember that the cantus firmus (C.F.) is the given melody; the counterpoint (Cpt.) is the melody provided by the student.

EXAMPLE 2–2 Species Counterpoint

FIRST SPECIES One note in the counterpoint for each note in the cantus firmus.
Dissonance is not allowed.

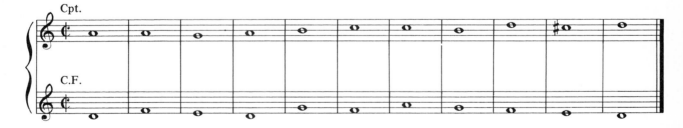

SECOND SPECIES Two notes in the counterpoint for each note in the cantus firmus.
Dissonance allowed on weak beats if prepared and resolved.

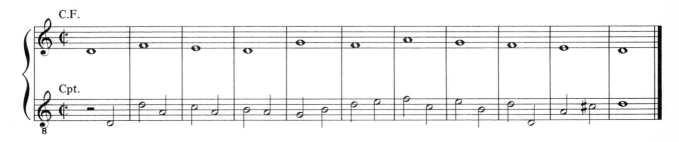

THIRD SPECIES Four notes in the counterpoint for each note in the cantus firmus.
Dissonance allowed on weak beats if prepared and resolved.

FOURTH SPECIES Two notes in the counterpoint for each note in the cantus firmus.
Syncopation and suspension figures are a feature of the style.

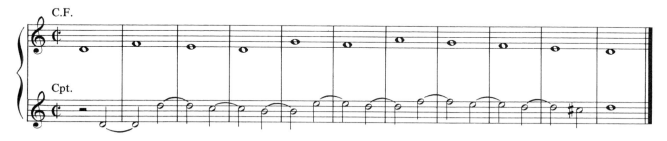

FIFTH SPECIES Free counterpoint with the given cantus firmus.

Two-Voice Tonal Counterpoint

The composition of a contrapuntally sound bass is one of the first steps in the harmonization of a melody. The success of the counterpoint depends primarily on three factors to be discussed in detail: *Voice Leading, Dissonance* and *Harmonic Structure.* Instead of proposing specific rules in the manner of a counterpoint text, this introduction will center on six CONTRAPUNTAL PRINCIPLES applicable to both vocal and instrumental writing.

VOICE LEADING

The movement of the individual contrapuntal lines is termed VOICE LEADING. In a stylistically faithful two-voice counterpoint, voice leading centers on two qualities: *Independence* and *Balance*.

INDEPENDENCE

Independence of voices is the essence of good contrapuntal writing. The finished product must never resemble a melody and accompaniment, but two *equal* melodic lines. To a large extent, voice independence is determined by the type of contrapuntal motion employed—parallel, similar, oblique, or contrary.

CONTRAPUNTAL PRINCIPLE 1	Contrary motion should predominate.

In a two-voice composition, four different types of contrapuntal motion are possible. Each permits a different degree of voice independence.

Parallel Motion

Contrapuntal motion is PARALLEL when both voices move by the same interval type and in the same direction.

Parallel motion contributes *least effectively* to melodic independence; if continued, one voice is heard as a harmonization of the other. In addition, *parallel motion by perfect intervals is forbidden* in two-voice tonal counterpoint.

Similar Motion

When voices move in the same direction but by different interval types, the contrapuntal motion is SIMILAR. Similar motion creates more part independence than parallel motion.

Oblique Motion

Contrapuntal motion is termed OBLIQUE if one voice remains stationary (or is rearticulated) while the other voice moves up or down. In general, oblique motion permits more part independence than either similar or parallel motion.

Contrary Motion

As early as the eleventh century, theorists advocated CONTRARY MOTION (movement of voices in opposite directions) in composing organum. Contrary motion permits maximum voice independence, and while other types of contrapuntal motion are employed for variety, voices should generally move in opposite directions.

<table>
<tr><td>CONTRAPUNTAL
PRINCIPLE 2</td><td>The range of each voice should be kept distinct.</td></tr>
</table>

In two-voice counterpoint, voices are kept distinct by employing contrary motion and by avoiding *voice crossing* and *voice overlap*.

Voice Crossing

Early polyphonic music was limited in range and often involved VOICE CROSSING—the movement of the upper voice to a position below the lower or *vice versa*. In the Common Practice Era, however, voice crossing was largely avoided (Example 2–3).

EXAMPLE 2–3   Voice Crossing[1]

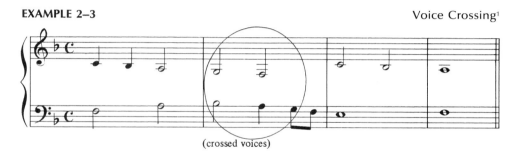

(crossed voices)

Voice Overlap

When two voices move in similar motion, one may temporarily intrude into the range of the other. In the fourth measure of Example 2–4, the soprano pitch (A_3) is *lower* than the previous bass pitch (Bb_3); the voices do not cross, but their ranges (and thus their individuality) are momentarily obscured. This situation is termed VOICE OVERLAP and should be avoided.

EXAMPLE 2–4   Voice Overlap

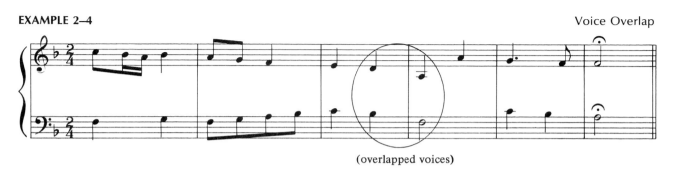

(overlapped voices)

[1]For present purposes, the counterpoint will be written as a bass below the given melody. The possibility of composing counterpoint above a given cantus firmus, however, should not be ignored; students are encouraged to try this approach as well.

BALANCE

A second important aspect of voice leading concerns the achievement of a balance between voices in terms of melodic, rhythmic, and implied harmonic elements.

CONTRAPUNTAL PRINCIPLE 3	The counterpoint must be complementary to the cantus firmus, but it must exhibit sound melodic and formal construction on its own.

Melodic Motion

While counterpoint conceived for vocal performance should move primarily by step, a balance between conjunct and disjunct motion is desirable. Constant stepwise motion results in a loss of momentum; well placed leaps (especially if countered by stepwise motion in the opposite direction) provide direction and balance. In addition, the counterpoint should possess an effective contour which complements that of the melody. The counterpoint in Example 2–5 is rather poor; it lacks contour and features too much stepwise motion.

EXAMPLE 2–5   Poor Melodic Motion

Awkward Melodic Intervals

The natural tendency of the leading tone to ascend to the tonic should be followed if possible. Likewise, the melodic augmented second should be avoided. Finally, unless the harmonic implications are clear, any leap involving an altered tone should be avoided. In Example 2–6, the D♯ in the first bass is heard as part of a dominant triad in E minor and thus is quite acceptable. In the second example, however, the harmony is ambiguous and the pitches G–D♯–B will be difficult to sing.

EXAMPLE 2–6   Awkward Melodic Intervals

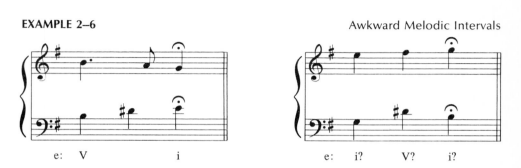

DISSONANCE

When Zarlino wrote in *Le Istituzioni armoniche* (1558) that "dissonance affords elegance," he was quick to add:

> . . . the composer . . . is not to understand by this that he is to use them [dissonances] in his counterpoint or compositions as they come to hand, without any rule or any order, for this would lead to confusion . . . .[2]

The treatment of dissonance is one of the most important factors in separating the style of one era from that of another. To ignore eighteenth-century attitudes toward dissonance, therefore, is to miss a crucial stylistic element.

CONTRAPUNTAL PRINCIPLE 4	Dissonance must be prepared and resolved in eighteenth-century style.

Consonance and Dissonance

In eighteenth-century tonal counterpoint, the following intervals are recognized as consonant:

Perfect Unisons
Perfect Octaves
Perfect Fifths
Major and Minor Thirds
Major and Minor Sixths

All other intervals are dissonant; they may be used only as nonharmonic tones in one of the patterns discussed previously. These nonharmonic tone categories are reviewed in Example 2–7.

EXAMPLE 2–7   Nonharmonic Tones

Prepared and Resolved by Step	*Prepared by Leap, Resolved by Step*
PASSING TONE	APPOGGIATURA
NEIGHBORING TONE	
	Prepared and/or Resolved through Oblique Motion
Prepared by Step, Resolved by Leap	ANTICIPATION
ESCAPE TONE	SUSPENSION
	PEDAL TONE

Dissonance in Two-Voice Counterpoint

Nonharmonic tones may be added to a counterpoint to improve the melody, embellish a pitch, or simply to provide variety. The basic first species counterpoint Bach composed as a bass to the chorale melody *Verleih' uns Frieden gnädiglich* (Example 2–8) shows a strong harmonic foundation; the addition of

[2]Oliver Strunk, *Source Readings in Music History* (New York, W.W. Norton and Company, Inc., 1950), p. 232.

nonharmonic tones, however, creates a smoother and more independent counterpoint (Example 2–9).

EXAMPLE 2–8   Reduction of Bass

EXAMPLE 2–9   Complete Bass

Nonharmonic tones cannot be added arbitrarily; while the addition of passing tones or other dissonances may improve the melodic line, new harmonic and/or melodic problems may be created at the same time.

IMPLIED HARMONIC STRUCTURE

A well-planned harmonic scheme is essential in counterpoint. In two voice writing, the harmony is implied rather than fully stated, and while the harmonic implications of a perfect fifth are clear, thirds and sixths (the predominant consonances) are subject to at least two different interpretations.

C: I   V   ii?   IV?   I?   iii?

Although linear movement in the counterpoint may clarify the harmony, the importance of quickly and consistently establishing a tonality through strong, well-defined progressions cannot be minimized.

CONTRAPUNTAL PRINCIPLE 5	The harmonic rhythm and tonality of the given melody must be established by the counterpoint.

One advantage of beginning the study of counterpoint with chorale melodies is that the harmonic rhythm, cadence structure, and implied tonal orientation are usually quite clear. Because some phrases can be harmonized in more than one key, however, several observations should precede the composition of a bass voice to a chorale melody. The following observations may be made about the melody *Herzliebster Jesu, was hast du* (Example 2–10).

EXAMPLE 2–10   *Herzliebster Jesu, was hast du*

1. Like most chorales, chords change every beat.
2. Where two or more pitches appear on the same beat of the melody, nonharmonic tones may occur (measures 1,4,5, and 7).
3. There is a variety of tonal possibilities for each phrase.

Choice of Tonality

While the tonality of some phrases is dictated by accidentals and characteristic melodic patterns, others present a variety of tonal possibilities. In order to make the best choice, the harmonic progressions within each possible key should be charted. Considering the first phrase of *Herzliebster Jesu*, the A♯ and G♯ in the first measure seem to dictate B minor, ending with a half cadence (measure 3). Another possibility, however, is a modulation from B minor to A major in measure 2 or 3; the cadence in the new key would be imperfect authentic. The second phrase might begin in B minor or A major. There are at least three possibilities for the cadence in measure 6: B minor, D major, or G major.

An inventory of tonal possibilities such as that shown in Example 2–11 is very valuable in selecting the most appropriate harmonic plan.

EXAMPLE 2–11   Tonal Inventory (First and Second Phrases)

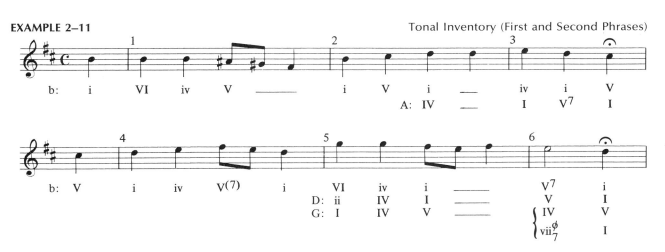

Any combination of keys shown in Example 2–11 represents an acceptable harmonic plan for the counterpoint. The choice of the key that ends each phrase should be made from among the several possibilities with attention to:

1. Harmonic and Cadential Variety.
2. The effect of any one tonality on an *overall* tonal plan.

The guidelines above arise from a study of Bach's chorale harmonizations. In one of his settings of *Herzliebster Jesu,* for example, Bach selects the tonic key (B minor) for the first, third, and fourth phrases; the second phrase provides contrast by concluding in the mediant key. The relationship between the tonic and mediant in minor, of course, is as close as that between the tonic and dominant in major. Bach's choices were not arbitrary, but intended to strengthen the overall tonality and the meaning of the text (Example 2–12).

EXAMPLE 2–12

J.S. Bach, Chorale Harmonization
Herzliebster Jesu, was hast du

The Harmonic Plan

To understand the simplicity of typical common practice progressions, it is helpful to view each tonic chord as an "arrival" and to study the route used to reach it. The progressions in the chorale above, for example, are listed in Example 2–13. The analysis shows not a wide variety, but a series of short progressions involving mostly dominant-tonic movements.

EXAMPLE 2–13   Progressions in Bach's
                                                    Herzliebster Jesu

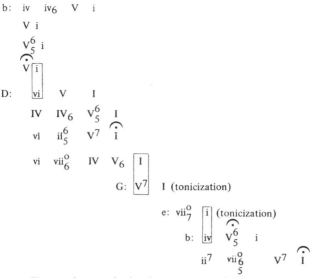

From the analysis above, several facts about Bach's harmonic choices are obvious:

1. Over two-thirds of the chords (28 of 39) have dominant or tonic function.[3]
2. Of the remaining 11 chords, 8 are of subdominant function and all but one of these precedes the dominant.
3. Submediant chords are rare.
4. The mediant triad is not used.

In short, the most typical chorale progressions are the most simple; variety comes through the use of inversions and nonharmonic tones.

Use of Inversions

While first inversion triads and chords may be employed at virtually any time (except the first chord in a work and chords at major points of cadence), *second inversion sonorities should be avoided* for the present. The stylistic use of second inversion chords will be discussed in Chapter 3.

IMPLIED SEVENTH CHORDS

In writing free counterpoint for two voices, the melodic seventh can be employed at will provided it resolves stepwise to a consonance. In Example 2–14, a seventh is seen in measure 1 as a passing tone and in measure 3 as part of a 7–6 suspension.

EXAMPLE 2–14   Melodic Sevenths

[3]Common chords are counted twice.

In addition to the two melodic sevenths, an implied *harmonic* seventh occurs at the asterisk. The final contrapuntal principle concerns the stylistic resolution of harmonic dissonance.

CONTRAPUNTAL PRINCIPLE 6	When voices combine to produce an implied harmonic seventh, the dissonance must be resolved by descending stepwise motion.

In the Renaissance, composers often employed a passing melodic seventh, especially at a cadence. By the time of Bach, this passing seventh had been incorporated into the triad as the first harmonic dissonance; retained from the original passing figure, however, was the descending stepwise resolution. Observe the resolution of the harmonic sevenths in Example 2–15.

EXAMPLE 2–15

J.S. Bach, Chorale Harmonization, *Wachet auf, ruft uns die Stimme*

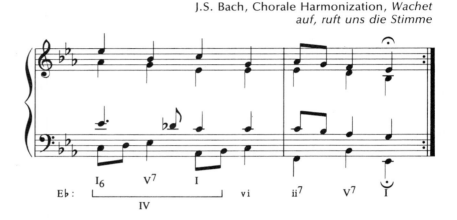

The resolution of the seventh when inverted is exactly the same: down by step. Study the resolution of the inverted sevenths in Example 2–16.

EXAMPLE 2–16

J.S. Bach, Chorale Harmonization, *Die Nacht ist Kommen*

The Implied Harmonic Seventh in Counterpoint

In two-voice writing, when a seventh chord is implied by either a seventh or second above the bass, care should be taken that it resolves characteristically. In Example 2–17 below, the implied seventh resolves correctly in the first version, but incorrectly in the second.

EXAMPLE 2–17 Implied Seventh Chords

Correct   Incorrect

Not all seconds and sevenths, of course, are heard as harmonic dissonances. In general, a minor seventh associated with a dominant triad is heard as harmonic; those associated with other chords may be heard as harmonic or melodic depending on the context.

Implied Sevenths in the Given Melody

Pitches in the melody can be harmonized as implied chordal sevenths provided that they resolve characteristically. Both correct and incorrect use of a pitch in the melody as a seventh is seen in Example 2–18.

EXAMPLE 2–18 Melody Pitches as Chordal Sevenths

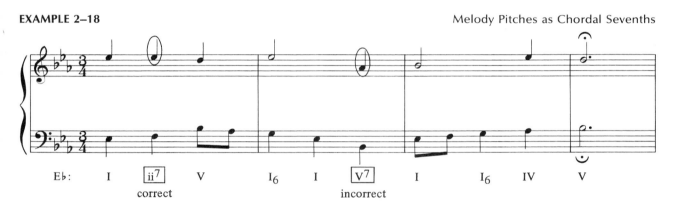

In the first measure of the melody, the E♭₅ is treated as a chordal seventh. Because the following pitch is D₅, the characteristic stepwise resolution is possible. In the second measure, however, the A♭₄ in the melody *may not* be harmonized as a seventh because the following pitch is a step higher, not lower.

When a harmonic seventh appears in one voice and recurs immediately in an adjacent voice, the resolution takes place in the second voice (Example 2–19).

EXAMPLE 2–19 Alternate Resolution of Seventh

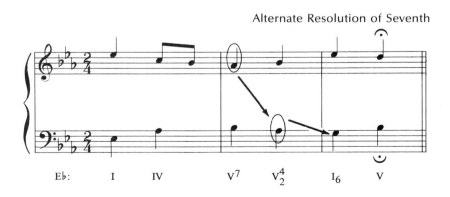

SUMMARY OF CONTRAPUNTAL PRINCIPLES

1. Contrary motion should predominate.
2. The range of each voice should be kept distinct.
3. The counterpoint must be complementary to the cantus firmus, but it must exhibit sound melodic and formal construction on its own right.
4. Dissonance must be prepared and resolved in eighteenth-century style.
5. The harmonic rhythm and tonality of the given melody must be established in the counterpoint.
6. When voices combine to produce an implied harmonic seventh, the dissonance must be resolved by descending stepwise motion.

Study the counterpoint Bach wrote for two chorale melodies (Examples 2–20 and 2–21). Analyze the counterpoint with special attention to the following:

1. Type of intervals employed (consonance and dissonance)
2. The use of nonharmonic tones
3. Type of contrapuntal motion
4. Degree of voice independence
5. Melodic motion, range, contour, and general style
6. Cadential and tonal structure

EXAMPLE 2–20
J.S. Bach, Chorale Harmonization, *Alle Menschen müssen sterben* (soprano and bass)

EXAMPLE 2–21
J.S. Bach, Chorale Harmonization, *Allein Gott in der Höh' sei Ehr'* (soprano and bass)

Many instructors will want their students to experience imitative writing both to reinforce contrapuntal principles and to stimulate the creative process. The canon is offered for this purpose.

IMITATIVE COUNTERPOINT: THE CANON

Popular with composers since the thirteenth century, the CANON is a composition for two or more voices in which a subject is stated in one voice and imitated in the other(s) after a brief interval. The imitating voice may appear at the octave (as in Example 2–22) or any other interval (Example 2–23).

EXAMPLE 2–22

Henry Purcell, Canon at the Octave

EXAMPLE 2–23

Robert Schumann, *Wann?*, Op. 113 (Canon at the fifth)

Two-Voice Canon at the Octave

To compose a two-voice canon at the octave (or unison), follow the simple procedure outlined below.

1. Compose a short subject that is melodically and rhythmically interesting and at the same time, clear in tonal structure.

Subject

2. Copy the subject in the second voice in either the same or a different octave. The length of the subject will determine the entry point of the second voice.

3. Compose new material for the first voice that forms a good counterpoint with the subject as it begins in the second voice. Remember that to be effective, the harmonic structure of the counterpoint must be clear. Copy the new material in the second voice as well.

4. Repeat step 3 and continue the process until the canon reaches the desired length. The final measure or two of the imitating voice may be altered to create a strong final cadence.

Analyze the following chorales harmonized by J.S. Bach. Note the counterpoint between bass and soprano, the use of dissonance, and the essential harmonic plan. If directed to do so, provide a reduction of some or all of the chorales showing only the soprano-bass counterpoint with appropriate harmonic analysis.

Bach, *In allen meinen Taten*

Bach, *O Traurigkeit*

Bach, *Jesu, der du meine Seele*

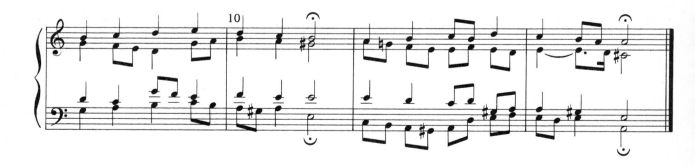

The following counterpoints contain various major and minor errors (like parallel fifths and incorrect use of dissonance) that should be located and identified. Errors in the first chorale phrase are marked.

G: I IV V I V I   I   V/V V₆ I IV₆ vi V   IV V   I

1. Parallel fifths
2. Unresolved harmonic dissonance
3. Unresolved melodic dissonance
4. Authentic cadence should be in root position.

g: i i₆ V VI IV V V₆   i   i VI V iv V i   V

Study the character and harmonic implications of the following chorale melodies. Determine an appropriate cadential and harmonic plan (include Roman numerals) and compose a bass that forms a good counterpoint. The bass should mainly be first species (note-against-note) although dissonance may be used if there are two or more pitches in the bass for one in the soprano. Melodic dissonance may not be used in first species.

Ach was soll ich Sünder machen

Weg, mein Herz, mit den Gedanken

Wenn wir in höchsten Nöten sein

Nun danket alle Gott

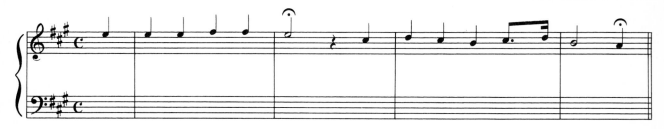

Ermuntre dich, mein schwacher Geist

Puer natus in Bethlehem

Ach Gott und Herr

ADDITIONAL CHORALE MELODIES

Vater unser im Himmelreich

Christ lag in Todesbanden

Wie schön leuchtet der Morgenstern

Christus, der ist mein Leben

Freu'dich sehr, o meine Seele

Jesu, der du meine Seele

Chapter 3
Harmonization of Chorale Melodies

The Lutheran chorale melodies harmonized in four parts by Bach and his contemporaries came from various sources: translations of Catholic hymns, German sacred and secular song, and newly composed materials. During the Reformation, Martin Luther composed or "improved on" many hymn tunes himself. In composing polyphonic chorale settings for congregational performance, Bach was preceded by several important German composers including Crüger (1598–1662) and Scheidt (1587–1654).

The study of the harmonization process begins with the four-voice texture itself, continues with a look at the distribution of pitches among the four voices, and culminates in an investigation of chord connection and partwriting procedure.

THE FOUR-VOICE TEXTURE

In chorale harmonizations, the four voices (soprano, alto, tenor, and bass) adhere closely to the ranges shown in Example 3–1.

EXAMPLE 3–1   Ranges in Four-Part Vocal Writing

Stem Direction

In VOCAL SCORE FORMAT, the soprano and tenor voices are written with stems up, alto and bass with stems down *regardless of the location of pitches on the staff*. Bass and tenor are written in bass clef; alto and soprano are notated in treble clef.

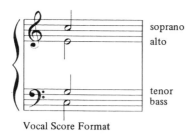

Vocal Score Format

Two voices in unison are indicated by double stems; unison whole notes are overlapped.

Vocal Scoring

A triad (with two roots in this case) can be spaced or "scored" in a number of ways, each having a distinct timbre (Example 3–2).

EXAMPLE 3–2   Spacing in C Major Triad

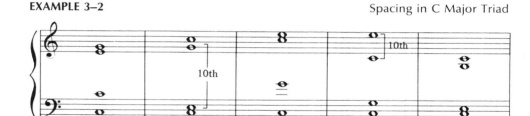

In four-part writing, the UPPER (THREE) VOICES (soprano, alto and tenor) are treated separately from the bass. *Rarely are any two adjacent upper voices separated by more than an octave.* While none of the chords in Example 3–2 above exceeds the normal ranges, chords B and D are not scored in a characteristic manner. In Example 3–2B, the tenor is a tenth below the alto; in 3–2D the soprano and alto are likewise separated by a tenth. The distance between tenor and bass, however, may correctly exceed an octave (Example 3–2C, for instance).

Open and Close Structure

STRUCTURE refers to the spacing of the upper three voices regardless of the position of the bass. In CLOSE STRUCTURE, the upper three voices are as close together as possible—the tenor and soprano are separated by less than an octave. In OPEN STRUCTURE, one or more chord tones are omitted between the upper three voices; the resulting spacing between tenor and soprano is an octave or more (Example 3–3). To repeat, structure refers to the distance between *tenor and soprano;* the bass is not considered. Each of the chords in Example 3–3 has two roots.

EXAMPLE 3–3   Open and Close Structure

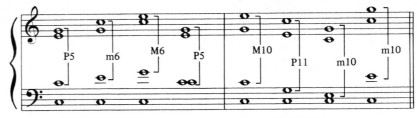

CLOSE STRUCTURE   OPEN STRUCTURE

An awareness of structure is important in connecting chords; certain problems in voice leading may be avoided by changing from open to close structure or the reverse.

DOUBLING

After a close study of the chorale harmonizations of J.S. Bach, Allen McHose, a modern theorist, was able to cite valuable statistics concerning doubling and other procedures.[1] DOUBLING refers to the duplication of one of the three triad members to accommodate a four-voice texture. McHose's findings concerning root position triads (Example 3–4) show that Bach's doubling was far from arbitrary.

EXAMPLE 3–4   Doubling in Root Position Triads[2]

| MAJOR TRIADS | | MINOR TRIADS | |
Percentage of Occurrence		Percentage of Occurrence	
Root Doubled	88%	Root Doubled	84%
Third Doubled	8%	Third Doubled	13%
Fifth Doubled	3%	Fifth Doubled	2%

(In 1 percent of major and minor triads, other arrangements were found—three roots, one third, for example)

From the statistics in Example 3–4, it is clear that Bach preferred to double the root in root position major and minor triads; this doubling, therefore, is considered conventional and should be the first choice in chorale harmonizations. A doubling of the third or fifth, however, is not necessarily an error. In the event that conventional doubling creates a stylistic problem (parallel fifths, for example), an alternate doubling may be a practical solution. As long as most chords follow conventional practice, exceptions can not only be tolerated, but may actually contribute richness to a chorale setting.

Major and Minor Triads

Conventional doubling in major and minor triads is shown below:

    Root Position: Double the ROOT
   First Inversion: Double the SOPRANO
  Second Inversion: Double the BASS

[1] Allen McHose, *The Contrapuntal Harmonic Technique of the 18th Century*, (New York: Appleton-Century-Crofts, Inc., 1947), p. 19.
[2] McHose, p. 19.

Study the doubling procedure employed in Example 3–5.

EXAMPLE 3–5 Doubling in Major and Minor Triads

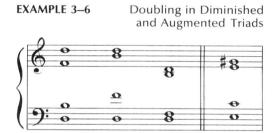

Root Position   First Inversion   Second Inversion

Tripled Root in Major and Minor Triads

Major and minor triads in root position sometimes occur with tripled root. In this case (which accounts for fewer than 1 percent of the triads in Bach's harmonizations), the fifth is omitted, *never* the third. A triad with tripled root occurs most often at an important cadence.

Diminished and Augmented Triads

Diminished triads are rarely found in root position. The tritone between the root and fifth of a diminished triad is less obvious when it appears in the upper voices, so the sonority is found most often in *first inversion* with *doubled third*. The same practice is followed in scoring augmented triads although they are rare in the common practice inventory (Example 3–6).

EXAMPLE 3–6 Doubling in Diminished and Augmented Triads

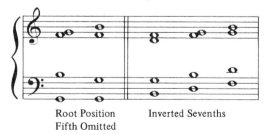

Seventh Chords

Because seventh chords include four discrete pitches, no doubling is mandatory. In root position, however, the fifth is often omitted so that the root may be doubled. Inverted sevenths occur typically with all four pitches present (Example 3–7).

EXAMPLE 3–7 Doubling in Seventh Chords

Root Position   Inverted Sevenths
Fifth Omitted

Active Tones

Due to its active nature, the leading tone is rarely doubled. Likewise, ALTERED TONES such as a raised sixth scale degree in minor or other chromatically altered pitches are not usually doubled.

While theorists generally agree that experience in four-voice chorale composition, commonly called PARTWRITING, should have a place in the undergraduate music curriculum, the scope of this study varies considerably. In some texts, practically all aspects of traditional harmony are introduced and studied through chorale analysis and composition. On the other hand, authors like Arnold Schoenberg (1874–1951) have summarized essential partwriting rules in a paragraph or two. In his book *Structural Functions of Harmony*, for example, Schoenberg writes:

> When connecting chords it is advisable that each of the four voices . . . should move no more than necessary. Accordingly, large leaps are avoided, and if two chords have a tone in common, it should, if possible, be held over in the same voice.
> This advice is sufficient to avoid the greatest mistakes in part leading, though special precautions are necessary to avoid open or hidden parallel fifths or octaves. Contrary rather than parallel motion is recommended.[3]

The Law of the Shortest Way

If all of the pages ever written about partwriting were condensed into one rule, it would probably be what Anton Bruckner is said to have advised his students: "Obey the Law of the Shortest Way." *Chords should be connected by the least possible movement—especially in the inner voices* (alto and tenor).

Acceptable partwriting is shown in Example 3–8 as the inner voices move by step. In Example 3–9, the many unnecessary leaps result not only in a difficult alto and tenor, but in several serious errors as well.

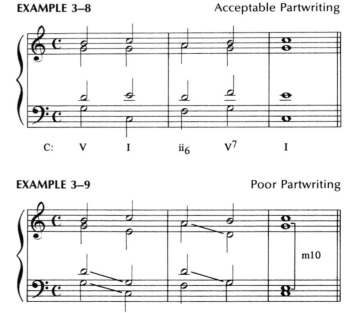

EXAMPLE 3–8   Acceptable Partwriting

C: V   I   ii₆   V⁷   I

EXAMPLE 3–9   Poor Partwriting

C: V   I   ii₆   V   I

[3]Arnold Schoenberg, *Structural Functions of Harmony.* (New York: W.W. Norton & Company, 1969), p. 4.

For greatest voice independence and to help avoid parallel fifths and octaves, the upper three voices should move generally in *contrary motion with the bass* (Example 3–10).[4]

EXAMPLE 3–10   Acceptable Voice Independence

In the passage above, the upper voices move predominantly, but not *entirely* in contrary motion with the bass. The procedures given in this chapter are not rules, but general guidelines of style extracted from the actual practice of Bach and others. Some of these guidelines can be ignored occasionally for either practical or aesthetic reasons.

Common Tones

When two triads have their roots a fifth apart, one pitch is a member of both triads; this pitch is known as a COMMON TONE and should be retained in the same voice whenever possible. If root movement is by third or sixth, two tones will be common. Similarly, both should be retained in the same voices. Where common tones are retained, the other voice (or voices) generally move stepwise in contrary motion with the bass (Example 3–11).

EXAMPLE 3–11   Retention of Common Tones

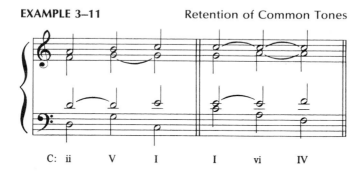

Root Movement by Second (or Seventh)

Chord roots related by second (or seventh) have no common tones. Most typically, upper voices move in contrary motion with the bass to the *closest* chord tones (Example 3–12).

---

[4]While parallel perfect octaves, fifths, and unisons are never permitted, parallel perfect fourths are acceptable in four-part writing. Some authorities object to perfect octaves or fifths even in contrary motion (Example 3–10, first measure, soprano and bass).

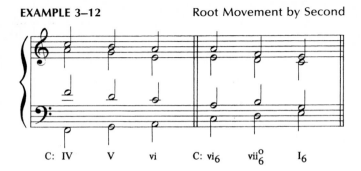

EXAMPLE 3–12   Root Movement by Second

C: IV   V   vi   C: vi₆   vii°₆   I₆

Change of Structure

If retention of common tones and/or contrary motion is impractical, an alternate approach to chord connection is to change structure from open to close or the reverse (Example 3–13).

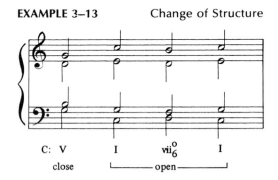

EXAMPLE 3–13   Change of Structure

C: V   I   vii°₆   I

close |——— open ———|

OTHER CONSIDERATIONS IN PARTWRITING

Cross Relation

Common practice composers avoided the use of diatonic and chromatically altered pitches in different adjacent voices. When chromatic movement is necessary, one voice should be assigned both pitches. A CROSS RELATION, as seen in Example 3–14B, should be avoided.

EXAMPLE 3–14   Chromatic Movement

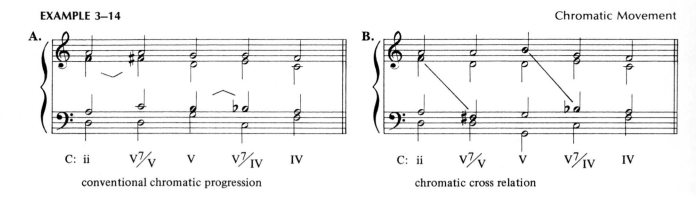

A.

C: ii   V⁷/V   V   V⁷/IV   IV

conventional chromatic progression

B.

C: ii   V⁷/V   V   V⁷/IV   IV

chromatic cross relation

Although examples of cross relationships occur in Bach's chorale harmonizations, they fall most often between phrases (Example 3–15).

EXAMPLE 3–15

Voice Crossing

As in counterpoint, voice crossing is best avoided in chorale harmonizations so that each of the voices maintains maximum independence. Likewise, voice overlap, although occasionally found in Bach's chorales, should be avoided in student work.

Unequal Fifths

The presence of UNEQUAL FIFTHS—the movement of a perfect fifth to a diminished fifth or vice versa—can reduce part independence as greatly as parallel perfect fifths. In general, a diminished fifth should not be followed by a perfect fifth.

Poor

A perfect fifth may be followed by a diminished fifth, however, *provided* the diminished fifth resolves in turn by contracting to a major or minor third.

Acceptable

If the diminished fifth does not resolve characteristically, the unequal fifths should be avoided.

Poor

SIX—FOUR CHORDS

When a triad is in second inversion, the instability of the perfect fourth between the bass and an upper voice is especially obvious. Accordingly, common practice composers were less free with their use of this sonority than they were with root position and first inversion triads. With only rare exceptions, all of the six–four chords in the common practice vocabulary fall into one of four categories: *Cadential, Passing, Arpeggiated,* or *Stationary.*

1. Cadential Six–Four

Discussed in Chapter 8 of Volume I, the CADENTIAL SIX–FOUR occurs as a tonic chord in second inversion that resolves *by step* to the dominant; the bass of the tonic six–four is sustained (or shifted an octave) to become the root of the dominant chord (Example 3–16).

EXAMPLE 3–16   Cadential Six-Four

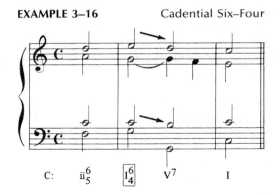

2. Passing Six–Four

A six–four sonority that occurs as the result of stepwise movement in the bass is the PASSING SIX–FOUR (Example 3–17). The three pitches (which ascend or descend) must *all* be chord tones.

EXAMPLE 3–17 Passing Six–Four

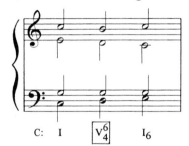

The passing six–four sometimes connects root position and first inversion chords (Example 3–17), although more often, the progression includes three different chords (Example 3–18).

EXAMPLE 3–18   Passing Six–Four
J.S. Bach, Chorale Harmonization,
Warum sollt' ich mich denn grämen

$$G: \quad V \quad I \quad IV_6 \quad \boxed{I_4^6} \quad ii_5^6 \quad V^7 \quad I$$

3. Arpeggiated Six–Four

When the same chord is reiterated with different chord members in the bass, a resulting six–four sonority is classified as ARPEGGIATED (Example 3–19).

EXAMPLE 3–19 Arpeggiated Six–Four

$$C: \quad I \quad I_6 \quad \boxed{I_4^6}$$

An arpeggiated six–four occurs in the second measure of Example 3–20. The dominant chord is heard in root position, second inversion, and finally third inversion as a seventh is added.[5]

EXAMPLE 3–20   Arpeggiated Six–Four
J.S. Bach, Chorale Harmonization,
Puer natus in Bethlehem

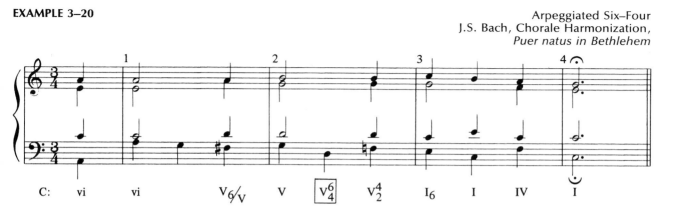

$$C: \quad vi \quad vi \quad V_6/V \quad V \quad \boxed{V_4^6} \quad V_2^4 \quad I_6 \quad I \quad IV \quad I$$

[5]The B♮ in the third measure of the soprano is analyzed as a passing tone. Others might consider it a harmonic dissonance (I[7]).

4. Stationary Six–Four

The STATIONARY SIX–FOUR occurs as the upper voices move over a stationary bass (Example 3–21).[6]

EXAMPLE 3–21   Stationary Six–Four

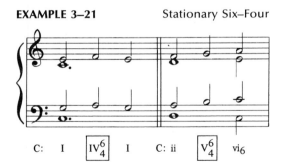

C: I   IV$^6_4$ I   C: ii   V$^6_4$ vi$_6$

In chorale harmonizations, the stationary six–four is not common; McHose cites only one example in his text (Example 3–22).[7]

EXAMPLE 3–22

Stationary Six–Four
J.S. Bach, Chorale Harmonization,
Beschränkt, ihr Weisen dieser Welt

A: V   I$^6_4$ ii$_6$ I$_6$ V^7 I   IV   ii^7 V   I
                                                        IV

Although the Stationary Six–Four is not common in Bach's chorale harmonizations, it is often seen in Classical and Romantic music.

Six–four sonorities other than the four types discussed here are extremely rare. Accordingly, students should avoid those which do not fit into one of the four categories.

Chorale Melody Harmonization

The successful harmonization of a chorale melody requires careful planning to select a harmonic scheme that complements the tonal implications of the melody, to allow a good counterpoint between soprano and bass, and to insure proper voice leading in the alto and tenor. A five-step procedure is recommended:

1. Analysis of the Melody
2. Selection of a Harmonic Plan for Each Phrase
3. Composition of the Bass
4. Composition of the Inner Voices
5. Critique and Revision

---

[6]Because of the melodic motion involved, the stationary six–four is also known as the NEIGHBORING SIX–FOUR and the AUXILIARY SIX–FOUR.

[7]McHose, p. 94.

While the harmonization discussed in this chapter is of a chorale melody, the same process is used with melodies in other styles. In fact, the harmonization of nonchorale melodies is easier in some ways because the harmonic rhythm is generally slower.

CHORALE MELODY HARMONIZATION: *JESU MEINE FREUDE*

Bach completed at least seven different harmonizations of Crüger's chorale melody *Jesu Meine Freude* (Example 3–23).

EXAMPLE 3–23   Johann Crüger, *Jesu Meine Freude*

I. ANALYSIS

Although each phrase of a chorale melody must be considered separately in terms of tonality, the overall tonal plan should emphasize one key or another. The key signature, accidentals, and melodic cadences in the first three phrases of *Jesu meine Freude* suggest D minor. Considered separately, however, several possibilities exist for most of the six major cadences. The range of tonal and cadential variety is shown in Example 3–24.

EXAMPLE 3–24   Tonal and Cadential Possibilities

Phrase	Possible Key(s)	Cadence Type
1	D minor	Perfect Authentic
	C major	Half
	F major	Deceptive
2	D minor	Half
	A major	Imperfect Authentic
3	D minor	Perfect Authentic
	C major	Half
4	D minor	Imperfect Authentic
	B♭ major	Plagal
	F major	Perfect Authentic
5	D minor	Half
	C major	Deceptive
	A minor	Perfect Authentic
6	D minor	Perfect Authentic

After studying all of the possibilities, a tonal plan should be devised which provides variety while strengthening the tonic through related keys. The relationships shown in Example 3–25 represent but one of several acceptable tonal plans.

EXAMPLE 3–25   Tonal Plan, *Jesu Meine Freude*

	Phrase					
	1	2	3	4	5	6
Key:	d	d	d	F	a	d
Cadence:	PAC	HC	PAC	PAC	PAC	PAC
Relationship:	Tonic	Tonic	Tonic	Mediant	Dominant	Tonic

II. HARMONIC PLAN

Within the key chosen for each phrase, all possibilities for harmonic function should be considered. The harmonic plan must not only establish each key area, but provide variety within it as well. Remember that pitches in the melody can be used as chordal sevenths *provided the appropriate pitch of resolution follows*. Study the harmonic possibilities of each phrase shown in Example 3–26. The chosen chords (circled) represent only one acceptable harmonic plan. These chords were chosen because they create a strong tonal effect while presenting adequate harmonic variety.

EXAMPLE 3–26   Harmonic Plan

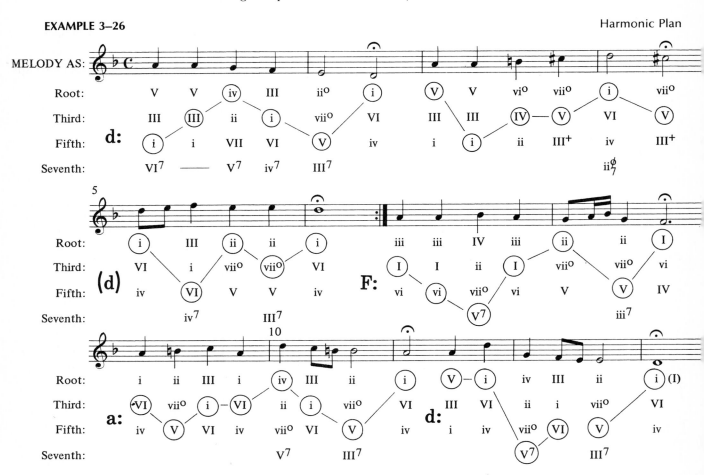

Secondary Function

Increased harmonic interest and variety are possible through the use of secondary function. Each major or minor chord in the harmonic plan represents an area of potential tonicization; the preceding pitch of the melody, however, must be one which belongs to the appropriate secondary dominant. Three possible areas of secondary function are shown in Example 3–27.

EXAMPLE 3–27   Secondary Function in Harmonic Plan

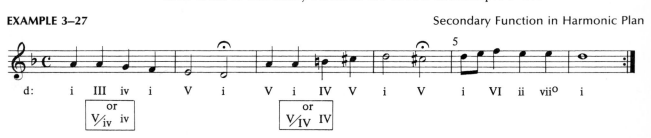

When secondary dominants and/or other color chords have been added where appropriate, the harmonic plan is complete. One must keep in mind, however, that the harmonic plan is original and if problems arise in the composition of the bass or inner voices, it may be changed if necessary.

III. COMPOSITION OF THE BASS

The bass must form a good counterpoint with the soprano. All six principles of contrapuntal writing apply, yet because the harmonic rhythm of a chorale is relatively fast, the bass occasionally may be assigned a wide or awkward leap for the sake of harmonic definition. Still, the employment of inversions and the addition of nonharmonic tones should permit a strong, but melodic bass line.

The choice of octave for the first bass note must be considered carefully to permit contrary motion. Because *Jesu meine Freude* begins with descending motion, the bass ideally should ascend. The pitch D_3, therefore, is preferable to D_4 as the first bass note. As the melody ascends or descends, bass notes should be chosen which permit a predominance of contrary motion. Special attention should be given to pitches across the barline; contrary motion is preferable, but in this instance, oblique motion is *least* effective.

Once the bass has been composed in note-against-note counterpoint with the soprano, nonharmonic tones can be added to provide contrary motion and to enhance the independence of the bass melody (Example 3–28).

EXAMPLE 3–28 Soprano–Bass Counterpoint

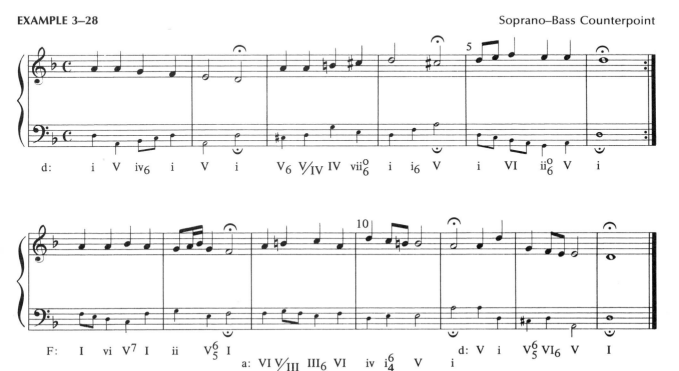

IV. COMPOSITION OF THE INNER VOICES

The fourth step in the harmonization process is the addition of the alto and tenor voices. The inner voices are added with attention to conventional doubling, the stated harmonic plan, and effective voice leading. Within this framework, problems will almost certainly arise. Although some may be solved simply through an alternate doubling or change of bass, others may require more extensive revisions in the harmonic scheme and necessitate the rescoring of several chords. Care should be taken that any change at this point does not create new problems with the chord(s) immediately preceding those changed.

After the inner voices have been composed in counterpoint with the soprano and bass, nonharmonic tones may be added where appropriate (Note: nonharmonic tones may *not* be added to the chorale melody). The completed chorale harmonization is shown in Example 3–29.

EXAMPLE 3–29 Preliminary Harmonization

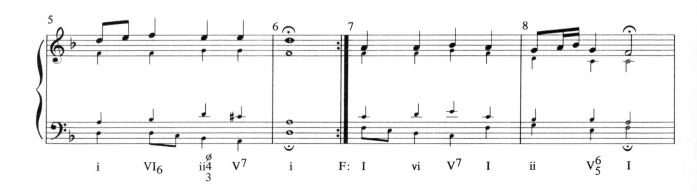

Comparing Example 3–29 with Example 3–28 (page 57), it should be observed that changes both in the bass and the harmonic plan were made during the composition of the inner voices. These changes were made to improve voice leading, avoid partwriting errors, add variety, or a combination of the three.

1. The V in measure 2 has become V^7.
2. The vii$^0_6$ in measure 3 is now V$^6_4$.
3. Passing tones have been added to the bass in measure 4.
4. The ii$^0_6$ in measure 5 has become ii$^6_3$.
5. Changes in measure 9 to avoid parallel fifths.
6. Sevenths have been added to measures 10 and 12.

V. CRITIQUE AND REVISION

Several aspects of the chorale in Example 3–29 could be criticized. The harmonization should be sung (or at least played on the keyboard) to locate any melodic problems and to check a final time for partwriting errors. Other questions may arise at this point. Are there too many nonharmonic tones? Too few? Is the tonality of each phrase clear? Is there too much harmonic variety? Not enough? Do six–four chords conform to one of the four categories? These and other questions should suggest areas for possible revision.

Compare the harmonization in Example 3–29 with two of Bach's settings of the same melody (Example 3–30 and 3–31). Analyze Bach's harmonizations and comment on differences between them.

EXAMPLE 3–30
J.S. Bach, Chorale Harmonization,
Jesu Meine Freude

EXAMPLE 3–31

J.S. Bach, Chorale Harmonization,
Jesu meine Freude

CHECKLIST FOR CHORALE MELODY HARMONIZATION

This checklist is intended as a ready reference when questions arise during the harmonization of a melody. While the summary may be of value in identifying conventions in the common practice style, it is not intended to be a set of rules for composition. One might follow every convention yet produce a dull and unmusical work. The many "atypical" procedures found in Bach's own work prove that the ultimate success of the music is judged according to its aesthetic qualities, not its conformity to a set of rules.

CHECKLIST FOR CHORALE MELODY HARMONIZATION

	QUALITIES TO WORK FOR	QUALITIES TO AVOID
I. SPACING AND RANGE	Appropriate timbres and comfortable ranges	More than an octave between adjacent upper voices Exceeding stated ranges
II. DOUBLING	Conventional Practice: *Triads: Major and Minor* Root Position: Double Root 1st Inversion: Double Soprano 2nd Inversion: Double Bass *Triads: Diminished/Augmented* Use 1st Inversion, Double Third *Seventh Chords* Root Position: All pitches present OR omit 5th, double root Inverted: All pitches present	Doubled Tritone Doubled Active Tone
III. MELODIC MOTION	Smooth, independent melodic lines with effective contour in bass	Melodic Tritone Augmented Second Other awkward intervals
IV. VOICE INDEPENDENCE	Contrary motion between bass and upper voices Ranges of four voices distinct	Parallel fifths, octaves Voice Crossing, Voice Overlap
V. CHORD CONNECTION	Obey "Law of the Shortest Way" Retain Common Tones where practical	Wide, awkward leaps Chromatic Cross Relationships

Score each triad for four voices by doubling the root. Write the chord first in open, then in close structure. Be sure that no two adjacent upper voices are separated by more than an octave.

SAMPLE

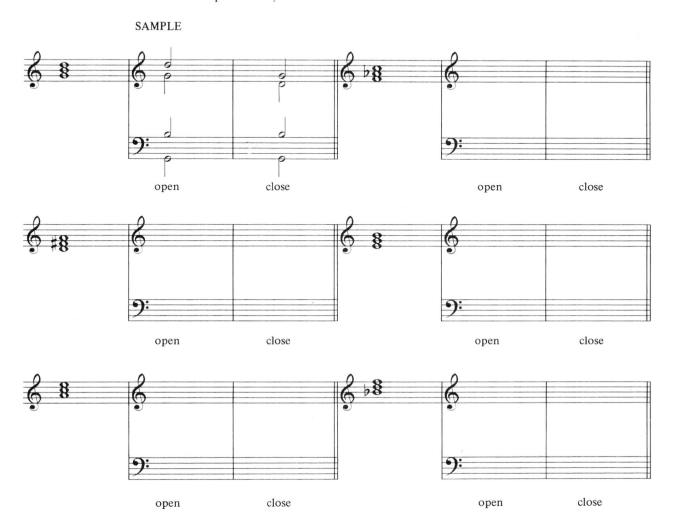

Score each of the following triads for four voices. Use first root position, then first inversion, and finally second inversion. Employ the conventional doubling for each chord. In the blank, identify the structure (open or close) that you choose.

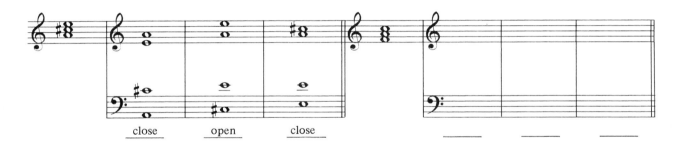

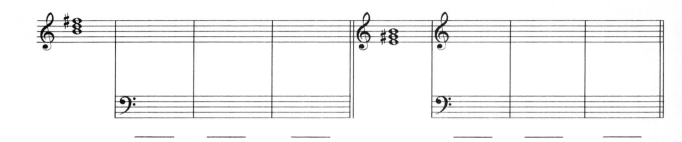

Fill in the inner voices in the following progressions. Maintain the same structure in both chords and use conventional doubling. Avoid parallel fifths and octaves.

Locate partwriting errors in the following chorales. Circle the error and explain below.

1. Parallel octaves.

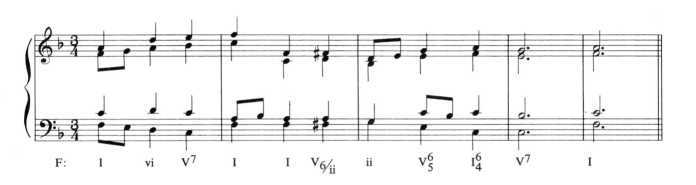

Using correct partwriting procedure, fill in the inner voices for the short progressions given. Change structure as necessary, but adhere to conventional doublings if possible.

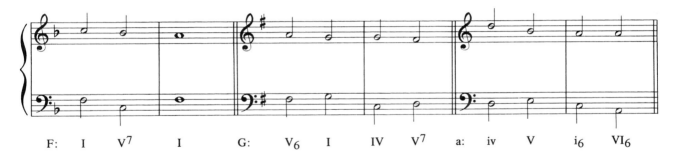

Bb: V^6_5 I   vii°$_6$ I_6 b: IV V^7 I   F: iii   vi   ii   V

Choose an appropriate harmonic plan for the given melodic fragments within the key indicated. Harmonize the melody in four parts following the steps outlined on pages 55–59. Provide Roman numeral analysis and identify any nonharmonic tones.

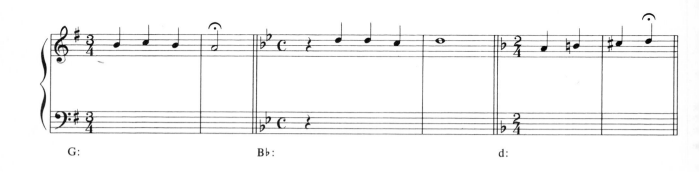

G: Bb: d:

C: f: e:

Continue as in previous exercise, but employ six–four chords of the types indicated.

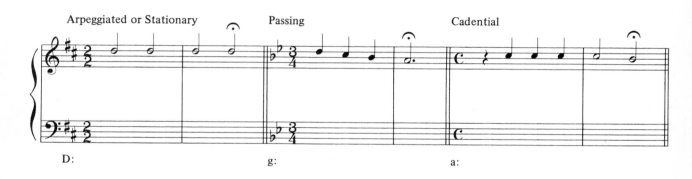

D: g: a:

For each phrase below, choose an appropriate key. Make a chart such as that given in Example 3–26, page 56 which shows all possible diatonic harmonic choices. Consider the melody pitch in turn as the root, third, fifth, and seventh of a chord. Remember that a melody pitch may not serve as the seventh of a seventh chord unless the next pitch represents the appropriate resolution. From among all the choices, select a harmonic plan that provides both function and variety.

Von Gott will ich nicht lassen

Root:
Third: **a:**
Fifth:
enth:

Nun preiset alle

Root:
hird:
'ifth: Key
enth:

Gott lebet noch

Root:
hird:
'ifth: Key
enth:

For each of the following melodic fragments, determine an appropriate harmonic rhythm and harmonic plan. Compose a bass in counterpoint with the soprano, then add the inner voices. Use inversions where appropriate. Be careful to limit six–four chords to one of the four types, and add nonharmonic tones to improve the melodic line of each voice.

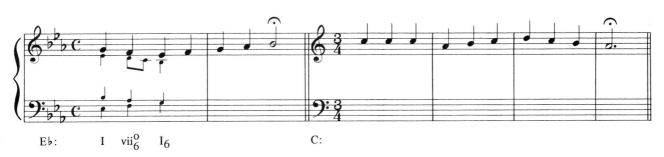

Harmonization of Chorale Melodies **67**

Jesu, du mein liebstes Leben
(first and second phrases)

Erschienen ist der herrliche Tag
(first and second phrases)

Jesu, Jesu, du bist mein

Keinen hat Gott verlassen

Wer nur den lieben Gott läßt walten

Chapter 4
Figured Bass

In the late sixteenth century, a group of Italian composers, poets, and intellectuals founded a new style of music *(Nuove Musiche)* based on a simple vocal melody accompanied by a strong bass and block chords. The group is known as the FLORENTINE CAMERATA and their music, which we call MONODY, grew into opera—one of the most important developments in the history of Western music.

Monody stands in stark contrast to the sixteenth-century madrigal, the most important secular form of the late Renaissance. The complex chromaticism and imitative counterpoint of the madrigal (which often rendered the text unintelligible) are seen in the following passage from *Io pur respiro* by Carlo Gesualdo (Example 4–1).

EXAMPLE 4–1

Carlo Gesualdo, *Io pur respiro* (1560–1613)

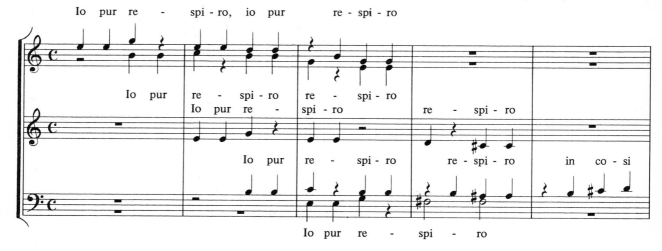

MONODY

Both as a reaction to the musical excesses of Gesualdo and his contemporaries, and as an attempt to exploit the dramatic possibilities of solo song, the composers of the Camerata developed an expressive melodic style designed to enhance rather than compete with the text.

As shown in Example 4–2, the accompaniments employed by the composers of the Camerata were quite simple; a violoncello, viola da gamba, or lute performed the bass line (often somewhat simplified) while a chordal accompaniment was supplied by a harpsichord or other keyboard instrument.

EXAMPLE 4–2   Jacopo Peri, *Le Musiche sopra l'Euridice*

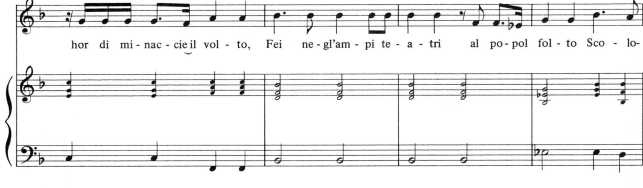

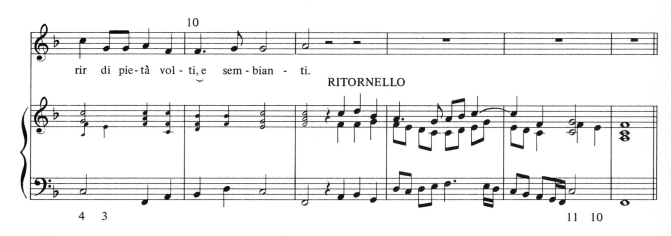

So much emphasis was placed on the soprano and bass, in fact, that the composers actually began to omit the chords from the score; numerals and other symbols were placed above (later below) the bass to indicate how the inner voices were to be filled in—a process known as REALIZATION. The FIGURED BASS seen in Example 4–3 is a characteristic of the Baroque Era and testifies to the recognition of the bass as the foundation of harmonic structure.

[1]This excerpt is a facsimile of the original 1700 edition of Corelli's Op. 5, No. 1. The work was probably printed from copper plates and is dedicated to the Electress Sophie Charlotte of Brandenburg. As was customary in slow movements, Corelli includes an ornamented version of the soprano above the soprano itself.

The Continuo

Keyboard players of the Baroque Era became proficient at reading a figured bass and realizing the inner voices at sight. The tradition of figured bass (also called THOROUGH BASS) accompaniment, however, was as much improvisation as score reading; performers were expected to add figuration (such as runs and arpeggios) and double or harmonize the melody as well as realize the harmonic and melodic details specified by the figures.

The two performers responsible for the realization (often a violoncello and harpsichord) constitute the CONTINUO. In Baroque music, the continuo was an indispensable unit and held a position not unlike that of the rhythm section in modern jazz.

The Study of Figured Bass

Although the practice of figured bass had essentially died out by the end of the eighteenth century, music students today must understand the concepts involved in order to interpret and perform scores from the Baroque and early Classical periods. While the realization of complex thorough bass accompaniments lies more in the field of musicology than theory, an ability to discern harmonic structure from a figured bass is essential. Moreover, figured bass symbols are commonly used with Roman numerals in the analysis of common practice music.

THE FIGURED BASS SYSTEM

Although the actual realization of a figured bass may be a complex task, the system itself is quite simple. Arabic numerals below the bass refer to intervals above it; rarely, however, do they designate a specific octave or voice. The numeral *3*, for example, indicates the presence of a *diatonic* third above the bass; the actual octave and voice in which it occurs is usually determined by the performer (Example 4–4).

EXAMPLE 4–4 Figured Bass

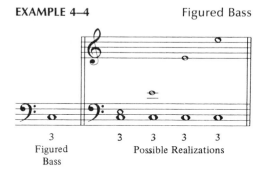

An entire chord in a four-voice texture can be indicated by giving the appropriate figured bass for the inversion and doubling desired.

Because the figured bass system is based on the indication of individual intervals, the designation of complete three or four note chords is somewhat cumbersome. A system of abbreviated figurations soon evolved through which not only intervals, but complete triads and chords were indicated by a figure or two.

Abbreviated Figured Bass for Triads and Chords

The *absence* of a figure beneath a bass note indicates a triad in root position. The numerals ⁵₃ (which would designate a fifth and third above the bass) are omitted. Conventional doubling to provide a fourth voice is assumed (Example 4–5).

EXAMPLE 4–5   Root Position Triads

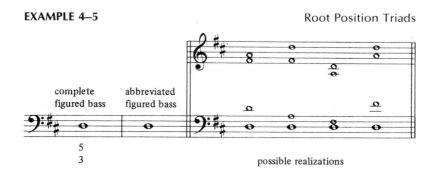

The numeral 6 indicates a triad in first inversion. Although the complete figure would be ⁶₃, the *3* is omitted. Again, conventional doubling is assumed (Example 4–6).

EXAMPLE 4–6   First Inversion Triads

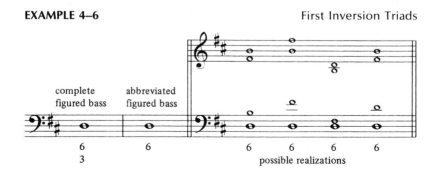

The numerals ⁶₄ indicate a triad in second inversion (Example 4–7).

EXAMPLE 4–7   Second Inversion Triads

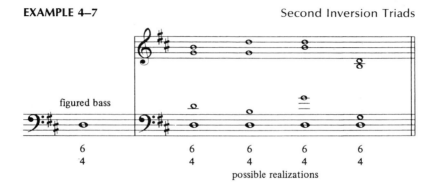

Seventh Chords

The figuration that indicates seventh chords, like that for root position and first inversion triads, is often abbreviated. The complete figured bass, its corresponding abbreviation, and one possible realization are shown in Example 4–8.

EXAMPLE 4–8   Seventh Chords

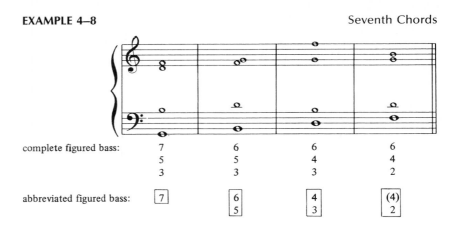

complete figured bass: 7   6   6   6
                        5   5   4   4
                        3   3   3   2

abbreviated figured bass: [7]   [6]   [4]   [(4)]
                                 [5]   [3]   [2]

When the complete figured bass is used for either triads or seventh chords, it is usually to specify an unusual doubling, or to identify pitches that are altered.

Accidentals

The intervals indicated above the bass are always *diatonic* intervals unless otherwise specified. A pitch raised or lowered outside the key signature is indicated in a number of ways:

6	⁶̸ +6	#6	♮6	♭6
Diatonic	Raised	Sharp	Natural	Flat
Sixth	└ One Half ┘	Sixth	Sixth	Sixth
	Step			

In Example 4–9, notice the use of the figured bass to designate both accidentals and unusual doubling.

EXAMPLE 4–9   Accidentals and Unusual Doubling

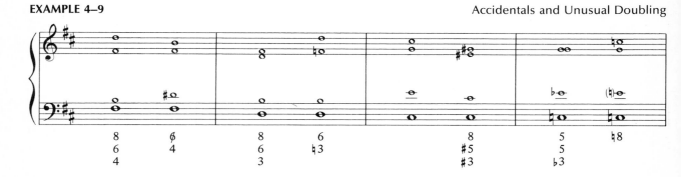

   8   ⁶̸   8   6   8   5   ♮8
   6   4   6   ♮3   #5   5
   4   3   #3   ♭3

The Third Above the Bass.   When the third above the bass is altered, the numeral *3* is often omitted. A flat, sharp, or natural sign *alone* always refers to the third above the bass (Example 4–10).

EXAMPLE 4–10   Altered Third

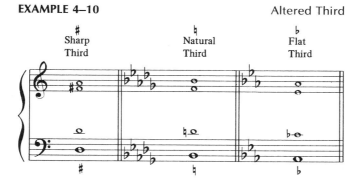

Linear Movement

Numerals that appear horizontally below a single bass note indicate linear movement in one or more upper voices. As usual, the particular voice and octave are not specified (Example 4–11).

EXAMPLE 4–11   Linear Movement in Upper Voices

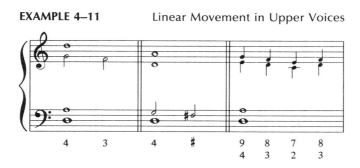

A horizontal line may be used to indicate one or more voices remaining stationary while another moves above the bass. The same process is used to indicate melodic movement in the bass itself (Example 4–12).

EXAMPLE 4–12   Linear Movement in Upper
                         Voices or Bass

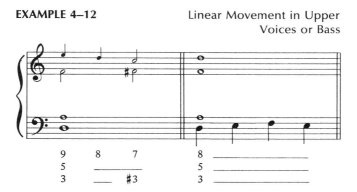

PRELIMINARY FIGURED BASS EXERCISES: VOCAL STYLE

Two-voice realizations in vocal style (soprano and bass given) are more exercises in partwriting than they are practical studies in the art of figured bass accompaniment. Nonetheless, the realization of inner voices with strict attention to the principles of chord connection forms an excellent introduction to the figured bass system. The procedures given in the previous chapter for the harmonization of chorale melodies apply equally well to the realization of a figured bass. One exception should be noted: *all* upper voice movement is specified by the figured bass; additional melodic movement should not be included.

A four-step procedure for figured bass realization will provide direction and minimize errors.

I. OBSERVATION
The figured bass (and melody if provided) should be scrutinized to determine:
    a. The basic harmonic rhythm and the location of any obvious nonharmonic tones in the bass.
    b. The relative complexity of the harmonic, rhythmic, and melodic activity as indicated by the figured bass.

II. ANALYSIS
A closer and more detailed inspection of the figured bass might include one or more of the following areas:
    a. A complete Roman numeral analysis.
    b. The location of suspensions and seventh chords that must be resolved characteristically.
    c. Pitches specified by the figured bass that appear in the soprano (if given).

III. REALIZATION
The actual process of realization is governed by the principles of chord connection outlined previously:
    a. Choose open or close structure, whichever is appropriate. (The position of the soprano, if given, may limit the choice).
    b. Compose the inner voices simultaneously.

IV. CRITIQUE AND REVISION
Many potential errors and stylistic inconsistencies will be spotted and avoided during the realization. An occasional set of parallel octaves or an awkward melodic leap, however, may be located only in the final phase.
    a. Sing or perform on the keyboard (as appropriate) all four parts to locate parallelisms, cross relations, etc.
    b. Sing the upper voices individually to check melodic style.
    c. Make a final comparison of the realization with the Roman numeral analysis to spot unresolved dissonance, misspelled chords, etc.
    d. Revise as necessary.

SAMPLE TWO-VOICE REALIZATION

Study the figured bass with given soprano in Example 4–13; follow the step-by-step realization.

EXAMPLE 4–13   Figured Bass with Given Soprano

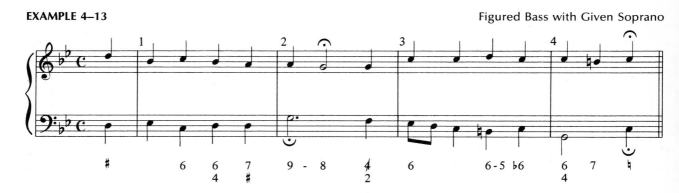

I. OBSERVATION
    1. Harmonic rhythm steady, predictable.
    2. Raised sevenths (F♯, B♮) may create augmented seconds if voiced incorrectly.
    3. Minimal inner voice movement.

II. ANALYSIS

1. Roman numeral analysis:

g: V   VI   ii°₆   i⁶₄   V⁷   i

c: V⁴₂   i₆   i   V₆   VI₆   i⁶₄   V⁷   I

2. Chordal sevenths (measures 1, 2, and 4) must resolve by step.
3. Cadential six–fours (measures 1 and 4) should resolve characteristically.
4. Second phrase modulates to C minor.
5. 9–8 suspension (measure 2) already present in given soprano.

III. REALIZATION

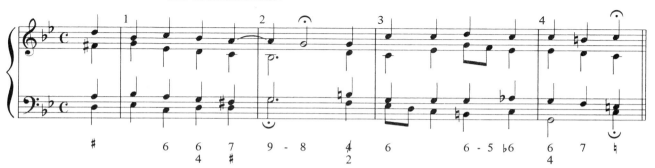

IV. CRITIQUE AND REVISION

1. Parallel fifths between tenor and bass (first two chords). *Solution:* Move tenor to G₃, double third.
2. Voice overlap (tenor and bass in fifth and sixth chords). *Solution:* exchange tenor and alto pitches.

Corrected Realization

FIGURED BASS REALIZATIONS WITHOUT GIVEN SOPRANO

The realization of a figured bass without given soprano may be approached in two ways:

1. as a continuation of partwriting exercises in a four-voice vocal format.
2. as a keyboard realization for study or performance purposes.

VOCAL MEDIUM

Four-voice chorale writing from a figured bass constitutes an excellent opportunity to apply the principles of voice leading and melodic construction within the limitations of a pre-conceived harmonic scheme. The necessity of creating a strong, independent soprano poses new and challenging problems.

The four-step procedure given on page 78 applies as well to realizations without given soprano. If composed simultaneously with the inner voices, however, the soprano may be dull. In the realization below, the soprano lacks direction (especially in the first two measures) and is awkward near the cadence. A seventh chord in measure 2 is resolved uncharacteristically. (Example 4–14.)

EXAMPLE 4–14   Realization: Poor Soprano

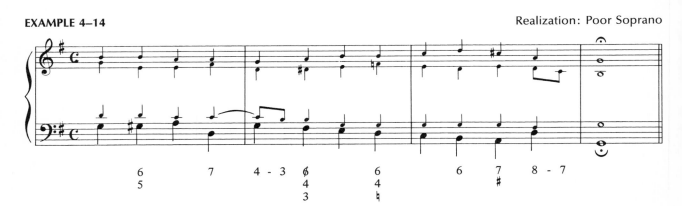

A better soprano is attained when it is composed first, as a counterpoint with the bass. The realization in Example 4–15 is substantially improved, and a set of unequal fifths (measure 2, Example 4–14) has been eliminated. Still, the realization might be criticized for its difficult tenor—especially in measure 2.

EXAMPLE 4–15   Improved Realization

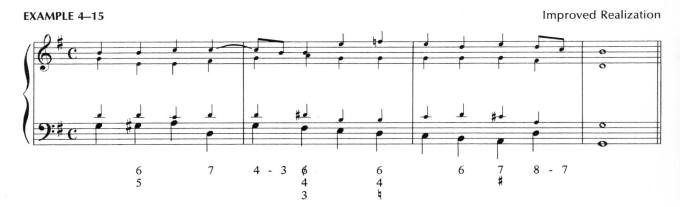

INSTRUMENTAL MEDIUM

When a realization is made for potential performance, a KEYBOARD FORMAT should be used. The bass is written in the bass clef with stems up or down as appropriate; the upper voices share a single stem which, again, is up or down depending on the location of the pitches. When the upper voices differ in rhythm, separate stems are employed (Example 4–16).

While the principles of chord connection are the same for both vocal and instrumental realizations, the latter is much more than a mechanical interpretation of the figures. A keyboard realization may vary in texture from two to four or more voices and include runs, arpeggios, rhythmic figures, and doubling or harmonization of the melody. Melodic and rhythmic figures, however, must be added with discretion; the purpose of the continuo is to complement, not compete with the solo part.

Many Baroque composers occasionally wrote out complete realizations of their own compositions, and because some of these have survived to the present day, scholars are able to make contemporary realizations with some authority. Invariably, however, different scholars come to different conclusions regarding the realization of the same figured bass. Study, for example, the three realizations of the opening phrase of Handel's *Sonata in G Minor for Flute and Continuo* (Examples 4–17, 4–18, and 4–19). Each is by a well known authority, yet each is unique in many ways. At the same time, however, the three realizations are consistent with one another in *style*.

EXAMPLE 4–17

G.F. Handel, *Sonata in G Minor*
Realization by Leigh Gerdine

EXAMPLE 4–18

G.F. Handel, *Sonata in G Minor*
Realization by Max Schneider

EXAMPLE 4–19

G.F. Handel, *Sonata in G Minor*
Realization by Louis Moyse

SUMMARY OF FIGURED BASS SYMBOLS

FIGURE	*REALIZATION*
(no figure under bass)	Root Position Triad
6	Triad in First Inversion
$^6_4$	Triad in Second Inversion
7	Root Position Seventh Chord
$^6_5$	Seventh Chord in First Inversion
$^4_3$	Seventh Chord in Second Inversion
2 (or $^4_2$)	Seventh Chord in Third Inversion
Diagonal line through Figure (6̸, 5̸, etc.)	Pitch Raised a Half Step
Sharp Sign with Figure (♯6, ♯5, etc.)	Pitch Sharped a Half Step
Flat Sign with Figure (♭6, ♭5, etc.)	Pitch Flattened a Half Step
Natural Sign with Figure (♮6, ♮5, etc.)	Pitch Natural
Sharp, Flat, or Natural Sign Alone (♯, ♭, ♮)	Third Above Bass Altered
"Plus" Sign with Figure (+6, +5 *or* 6+, 5+, etc.)	Pitch Raised a Half Step

Realize the following figured basses with given soprano. Use conventional doublings although exceptions can be made to avoid partwriting errors. Provide Roman numeral analysis.

Gelobet seist du, Jesu Christ

Von Gott will ich nicht lassen

Name _____

Realize the following figured basses with given soprano. Provide harmonic analysis.

Ach Gott, wie manches Herzeleid

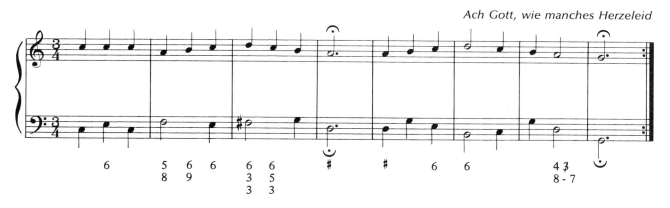

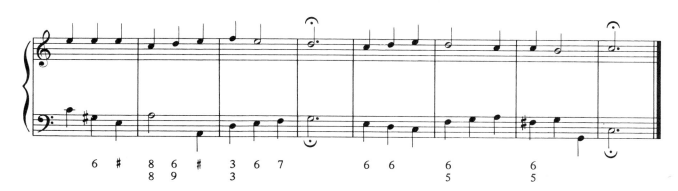

Realize the following figured basses for vocal performance. First compose an appropriate soprano in counterpoint with the bass; next, realize the inner voices. Provide Roman numeral analysis.

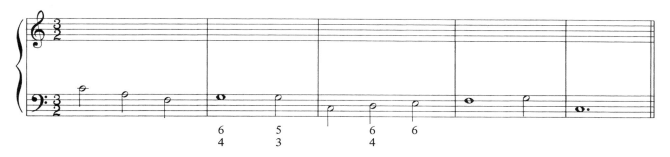

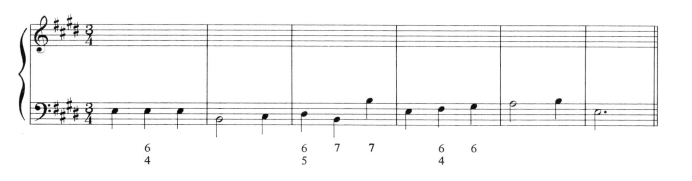

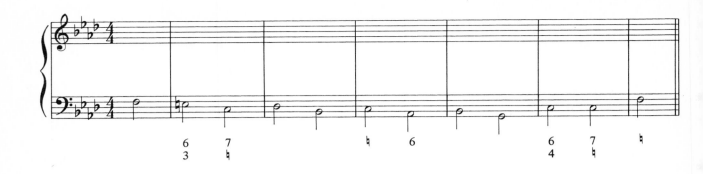

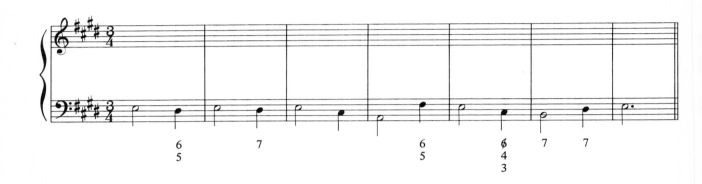

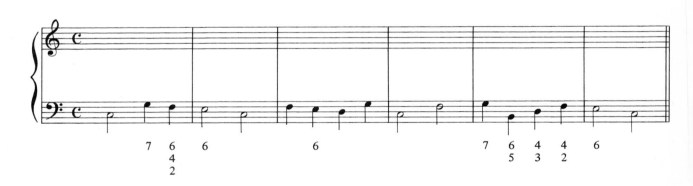

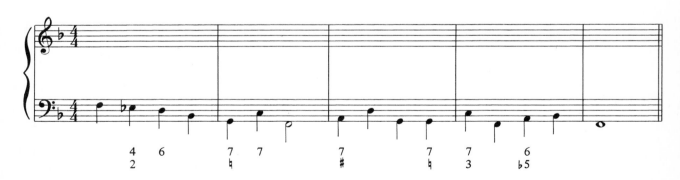

Arcangelo Corelli, *Sonata in D Minor* (Follia)

Chapter 5
The Variation Principle

As a means of extending a motive into a longer melodic unit, the VARIA-TION PRINCIPLE predates the development of imitative counterpoint. Even before the *Ars Nova,* composers sometimes organized sections of a work by pre-senting a musical idea and then altering it so that the variety offered by new material was combined with the structural advantages of material previously heard. In the late Renaissance, a new use of the variation principle emerged in which not a fragment, but a complete theme was presented and varied in a number of ways. Such a series of complete variations constitutes not only a technique, but a *form.*

Two types of variation form occur in the Common Practice Era: series of variations that are continuous and those that are sectional. SECTIONAL VAR-IATIONS are each self-contained movements in which one or more aspects of the original theme are subject to variation. CONTINUOUS VARIATIONS, on the other hand, generally follow one another without pause and are often based on a single recurring element heard more or less unchanged in each variation.

CONTINUOUS VARIATIONS

The most important continuous variations of the Common Practice Era are those based on a BASSO OSTINATO (or GROUND BASS)—a recurring me-lodic and rhythmic pattern used throughout a movement or section. The ostin-ato occurs in Western music as early as the thirteenth century and is found regularly throughout the Renaissance. In the Baroque Era, the ostinato pat-tern serves as a unifying device for a series of variations while other aspects of the original material are altered.

The Basso Ostinato

Usually (but not always) in the bass, the ostinato pattern is often nothing more pretentious than a descending tetrachord.

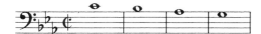

On the other hand, many composers employ longer and more complete ostinato patterns. Two such patterns are shown in Example 5–1.

EXAMPLE 5–1   Ostinato Bass Patterns

J. S. Bach, *Passacaglia and Fugue in C Minor*

Henry Purcell, *Dido and Aeneas*

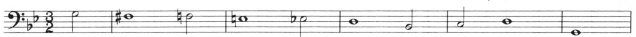

THE PASSACAGLIA

Apparently derived from certain sixteenth-century dances, the most important ostinato bass form of the Common Practice Period is the PASSACAGLIA—a melodic bass pattern which unifies a series of continuous variations. The ostinato pattern is usually heard several times although it may or may not coincide with the periodic structure of the upper voices.

A number of passages from Bach's *Passacaglia and Fugue in C Minor* are shown in Example 5–2. The eight measure ground bass that opens the work unifies the following variations. Notice the variety of material that Bach uses to accompany the ground bass.

EXAMPLE 5–2   J. S. Bach, *Passacaglia and Fugue in C Minor*

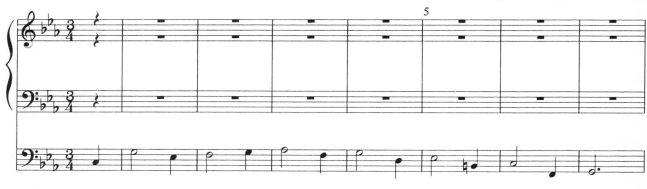

Measure 33

Measure 49

Measure 81

Measure 89

Measure 121

THE CHACONNE

A CHACONNE is based not on a melodic ostinato, but on a recurring *harmonic* pattern. While a passacaglia features a repeated bass and varied harmonies, the chaconne is the opposite—a fixed harmonic scheme with variable bass. Baroque composers often used the two terms interchangably, but today, a distinction between them is generally made.

The first nine variations (of fifty-two!) of Handel's *Chaconne in G Major* are shown in Example 5–3. The simple harmonic progression is unchanged throughout the work and even the bass, though ornamented, is left basically intact. Thus the confusion between the terms "passacaglia" and "chaconne" is easy to understand; Handel's work combines the essential features of both.

EXAMPLE 5–3

G. F. Handel, *Chaconne in G Major*

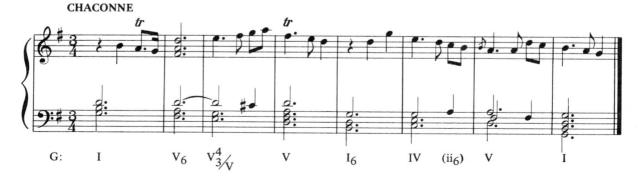

SECTIONAL VARIATIONS

Although each of the variations in the previous example is clearly defined, they are considered continuous because they are brief and cannot stand alone. Sectional variations, on the other hand, are usually based on material of at least a double period in length and can be heard as more or less complete.

THEME AND VARIATIONS

As a form, the THEME AND VARIATIONS developed during the seventeenth century from, among other influences, the practice of composing a variation or *double* to a movement in a suite of stylized dances. In Bach's *English Suite No. 1,* for example, the second of two Courantes is followed by two doubles clearly related to the original. The beginning of the Courante and of the two variations is shown in Example 5–4A, B, and C.

EXAMPLE 5–4   J. S. Bach, *English Suite No. 1*

A. Courante II

B. Double I

C. Double II

The theme and variations was an important form throughout the Common Practice Era. While in the eighteenth century a composer might write as many as thirty or more variations to a theme (with the performer at liberty to select from among them), Classical and Romantic variations are more often one complete, symmetrical composition. All of the movements are generally performed and in the sequence specified.

Fixed and Variable Elements

Because the simultaneous alteration of too many elements might cause disorientation, composers typically leave one or more parameters associated with the theme *fixed* while others are *varied*. A balance between fixed and variable elements helps create a unified composition based on a single theme rather than a succession of loosely related movements.

The Theme

Either newly composed or borrowed from an existing work, the theme upon which a set of sectional variations is based is often a complete, periodic melody with clearly defined melodic, harmonic, and rhythmic parameters. The formal construction is often binary with the repetition of one or both sections.

TECHNIQUES OF VARIATION

While two or more parameters may be varied simultaneously, one is usually dominant and determines the character of the movement. The most commonly varied elements are melody, rhythm, and harmony.

Melody as a Variable Element

The melodic variation of a theme is often as simple as the addition of nonharmonic tones. The melody *God Save The King (America),* for example, takes on a new perspective when embellished (Example 5–5).

EXAMPLE 5–5   *God Save the King,* Melodic Variation

Scale passages and other figuration provide another approach to melodic variation within the same harmonic scheme (Example 5–6).

EXAMPLE 5–6   Figural Variation

In both of the previous examples, the pitches of the melody are easy to identify although their metric positions are sometimes shifted.

Rhythm as a Variable Element

The theme may be varied by creating a new rhythmic figure which completely changes its character. Both syncopation and dotted rhythms provide distinctive contrast with the original material (Examples 5–7 and 5–8).

EXAMPLE 5–7   Rhythmic Variation: Syncopation

EXAMPLE 5–8   Rhythmic Variation: Dotted Rythms

A change of meter transforms the melody into a march (Example 5–9).

EXAMPLE 5–9   Rhythmic Variation: Metric Change

Harmony as a Variable Element

A change of mode occurs at some point in most sectional variations. Often clearly labeled "major" or "minor," a shift to the parallel key provides stark contrast even if the other parameters of the theme remain fixed (Example 5–10).

EXAMPLE 5–10   Harmonic Variation: Change of Mode

The variation of melody, rhythm, and harmony, used separately and in combination, as well as the alteration of other parameters (texture, for example) are seen in the seven variations Beethoven wrote on the tune *God Save the King*.

L. VAN BEETHOVEN, *SEVEN VARIATIONS ON GOD SAVE THE KING*

Like many of Beethoven's piano variations, those on *God Save the King* are of moderate technical difficulty but exhibit a wide range of variation techniques. The theme is comprised of a six measure repeated phrase followed by an eight measure repeated period. The harmonic setting is simple and chordal (Example 5–11).

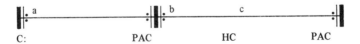

EXAMPLE 5–11   Theme

Variation I

The first variation is one of the most complex. Independent voices create a thick *contrapuntal texture* in which the melody, slightly embellished, remains distinct and in the uppermost voice. The simple beat division of the original is maintained, but the use of *syncopation* (measures 4 and 15) varies the rhythmic effect. In terms of cadential structure, the harmony remains fixed although there is more color provided by secondary dominants and chromatic nonharmonic tones (Example 5–12).

EXAMPLE 5–12   Variation 1

Variation II

Without pause, the second variation begins with a two-voice texture that alternates between counterpoint and accompanied melody. Compared to the first variation, the *change in texture* is dramatic. Despite a highly embellished melody, the theme is not difficult to identify. Harmony, rhythm, and form remain basically intact (Example 5–13).

EXAMPLE 5–13   Variation II

Variation III

Similar to the second variation in texture, Variation III features an *Alberti bass accompaniment*. The melody is fragmented through *rhythmic figuration* and *changes in register*. Again, form and harmony are fixed (Example 5–14).

EXAMPLE 5–14   Variation III

Variation IV

The chordal fourth variation provides *textural contrast* to the previous movements. The melody is spaced through *several registers* and *rhythmic figuration* creates an agitated effect (Example 5–15).

EXAMPLE 5–15   Variation IV

Variation V

Changes in *mode* and *character* dominate the fifth variation. The lyric nature of the movement *(con espressione)* contrasts sharply with the fourth variation. The use of the *borrowed division* of the beat likewise provides welcome relief. The harmonic plan includes a number of seventh chords and a Neapolitan six (Example 5–16).[1]

EXAMPLE 5–16   Variation V

[1]The Neapolitan Six, a major triad built on the lowered second scale degree, is discussed in Chapter 6.

Variation VI

Returning to the major mode, the sixth variation features a *change of meter*. The movement is set as a march with dotted rhythms providing yet another approach to the theme. The sixteenth note figuration in measure 13 anticipates the seventh variation which begins without pause (Example 5–17).

EXAMPLE 5–17   Variation VI

Allegro, Alla marcia

Variation VII

The finale is typical in that it is a *free variation* of the theme and includes an extended CODA (a section designed to create a sense of finality). Thus for the first time in the work, *form* appears as a variable element. The first phrase (ornamented with arpeggiated triads) is not repeated as before; the second and third phrases are not merely repeated, but varied with significant changes in *rhythm* and *accompaniment*.

The coda begins in measure 22 with a continuation of the sixteenth note figuration, but is interrupted by an Adagio setting in F major. A final flourish follows the return to the original meter and features the rhythmic complexity of two-against-three. A tonic pedal persists through a statement of part of the theme in the bass (Example 5–18).

EXAMPLE 5–18   Variation VII

Beethoven's *Variations on God Save the King* are a study in contrast, clarity, and economy. No movement features too much variety, yet each is unique. Especially in terms of texture, the work moves from complex to simple, and back again. The melody is embellished, broken, and transposed but remains always clear. The harmony and rhythm are varied, yet the original structures are always close at hand. Dramatic variations in mode, meter, and form are reserved for the final three variations respectively.

SUMMARY

Composers of the twentieth century have neglected neither the continuous nor the sectional variation forms. Hindemith, Piston, Copland, Schoenberg, and Webern, among others, have all contributed important works. In general, the following list of potential variable elements is valid for common practice and twentieth-century works alike (Example 5–19).

EXAMPLE 5–19   Potential Variable Elements

Melody	Key/Mode
Rhythm	Tempo
Form	Meter
Harmony	Dynamics
Texture	Register
Timbre (instrumentation)	Character (mood)
Accompaniment	

Discuss the variation form beginning in measure 9 of an aria from Henry Pucell's opera *Dido and Aeneas*.

Henry Purcell, *Dido's Lament*

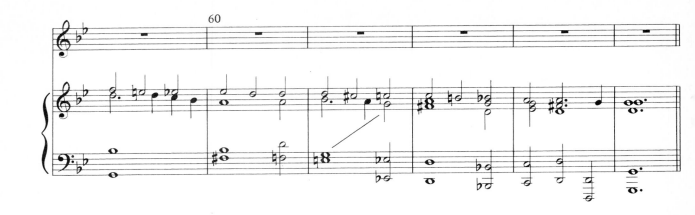

Name _____

Provide analysis as directed.

G. F. Handel, *Chaconne in G Major.*
Variations 1–5 (of 21)

von Weber, *Andante with Variations*

Provide analysis for the following theme and variations. Discuss the variation techniques employed as well as the overall balance between fixed and variable elements. Only the first portion of each variation is given.

Franz Schubert, *Ten Variations for Piano*

Chapter 6
Chromatic Resources

Introduction to Chapters 6 to 10: Materials of the Classical and Romantic Eras

Just as the chromatic experiments of the late sixteenth century had anticipated the end of the modal era, in the nineteenth century a number of factors led to a gradual dissolution of the tonal system. First, the chromatic embellishment of certain diatonic chords fostered a more liberal view of tertian materials. Second, traditional key relationships were enriched through remote and enharmonic modulations so that the formal implications of the dominant (in major) and the mediant (in minor) were lessened. Finally, experiments with nonfunctional and nontertian harmony paved the way for composers like Debussy, Stravinsky, and Bartók to found a new music for the twentieth century.

Lending stability to much music of the turbulent nineteenth century, however, were two great formal principles. Rooted in the dance, refined by Scarlatti and others, and synthesized in the works of Haydn and Mozart, the SONATA PRINCIPLE became the most dominant formal structure of the common practice era. The RONDO PRINCIPLE, Medieval in origin, reached full development in the eighteenth and nineteenth centuries. More than mere forms, these *principles* represent alternate means of balancing tension and relaxation, momentum and stasis, shape and growth.

After the complex and highly chromatic art of the Italian madrigalists went out of vogue during the early seventeenth century, composers were content for a time with the resources of diatonic harmony. While chromaticism is prevalent in the music of many Baroque and Classical composers, it most often stems from the use of materials that *embellish* rather than supplement diatonic triads. In short, the first two hundred years of the Common Practice Period was a time of conservative harmony. Enriching the traditional vocabulary, however, were several classes of chromatic chords that appeared throughout the Common Practice Era. *Borrowed Chords*, for example, exploit the close relationship between major and parallel minor keys; the *Diminished Seventh Chord* creates variety as well as harmonic tension; and certain *Altered Chords* (specifically those of subdominant function) allow a chromatic embellishment of the dominant.

BORROWED CHORDS

In the late Renaissance, before the major–minor system was firmly entrenched, composers routinely varied the mode of many triads. The dominant and subdominant triads, for example, appeared as both major and minor; the subtonic and leading tone triads were virtually interchangeable. In Example 6–1, the tonic, subdominant, and dominant triads appear as both major and minor. Notice also the use of the subtonic triad.

EXAMPLE 6–1   Guillaume Costeley, *Allon, Gay, Gay*

As the tonal system gained momentum during the seventeenth century, composers generally adhered to the materials of *either* the major or minor mode. One of several conventional exceptions to diatonic harmony, however, is the so-called "borrowed" relationship—a free exchange ("borrowing") of triads between major and parallel minor keys.[1] Most often, a BORROWED CHORD is one altered only in mode. The function of the triad is unchanged while at the same time, new color is introduced.

One example of a borrowed chord has already been discussed: the Picardy Third. While this major tonic was used in a minor key for practical reasons (to avoid intonation problems), other triads were sometimes borrowed simply for the sake of their color.

Haydn, for example, suddenly introduces a minor tonic in his *Sonatina in C Major* (Example 6–2). Without a loss of tonality, there is a dramatic change in color.

EXAMPLE 6–2   Joseph Haydn, *Sonatina in C Major*

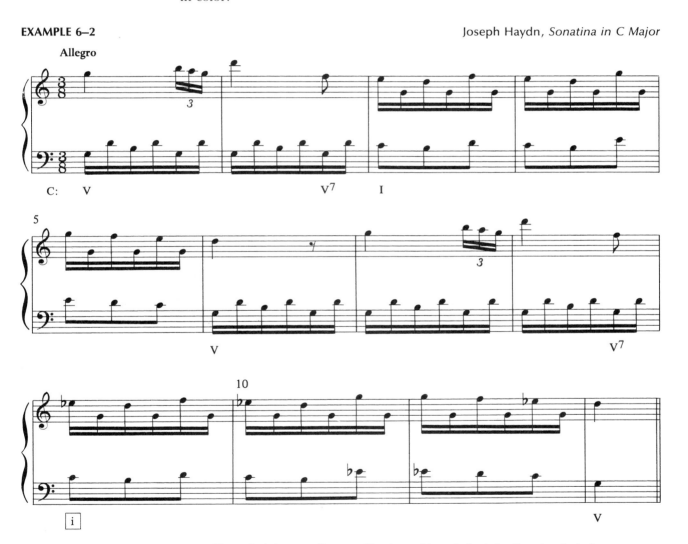

---

[1]Some find the term "borrowed" to be problematic for it implies, they feel, that composers somehow felt it necessary to justify their use of chromatic materials. This is not true, of course; composers of common practice music made harmonic choices based on the way they wanted the music to sound (as we have seen, for example, they used the leading tone in minor keys). The term "borrowed," however, reflects the fact that many (not all) of the chromatic materials employed in the Common Practice Period do have a close relationship with the parallel major/minor keys. The term has become a fairly standard way of expressing this relationship.

Composers sometimes chose to employ borrowed chords altered not only in mode, but those having a raised or lowered root as well. In major, the borrowed submediant and mediant were especially common.[2]

C: I   ♭III   ♭VI

Chromatic Mediants

Used in major, the chords above (borrowed mediant and submediant) are examples of altered or CHROMATIC MEDIANTS. The term "mediant" here refers to a root relationship that includes both the mediant proper, and the submediant. These chords are examples of THIRD RELATION—a root movement (or key relationship) by third which produces a chromatic cross relationship. In addition to chords borrowed from the parallel minor (less often the parallel major), composers employed chromatic mediants without the "borrowed" relationship. In C major, for example, an A major or an E major chord (used as other than a secondary dominant) is neither diatonic nor borrowed. By 1825, third relation (including both borrowed and other chromatic root movement by third) was employed regularly as an expansion of diatonic resources (Example 6–3).

EXAMPLE 6–3   Third Relation

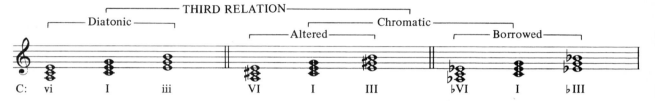

In the example below, Brahms contrasts diatonic triads in C major with subdominant and submediant triads borrowed from the parallel minor (Example 6–4).

EXAMPLE 6–4   Johannes Brahms,
Symphony No. 3 in F Major, Op. 90

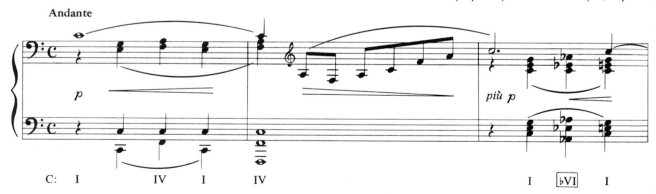

[2]In analysis, a lowered root is indicated by placing a flat (or natural) sign before the Roman numeral. The quality of the triad is indicated in the usual way. A sharp sign before a Roman numeral or a diagonal line through it indicates a raised root.

C: ♭VI   C: III   C: I̸V

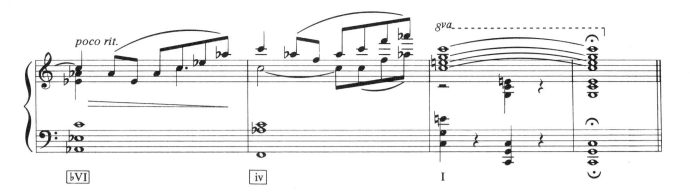

A number of composers were fond of ending a work with a plagal cadence borrowed from the parallel key. In Example 6–5, Brahms chooses the diminished (rather than minor) supertonic for its unique plagal effect.

EXAMPLE 6–5

Johannes Brahms, *Die Mainacht*

Voice Leading in Borrowed and Other Altered Chords

In four-part vocal composition, traditional guidelines for the introduction and resolution of altered tones apply: they are approached and resolved by step. Cross relationships should be avoided, and in most cases, doubling is limited to diatonic pitches. Notice the tonicization of the minor subdominant in Bach's harmonization of the chorale melody *Ach Gott und Herr* (Example 6–6).

EXAMPLE 6–6

J.S. Bach, Chorale Harmonization,
Ach Gott und Herr

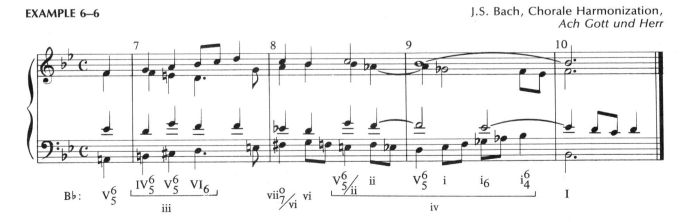

Although borrowed chords are often used for the value of their harmonic color, just as often, they initiate a remote tonal shift. Modulation through change of mode will be discussed in Chapter 7.

THE DIMINISHED SEVENTH CHORD

Because the fully diminished leading tone seventh chord is diatonic to the minor mode, its use in major constitutes another category of borrowed chord.

By the end of the seventeenth century, the fully diminished seventh was a common substitute for the dominant in both major and minor keys. Although the chord contains two tritones, the resolution often includes a leap in one or more voices (Example 6–7). Another common resolution of the diminished seventh chord is by step to a chord with doubled third; both of the tritones expand or contract characteristically (Example 6–8).

EXAMPLE 6–7

J.S. Bach, Chorale Harmonization,
Für Freuden laßt uns springen

EXAMPLE 6–8

J.S. Bach, Chorale Harmonization,
Mach's mit mir, Gott, nach deiner

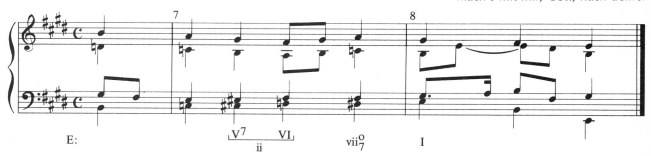

In the Classical Era, the diminished seventh was equally prevalent. Mozart, for example, uses it to tonicize the dominant area in B♭ major (Example 6–9). Despite the numerous accidentals and the chromatic melody, however, the progressions in measures 16 and 18 render the tonality secure.

EXAMPLE 6–9

W.A. Mozart, *Sonata in E♭ Major, K. 282,*
Second Movement

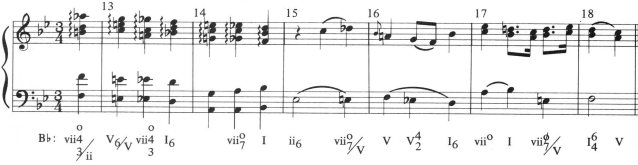

As the taste for chromaticism and the tendency toward some tonal ambiguity increased during the nineteenth century, composers did not overlook enharmonic interpretations of the diminished seventh chord (discussed in Chapters 7 and 10).

ALTERED CHORDS OF SUBDOMINANT FUNCTION

The embellishment of diatonic triads with chromatic neighboring and passing tones led to two very common types of altered chord—the Augmented Sixth and the Neapolitan.

AUGMENTED SIXTH CHORDS

AUGMENTED SIXTH CHORDS evolved through chromatic linear motion in the progression iv_6–V in minor. A chromatic passing tone provided a leading tone to the dominant pitch and created the interval of an augmented sixth with the bass (Example 6–10A). Later, the chromatic pitch was incorporated into the chord itself (Example 6–10B).

EXAMPLE 6–10   Development of the Augmented
Sixth Chord

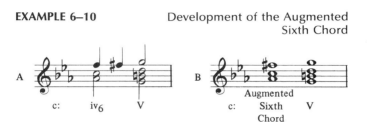

There are three varieties of augmented sixth chord. Although the origin of the names is obscure, they are known almost universally as *Italian, French,* and *German* respectively. The basic triad seen in Example 6–10B above appears in all three varieties. The most characteristic element, however, is the augmented sixth itself which expands to the octave in contrary motion:

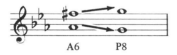

Unfortunately, there are no uniform analytical symbols for augmented sixth chords. In some texts, a conventional Roman numeral with figured bass is employed; in others, the geographical name is abbreviated. While the latter designation has the advantage of simplicity and will be used in this text, students must not ignore the important relationship between the root of the chord and the diatonic scale (See footnote, page 141).

The Italian Six $\boxed{It_6}$

The basic augmented sixth sonority is the ITALIAN SIX; its root is the *raised* fourth scale degree. The third and fifth are diatonic in the minor key.

When inverted, the diminished third (F♯–A♭ in the example above) becomes the characteristic augmented sixth and in resolution, expands to the octave. It is worth noting that augmented sixth chords are the only chords in the common practice vocabulary that include a diminished third.

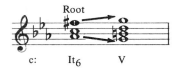

Construction. The construction of an Italian six in minor is a three step process: begin with the subdominant triad, raise the root, and write in first inversion.

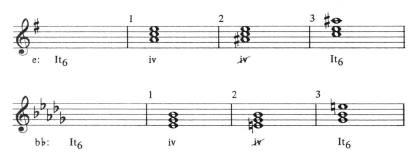

In major, the Italian six is constructed the same way beginning with the subdominant triad *borrowed* from the parallel minor.

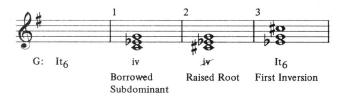

Use of the Italian Six. The Italian six usually progresses to the dominant or tonic six–four. Notice that in Example 6–11 the outer voices (the augmented sixth) expand to the octave; the remaining voice moves stepwise.

EXAMPLE 6–11   Joseph Haydn, *Sonata in G Major,*
First Movement

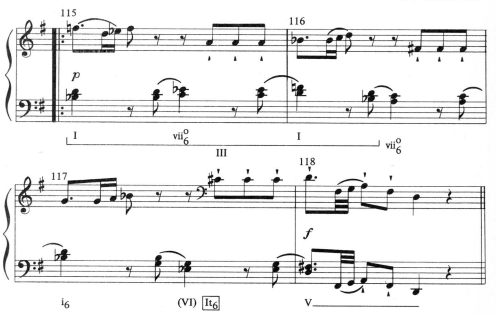

When the Italian six resolves to a dominant seventh, the octave expansion of the augmented sixth is sometimes abandoned (Example 6–12).

EXAMPLE 6–12

L. van Beethoven,
Die Ehre Gottes aus der Natur

Their sound rings out His Ho - ly Name.
That Na - ture hath for us un - furl'd.

B♭:   It₆   V⁷   I

Because they are strongly subdominant in function, augmented sixth chords are often included in tonicizations. Beethoven, for example, opens his *Sonata in E♭ Major* (Op. 81a) with a tonicization of the submediant that includes an Italian six (Example 6–13).

EXAMPLE 6–13

L. van Beethoven, *Sonata in E♭ Major*, Op. 81a, First Movement

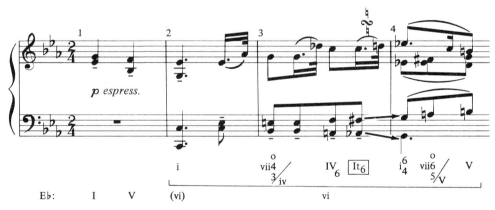

E♭:   I   V   (vi)   vi

The German Six–Five Gr^6_5

Like the Italian six, the root of the GERMAN SIX–FIVE is the raised fourth scale degree. In addition to the three basic pitches of the Italian six, the German six–five includes a diminished seventh above the root:

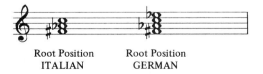

Root Position   Root Position
ITALIAN   GERMAN

As the name indicates, the German six–five is found typically in first inversion:

Root

Construction. In minor, the construction of a German six–five is again a three step process: begin with a subdominant *seventh,* raise the root, and write in first inversion.

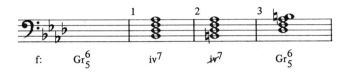

In major keys, construction of the German six–five begins with the borrowed subdominant and follows the same process.

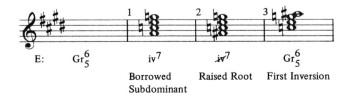

Use of the German Six–Five. The most typical resolution of the German six–five is not to dominant, but to tonic six–four. If the augmented sixth is resolved characteristically in a progression to the dominant, an inner voice must move either in parallel perfect fifths with the bass or leap a diminished fourth to the leading tone (Example 6–14). Neither possibility was favored by common practice composers.

EXAMPLE 6–14

Problems of Voice Leading
in the German Six–Five

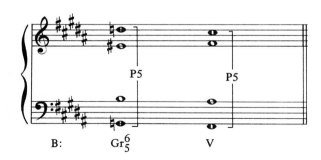

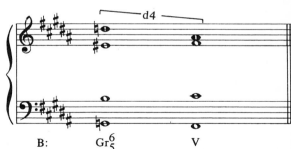

To avoid these problems of voice leading, composers most often precede the dominant by tonic six–four (Example 6–15).

EXAMPLE 6–15 Resolution of German
Six–Five to Tonic Six–Four

Passages in which the German six–five resolves to tonic six–four are shown in Examples 6–16A and 6–16B.

EXAMPLE 6–16A

Franz Schubert, *Am Grabe Anselmos*
Op. 6, No. 3

EXAMPLE 6–16B

Robert Schumann, *Waltz* from *Albumblätter*
Op. 124, No. 2

Composers found individual solutions to the problem of voice leading when a progression of the German six–five to dominant was desired. An arpeggiation (Example 6–17) permits all chord members to be sounded, yet spaced so that the perfect fifths are several beats apart.

EXAMPLE 6–17

W.A. Mozart, *Sonata in D Major*, K. 284,
First Movement

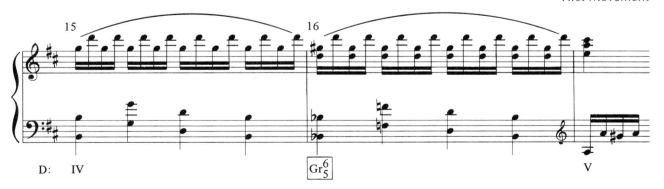

In Example 6–18, Mozart omits the fifth of the dominant seventh that follows a German six–five.

EXAMPLE 6–18

The Enharmonic German Six–Five

In major keys, the German six–five occurs occasionally with the perfect fifth above the bass spelled enharmonically as a doubly augmented fourth.

In a resolution to the dominant, the unusual spelling of the German six–five avoids the visual (but not the aural) effect of parallel fifths (Example 6–19).

EXAMPLE 6–19 Enharmonic German Six–Five

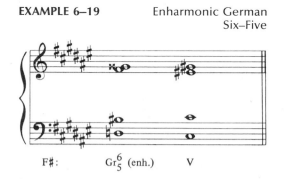

An enharmonic German six–five opens Schumann's *An Leuchtenden Sommermorgen* (Example 6–20).

EXAMPLE 6–20

Robert Schumann,
Am Leuchtenden Sommermorgen

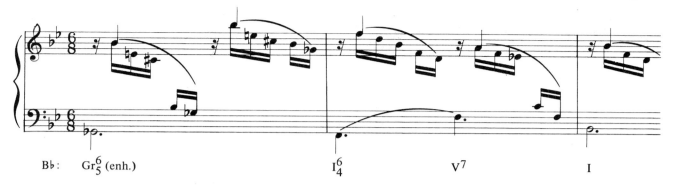

Bb: Gr$_5^6$ (enh.)   I$_4^6$ V^7 I

The French Four–Three $\boxed{\text{Fr}_3^4}$

The FRENCH FOUR–THREE differs from both the Italian and German augmented sixth chords in that the raised fourth scale degree is not the root, but the third. The second scale degree is the root; the other three pitches are those of the Italian six.

c: Root Position   Root Position   Root Position
       ITALIAN   GERMAN   FRENCH

The French four–three is usually employed in second inversion:

c: Fr$_3^4$

Construction. The French four–three is constructed in major or minor by beginning with a half diminished supertonic seventh (a borrowed chord in major), raising the *third*, and writing in *second* inversion.

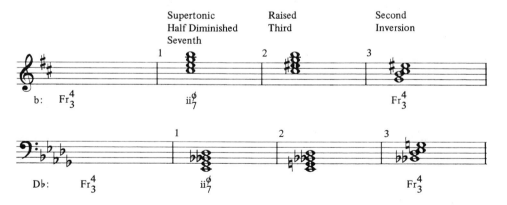

Use of the French Four–Three. The typical resolution of the French four–three is the same as that of the other augmented sixth chords: to the dominant or tonic six–four. In example 6–21, Schubert employs the French four–three to add color to a half cadence.

EXAMPLE 6–21

Franz Schubert, *Der Kreuzzug*

In the well-known passage below, the Fr$_3^4$–V^7 progression is obscured by lengthy appoggiaturas (Example 6–22).

EXAMPLE 6–22

Richard Wagner, *Tristan und Isolde*, Prelude

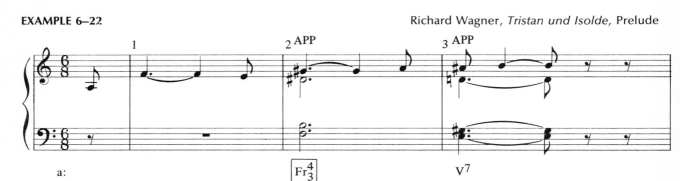

An alternate resolution of the French four–three to tonic six–four is seen in Example 6–23.

EXAMPLE 6–23

Frédéric Chopin, *Nocturne*, Op. 48, No. 2

Voice Leading in the Augmented Sixth

The key to a characteristic use of augmented sixth chords is the resolution of the augmented sixth to the octave. Other voices are retained (in a progression to tonic six–four) or resolved stepwise (to dominant or dominant seventh).

Doubling. All four chord tones should be present in the German six–five and the French four–three. The fifth is normally doubled in the Italian six.

THE NEAPOLITAN SIX CHORD $\boxed{N_6}$

Like the augmented sixth chords, the NEAPOLITAN SIX evolved through linear motion in the progression iv–V in minor. A chromatic upper neighbor eventually became incorporated into the chord as a new root. (Example 6–24).

EXAMPLE 6–24   Development of the Neapolitan Six

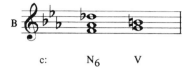

Construction of the Neapolitan Six

The Neapolitan six is a major triad built on the *lowered* second scale degree; it typically occurs in first inversion.[3]

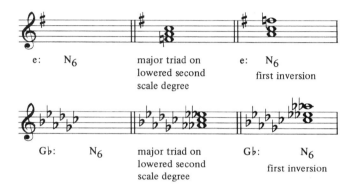

Use of the Neapolitan Six

Subdominant in function, the Neapolitan six resolves to dominant or tonic six–four. Like other chromatic chords, it frequently occurs as a passing sonority between diatonic triads. In the following example, the Neapolitan six connects the subdominant and dominant chords in a stepwise progression (Example 6–25).

EXAMPLE 6–25   G.F. Handel, *Suite in G Minor*, Chaconne
(Variation 13)

[3]Chromatic chords identified in this text with geographical abbreviations are sometimes shown in other sources as altered Roman numerals with appropriate figured bass.

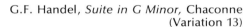

iv N_6 V^7 i   V   i

Nonharmonic tones add color to the passage below which features a Neapolitan six in a resolution to tonic six–four (Example 6–26).

EXAMPLE 6–26

Johannes Brahms, *Intermezzo in A Major,*
Op. 118, No. 2

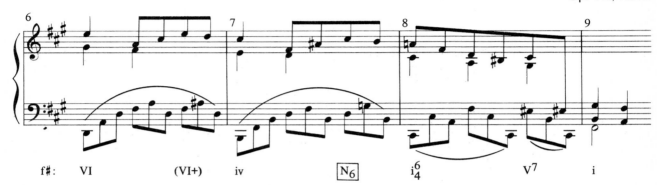

f#:   VI   (VI+)   iv N_6 i_4^6 V^7 i

In the example below, the Neapolitan six follows the tonic and progresses to tonic six–four (Example 6–27).

EXAMPLE 6–27

L. van Beethoven, *Sonata No. 23 in F Minor,*
Op. 57, First Movement

Ab: I V^7 I_6

N_6 I_4^6 V^7

The Root Position Neapolitan

Although the Neapolitan is most often found in first inversion, composers sometimes employed it in root position as well. Chopin's brief but harmonically interesting *Prelude* Op. 28, No. 2 includes a progression of the root position Neapolitan to dominant seventh (Example 6–28).

EXAMPLE 6–28   Frédéric Chopin, *Prelude*, Op. 28, No. 2

As composers began to experiment with new tonal relationships in the mid–nineteenth century, the Neapolitan region was sometimes tonicized. In Example 6–29, the root position Neapolitan is preceded by its dominant seventh.

EXAMPLE 6–29   Frédéric Chopin, *Mazurka*, Op. 7, No. 2

Voice Leading in the Neapolitan Six

Composers of the Common Practice Period adopted a standard approach to voice leading in the Neapolitan six.

1. The third (the bass) is doubled most consistently.
2. In a progression to dominant, one voice moves by descending diminished third—from the lowered second scale degree to the leading tone.

b: VI   N₆   V

Typical Resolution of N$_6$ to V

The cross relationship between C and C♯ in the example above was considered preferable to a resolution involving an augmented second.

b: VI   N₆   V

Unusual Resolution of N$_6$ to V

When the Neapolitan six progresses to tonic six–four before resolving to the dominant, both the cross relationship and the awkward augmented second are eliminated. Missing too, however, is the striking tritone root relationship.

SUMMARY

Together with secondary dominants, the diminished seventh as well as borrowed and altered chords constitute the major chromatic resource in the Baroque and Classical periods. Typically resolved to diatonic harmonies, these chords provided variety without seriously obscuring tonality. While later composers expanded the chromatic vocabulary, Bach, Mozart, and even Beethoven limited themselves largely to these few alternatives to diatonic triads.

Name _____

In four-part vocal style, construct and resolve the chords indicated.

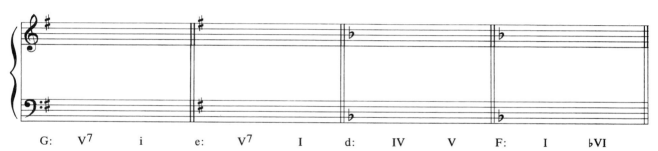

G: V⁷ i e: V⁷ I d: IV V F: I ♭VI

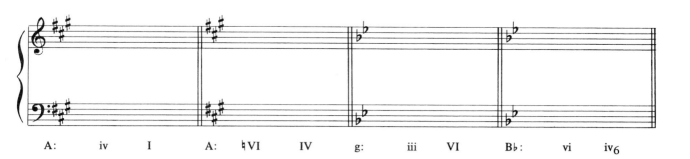

A: iv I A: ♮VI IV g: iii VI B♭: vi iv₆

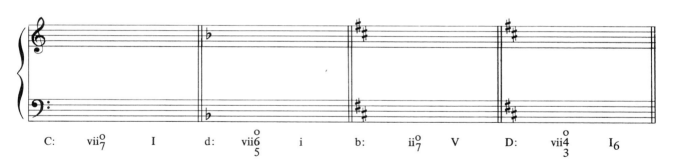

C: vii°₇ I d: vii°⁶₅ i b: ii°₇ V D: vii°⁴₃ I₆

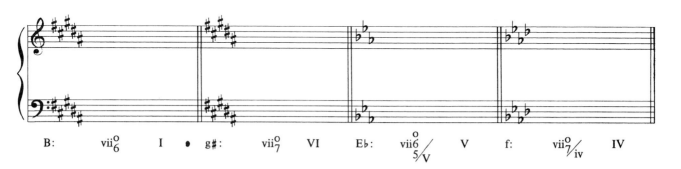

B: vii°₆ I g♯: vii°₇ VI E♭: vii°⁶₅/V V f: vii°₇/iv IV

Construct and resolve the following chords in four-part vocal style.

d: It$_6$ V   D: It$_6$ I$_4^6$ a: It$_6$ V   C: It$_6$ I$_4^6$

f#: Gr$_5^6$ i$_4^6$ B♭: Gr$_5^6$ I$_4^6$ g: Gr$_5^6$ V^7 G: Gr$_5^6$ (enh.)   I$_4^6$

b♭: Fr$_3^4$ i$_4^6$ E: Fr$_3^4$ V   d: Fr$_3^4$ V^7 E♭: Fr$_3^4$ I$_4^6$

g#: N$_6$ V   a: N$_6$ i$_4^6$ A♭: N$_6$ V   e: N$_6$ i$_4^6$

Identify the following triads and chords in the keys indicated. Consider all chromatic possibilities: secondary dominants, diminished and half diminished seventh chords, borrowed and altered chords.

d: _____   d: _____   d: _____   B: _____   B: _____   B: _____

Ab: _____   Ab: _____   Ab: _____   e: _____   e: _____   e: _____

b: _____   b: _____   b: _____   Bb: _____   Bb: _____   Bb: _____

c#: _____   c#: _____   c#: _____   F: _____   F: _____   F: _____

g: _____   g: _____   g: _____   C: _____   C: _____   C: _____

Provide harmonic analysis for the following.

Robert Schumann, *Waltz* from *Albumblätter*

Provide harmonic analysis for the following passage.

Robert Schumann, "The Poet Speaks" from
Scenes from Childhood

Provide harmonic analysis for the following passages.

Franz Schubert, *Sonata in E♭ Major,* Third
Movement

c:

L. van Beethoven, *Sonata in C♯ Minor,*
Op. 27, No. 2, First Movement

Continue as in the preceding exercises.

Johannes Brahms, *Wie Melodien zieht es mir*,
Op. 105, No. 1

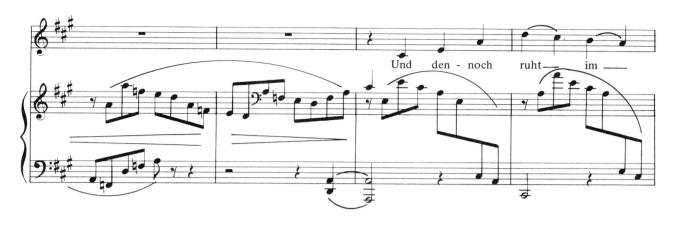

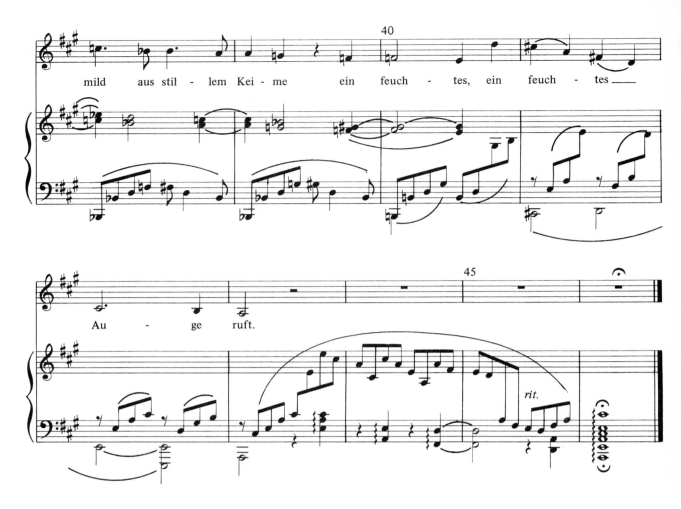

mild aus stil - lem Kei - me ein feuch - tes, ein feuch - tes _____

Au - ge ruft.

Franz Schubert, *Mass in E♭ Major*

do - na no - bis pa - cem, do - na

do - na no - bis pa - cem,

do - na no - bis pa - cem, do - na

do - na no - bis pa - cem,

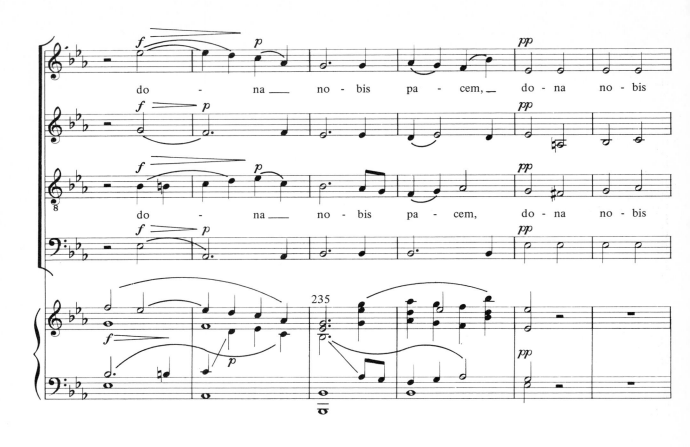

Chapter 7
Chromatic and Enharmonic Key Relationships

When composers of the seventeenth and eighteenth centuries changed keys during the course of a work, they most often chose those that were closely related. While a Baroque or Classical composer might touch upon a number of foreign keys during the development of a theme, the keys of the themes themselves were usually closely related. Bach, Mozart, and even Haydn were tentative in their use of remote keys. While lingering intonation problems account for some of this conservatism, just as limiting was the traditional use of certain key relationships in defining formal structure.

In the nineteenth century, however, a number of new tonal relationships gained favor—particularly that between the tonic and a chromatic mediant. Where Mozart would have modulated from C major to G major, Beethoven was just as likely to state a new theme in E, E♭, A, or A♭ major. By 1825, improvements in the construction of instruments and the increasing use of Twelve Tone Equal Temperament made modulation to any key feasible. More than any technical improvement, however, it was the composers' desire to revitalize tertian materials that led to the employment of innovative key relationships.

MODULATION THROUGH CHANGE OF MODE

For the return of the second theme in his *Sonata in C Major* (Op. 53), Beethoven chooses the chromatic submediant (A major). The new key is fresh and welcome, yet because the formal structure of a sonata-form depends upon a return to the tonic key (See Chapter 8), Beethoven shifts abruptly to C major by changing the mode of the tonic triad in the old key (A major) and using it as a common chord in the modulation.

$$\text{A:} \quad \text{I}_4^6 \quad \text{V}^7 \quad \boxed{\begin{array}{c}\text{i} \\ \text{vi}\end{array}}^{\text{change of mode}} \quad \dots \text{I}_4^6 \quad \text{V}^7 \quad \text{I}$$

Without the change of mode, a rapid modulation to C major would be less smooth. Upon hearing the A minor triad (Example 7–1, measure 200), the listener *immediately* accepts the change of mode; there is no tonal disorientation.

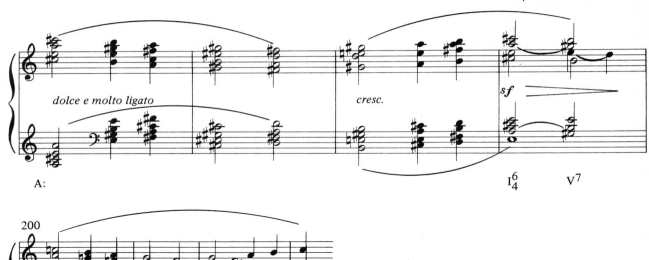

A:
I_4^6 V^7

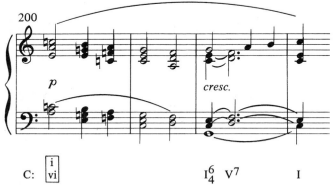

C: [i / vi]
I_4^6 V^7 I

The passage above illustrates MODULATION THROUGH CHANGE OF MODE—a modulation by common chord borrowed from the parallel key. In order to more fully appreciate the potential role of borrowed chords in remote modulation, it is helpful to review the close relationship between the triads in parallel keys.

1. The DOMINANT and LEADING TONE triads are identical in major and parallel minor:

E: V viiᵒ   e: V viiᵒ

2. The TONIC and SUBDOMINANT triads differ only in quality:

E: I IV   e: i iv

3. Depending on the form of minor employed, the SUPERTONIC triads may be the same or different in quality:

E: ii   e: iiᵒ ii

4. The MEDIANT and SUBMEDIANT triads have different roots and differ in quality:

E: iii   vi   e: III   VI

Any triad from the parallel key can be used as a borrowed pivot chord, but the tonic and subdominant are especially common. Once the borrowed chord is introduced and reinterpreted in the parallel key, a significant change in diatonic material has been made *without a loss of tonality*.

In Example 7–2, Schubert modulates from G major to E♭ major through change of mode. The two keys are remote, yet by introducing a minor tonic in the old key, the composer provides a closely related link with the new key—E♭ major.

G: ii₆   V   [i]
E♭:   [iii]   . . .   I₄⁶   V⁷   I

EXAMPLE 7–2   Franz Schubert, *Sehnsucht*, Op. 8, No. 2

In Example 7–3, a change of mode in the tonic chord (D major to D minor) introduces a new key—B♭ major. A further tonal shift to G minor is through conventional common chord.

EXAMPLE 7–3

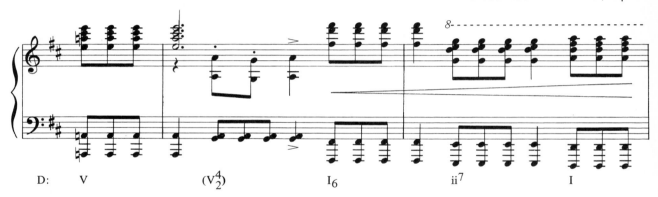

D: V   (V$^4_2$)   I$_6$ ii^7 I

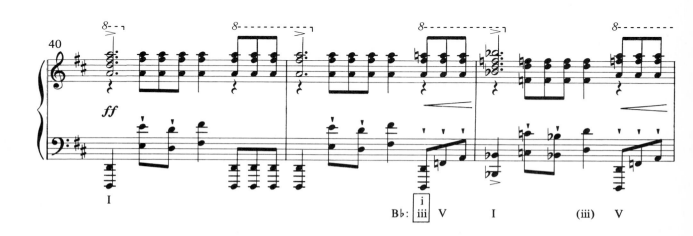

ff

I

B♭: iii | i | V   I   (iii)   V

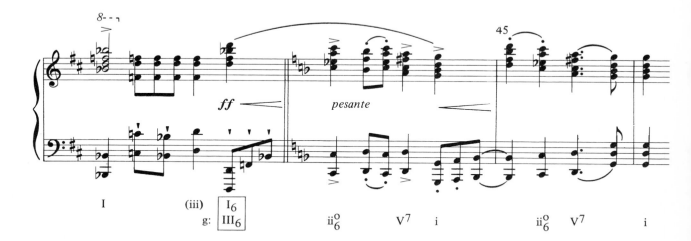

ff   pesante

I   (iii) | I$_6$ |
       g: | III$_6$ | ii$^o_6$ V^7 i   ii$^o_6$ V^7 i

In another example from Schubert's richly varied *lieder*, a change of mode initiates a modulation from B♭ major to G♭ major and back again. The G♭ major chord is first heard as a borrowed submediant; as the progression continues, however, its role as a temporary tonic is clear. The return to B♭ major is accomplished by reversing the process: the B♭ major chord is heard as a chromatic mediant in G♭ major (Example 7–4).

EXAMPLE 7–4   Franz Schubert, *Die Sterne*, Op. 96, No. 1

ENHARMONIC MODULATION

While borrowed chords and chromatic mediants facilitate modulation to foreign keys, nineteenth-century composers, just as often, chose ENHARMONIC RELATIONSHIPS to initiate sudden tonal shifts. Chopin, for example, moves away from B minor giving the impression that F# minor is the tonal goal; a sudden reinterpretation of the C# major triad (V in F# minor) as a Db major triad, however, introduces F minor and by change of mode, F major (Example 7–5).

EXAMPLE 7–5   Frédéric Chopin, *Etude*, Op. 25, No. 3

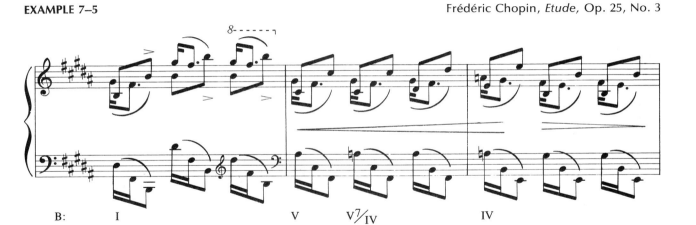

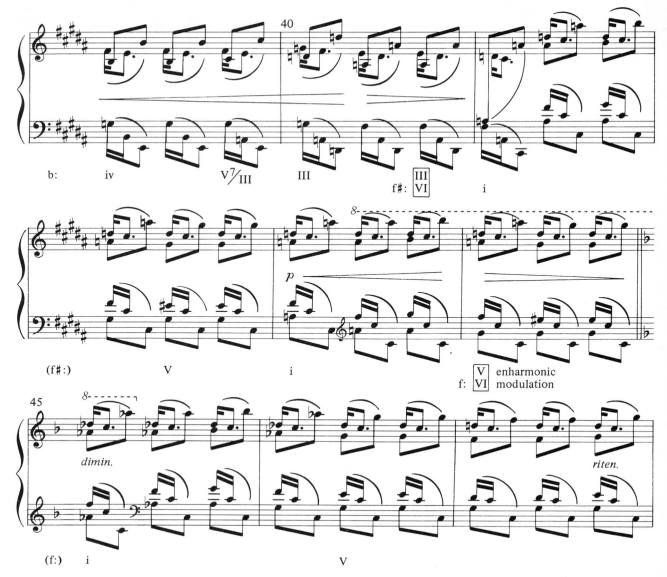

The striking harmonic changes seen in the example above became increasingly popular during the nineteenth century. In addition to such free enharmonic relationships, however, several specific chords were regularly employed as pivots in modulations to foreign keys: the *diminished seventh chord*, the *German six–five,* and the *Neapolitan six.*

THE DIMINISHED SEVENTH AS ENHARMONIC PIVOT

The fully diminished seventh is one of the most ambiguous and colorful chords in the common practice vocabulary. Because it is constructed entirely of minor thirds, inversions cannot be discerned aurally. The chord has only two half step transpositions before the pitches of the original sonority are duplicated enharmonically.

In conventional use, the diminished seventh is built on the leading tone of the key in which it has dominant function; the resolution is to tonic.

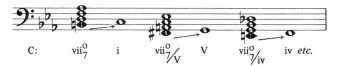

Because the function of the leading tone is identified only *through resolution,* each of the four pitches in a given diminished seventh chord has the potential of functioning as a leading tone and thus establishing a different tonic. In other words, a single diminished seventh chord has potential dominant function in at least eight different keys—four major, and four minor.

To illustrate this phenomenon, consider the diminished seventh chord on B. The characteristic resolution would be to a C major or minor triad:

Inverted, the diminished seventh on B has a similar resolution: to a root position or inverted C major or minor triad:

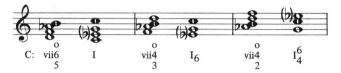

To the listener, however, the first inversion diminished seventh on B has the same *sound* as a root position diminished seventh on D. The chord on D would function in the key of E♭ (major or minor) and regardless of how the chord is actually notated on the printed page, a resolution to E♭ major *or* minor is an alternate possibility.

Likewise, the second and third inversions of the diminished seventh on B have enharmonic interpretations as well.

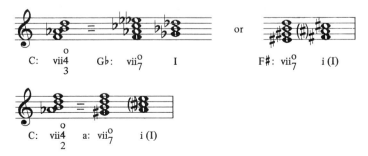

While enharmonic interpretations of the diminished seventh were not unknown in the seventeenth and eighteenth centuries, it was in the Romantic Era that the ambiguity of the chord was more fully exploited.

In the first movement of his *Sonata in C Minor* (Op. 13), Beethoven employs the diminished seventh in an enharmonic relationship to modulate from G minor to E minor. Naturally, the change of spelling in measure 135 of Example 7–6 is not evident to the listener; when an E minor chord appears instead of the expected G minor, however, the former is accepted as a new tonic.

EXAMPLE 7–6

L. van Beethoven, *Sonata in C Minor,*
Op. 13, First Movement

Not all composers actually respelled the chord in the new key as Beethoven did in the previous example. Mendelssohn uses a similar progression to tonicize the mediant in F♯ minor, although the spelling is not changed (Example 7–7).

EXAMPLE 7–7

Felix Mendelssohn, *Capriccio,* Op. 5

While Mendelssohn returns immediately to F♯ minor, the shift to A major just as easily could have gone on indefinitely. As has been discussed previously, modulation depends less on *means* than on the duration of the new area.

THE GERMAN SIX–FIVE AS ENHARMONIC PIVOT

While the German six–five was an important color chord throughout the Common Practice Period, not until the nineteenth century was the enharmonic potential of the chord fully realized. The German six–five is a major triad with augmented sixth above the bass; its *sound* is the same as that of dominant seventh chord (a major triad with minor seventh above the bass).

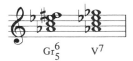

The listener is not aware of the function of the German six–five/dominant seventh sonority until it is resolved; both resolutions are familiar and *either* is accepted. In C minor, for example, the German six–five may resolve traditionally to tonic six–four, *or* it may function enharmonically as the dominant seventh of Db major.

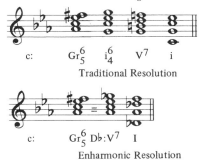

The enharmonic progression sketched above is seen in Example 7–8. Although spelled as a dominant seventh, the pivot is heard first as a German six–five in C minor. When the Db major triad follows, however, the enharmonic dominant role is clear.

EXAMPLE 7–8

Frédéric Chopin, *Prelude in D Minor,*
Op. 28, No. 24

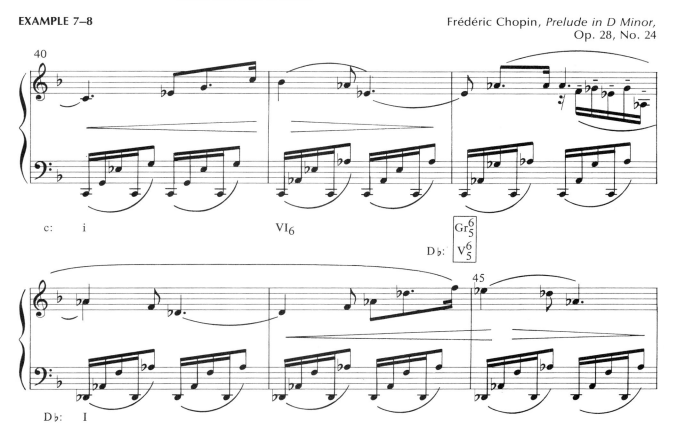

Any dominant seventh chord can be reinterpreted enharmonically as a German six–five. In C♯ minor, for example, the dominant seventh may form an enharmonic pivot in a modulation to C major (or less smoothly, C minor).

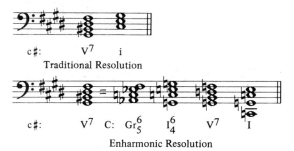

c♯:   V⁷   i

Traditional Resolution

c♯:   V⁷   C: Gr⁶₅   I⁶₄   V⁷   I

Enharmonic Resolution

A *secondary* dominant seventh/German six–five relationship may be used to introduce still other remote key areas. In E major, for example, a tonicization of the subdominant is no surprise; reinterpreted enharmonically, however, V⁷/IV becomes a German six–five in A♭ major.

E: V⁷   I | V⁷/IV |
         A♭: | G⁶₅ | I⁶₄   V⁷   I

The progression above is taken from Chopin's *Nocturne in C♯ Minor* (Example 7–9). Heard first as a secondary dominant seventh, the chord on the final beat of measure 48 is resolved as if it were a German six–five in A♭ major.

EXAMPLE 7–9   Frédéric Chopin, *Nocturne in C♯ Minor*,
                                                                Op. 27, No. 1

Ab: V⁷   I

Sometimes the German six–five is used enharmonically in other than its standard first inversion form. In *Todessehen*, Brahms moves from A major to F major through a chromatic mediant/dominant relationship. Once F major has been established, the dominant seventh in measure 48 is used as an enharmonic German six–five (actually in root position) in E major (Example 7–10).

EXAMPLE 7–10

Johannes Brahms, *Todessehen*,
Op. 86, No. 6

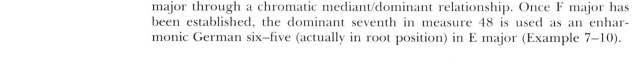

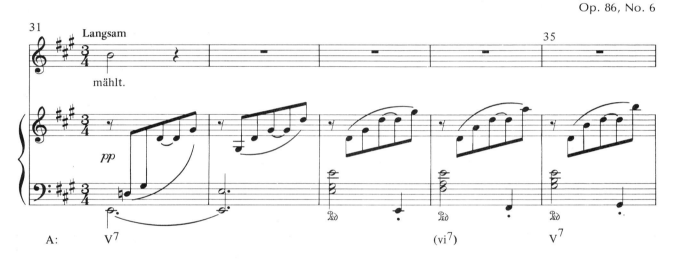

THE NEAPOLITAN SIX AS ENHARMONIC PIVOT

The Neapolitan six offered nineteenth-century composers an additional opportunity to use old materials in new ways. Like all major triads, the Neapolitan six has the potential of dominant function. Reinterpreted literally as a dominant, the chord serves as the pivot in a modulation up or down a tritone from the original key.

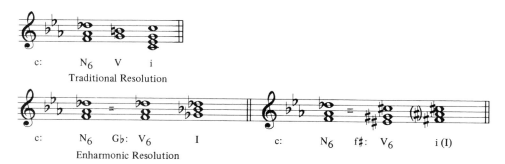

c: N₆   V   i

Traditional Resolution

c: N₆   G♭: V₆   I   c: N₆   f♯: V₆   i (I)

Enharmonic Resolution

Naturally, the process can be reversed with a major triad being reinterpreted as a Neapolitan six. In the passage below, the D♭ major triad before the double bar is heard as tonic. When a dominant seventh on G follows, however, the D♭ major chord is heard retroactively as a Neapolitan (in root position) in C major. The modulation to C major is short lived, but distinct nonetheless (Example 7–11).

EXAMPLE 7–11

Robert Schumann, *Phantasiestücke,*
Op. 12, No. 3

D♭:   V⁷/vi   vi   vii°₇/V   V/V   V⁷   C: I / N

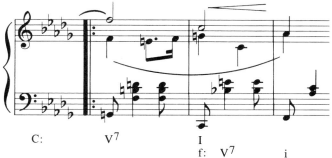

C: V⁷   I   f: V⁷   i

SUMMARY

By the end of the third quarter of the nineteenth century, composers were no longer limited to the diatonic chords in any one major or minor key. Augmented sixth, Neapolitan, and diminished seventh chords provided variety as they facilitated modulation to remote areas. The freedom composers allowed themselves to progress less in terms of function than color gradually led to a questioning of the tonal system itself. In addition to the enharmonic relationships discussed in this chapter, other chromatic and altered chords, extended tertian structures, unresolved dissonance, and nonfunctional progressions helped pave the way for the final dissolution of the common practice style.

Study the model and sketch similar modulations using borrowed chords of various types. Use a variety of chords to establish the old and new keys. Include all accidentals and Roman numeral analysis.

A major to C major—change of mode in tonic triad

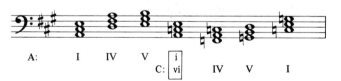

A: I   IV   V | i |
                               C: | vi | IV   V   I

a. *G major to E♭ major*—change of mode in tonic triad

G:

b. *C major to F minor*—change of mode in subdominant triad

C:

c. *B minor to G♯ minor*—change of mode in subdominant triad

b:

d. *C major to D♭ major*—use a borrowed submediant

C:

e. *A major to B♭ major*—use an altered submediant

A:

f. *E major to G major*—use an altered mediant

E:

For each diminished seventh given, respell the first, second, and third inversions as enharmonic root position diminished sevenths in other keys. Follow the model.

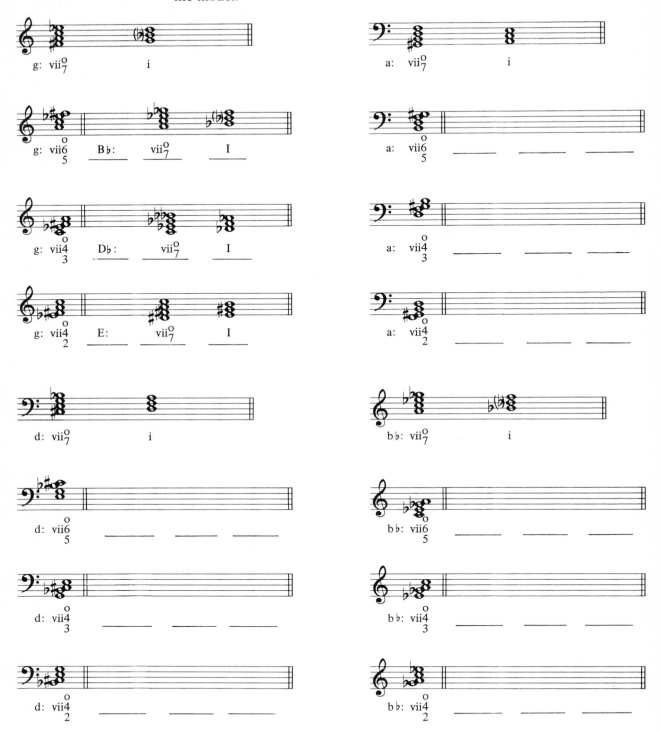

Complete the composition below for flute, oboe, or violin. Study the character and harmonic rhythm of the opening phrase. Next, plan a modulation to E major using an enharmonic interpretation of a diminished seventh chord (or other appropriate chord) as the pivot. The work should be a small binary form with E major as the related key. Return to C major through change of mode.

1. Write a brief four-part chorale that illustrates the use of a German six–five as an enharmonic pivot.

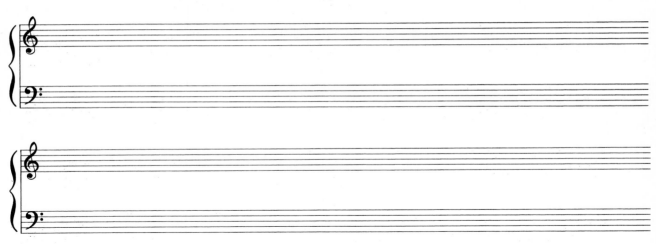

2. Continue the following piano composition to include a remote modulation using a Neapolitan six as the pivot.

Provide harmonic analysis for the following:

Franz Schubert, *Impromptu in C Minor*, Op. 90

Johannes Brahms, *Treue Liebe dauert lange*

Stund,   und kein Zwei -   fel macht sie ban - ge,   im - mer
hour,   'gainst all doubt   and fear as - sur - éd,   los - eth

mut   Sturm   und   Tod,   setzt den Ge - fah - ren   Lieb___
part,   *e'en*   *to*   *death,*   *'mid foes as - sail - ing,*   *love___*

___   ent - ge - gen,   treu - es___ Blut.
___   *will keep___ his   loy - al___ heart.*

Provide harmonic analysis.

Franz Schubert, *Sonata in A Minor*, Op. 164,
First Movement

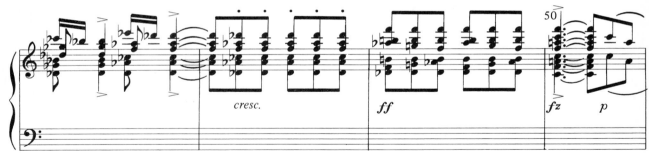

Chapter 8
The Sonata Principle

The term *sonata* is most closely associated with multi-movement works for piano, or solo instrument with piano accompaniment. *Sonata-form,* on the other hand, designates the formal construction often employed in the first movement of a sonata. Sonata-form is one of the most influential developments in Western music. From its origin in the binary dances of the Baroque suite to the twentieth-century efforts of Hindemith, Stravinsky, and others, the sonata principle has provided a structure for a movement of any length, style, or tempo.

When Haydn, Mozart, and Beethoven wrote sonatas, they were not so much adhering to a preconceived sequence of tonal relationships and themes as they were innately balancing musical and dramatic elements both in a broad sense and in minute detail. As Charles Rosen has observed, "sonata-form could not be defined until it was dead."[1] By the time young composers could read about how they "ought to compose sonatas," the "classical" form, extracted from the works of the Viennese Classicists, essentially had ceased to exist. What remained was the sonata *principle*—not a form, but a philosophy of balance and symmetry that has survived intact to the present day.

The sonata principle represents a logical means of controlling opposing elements: tension and stability, the familiar with the unknown. A symmetrical theme may constitute stability whereas the fragmentation of that theme would represent tension. The tonic key is a point of stability; a movement away from it creates tension.

Key Relationships

While sonata-form is traditionally discussed in terms of themes, in a broader sense, key relationships govern structure. The establishment of a tonic, a digression, and an eventual return represent the most general outline of the form. In the Classical Era, the first and most important tonal digression is to the dominant; in a work in the minor mode, the relative major is the most likely secondary area.

| ESTABLISHMENT OF TONIC | DIGRESSION TO RELATED KEY[2] | RETURN TO TONIC |

[1]Charles Rosen, *The Classical Style* (New York: W.W. Norton and Company, 1971), p. 30.
[2]The term "related key" is used to describe the tonal digression in sonata-form whether it be to the dominant, relative major, or another key.

Thematic Relationships

The growth of a melody from motive and sub-phrase to phrase and period establishes a hierarchy of formal elements producing a unified (but not always symmetrical) whole. The thematic structure of a sonata movement mirrors the establishment–digression–return sequence found in key relationships. The first theme is presented in the tonic key. The second theme or themes appear soon after in a related key and represent both tonal and thematic digression. Following further digression (involving modulation to other related keys), the first and second themes return in the tonic (Example 8–1).

EXAMPLE 8–1   Establishment, Digression, and Return in Sonata-Form

ESTABLISHMENT	DIGRESSION		FURTHER DIGRESSION	RETURN
Tonic Key	Related Key		Modulations	Tonic Key
First Theme	Second Theme			First and Second Themes

The importance of tonal digression and subsequent resolution is emphasized by the fact that some composers (Haydn, for example), often employ only one theme, stated first in the tonic then reinterpreted at the level of the dominant or other related key. Thus in principle, it is the *key* of the theme more than the theme itself that contributes to a sense of stability or tension.

THE "CLASSICAL" SONATA

While most sonatas, especially those of the Classical Era, share a central philosophy as well as certain formal characteristics, an attempt to study structure from conformity to a model is invariably frustrated by elements which are "atypical." Yet if students begin with an understanding of the broadest outlines of stability and tension and keep them in mind while viewing the specific, the analysis of sonata-form through themes is less problematic.

The Binary Structure

Although often discussed in terms of three major sections, sonata-form is inherently binary. The digression to a related key at the end of the first part, the organization of themes, the relative proportions, and the return to the tonic are all characteristics of binary or rounded binary form. The ternary principle is sometimes incorrectly applied to sonata-form because there are three distinct internal divisions: *Exposition, Development,* and *Recapitulation.* Especially in later sonata movements, the proportions of the three divisions are more or less equal; in form, however, the exposition is balanced by the development and recapitulation *together* (Example 8–2).

EXAMPLE 8–2   Binary Structure in Sonata-Form

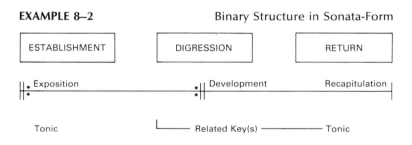

The Themes and Their Roles

Themes are not the essence of sonata-form. As discussed previously, the form is a series of three events: establishment, digression, and return. The themes serve to dramatize or *articulate* each event. In the exposition, the tonic key is articulated by the first theme. After a modulatory transition, the digression to a related key is articulated by the second theme.

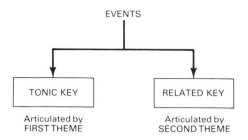

A major problem with a formal analysis of sonata movements is the description of themes and events with terms that are misleading. The first theme of a sonata-form, for example, is often referred to as the "principal" or "primary" theme; the theme associated with the digression is described as "secondary" or "subordinate." In fact, however, the themes of a sonata movement are more often equal in weight and any of them may be developed extensively. Students should avoid associating with any theme a specific set of characteristics. The first theme or theme group merely occurs first; the second theme occurs second and in a related key; another theme often concludes the exposition. Whichever terms are used to discuss sonata-form, they refer to order and tonal level—not character or importance.

Formal Analysis

The formal analysis of sonata-forms can be as general or as detailed as necessary. In most cases, it is sufficient to identify the major events and the transitions which link them. Jan LaRue's system of formal analysis (*Guidelines for Style Analysis,* 1970) has been adapted for use in this book because it is the most complete and flexible available. Upper case letters are used to identify major themes and theme groups. Arabic numerals refer to the order of themes within each group (the second theme, for example, might consist of two themes identified *1S* and *2S* respectively).

Material	*Designation*	*Subsequent Themes in Same Role*
FIRST THEME[3]	1F	2F, 3F, etc.
SECOND THEME	1S	2S, 3S, etc.
"CLOSING" THEME	1K	2K, 3K, etc.

Material which is introductory or transitional is identified in a similar manner:

Material	*Designation*	*Subsequent Themes in same Role*
TRANSITION	1T	2T, 3T, etc.
INTRODUCTION	1I	2I, 3I, etc.

[3]LaRue identifies the first theme as "Primary" (1P) and the second theme as "Secondary" (1S). To maintain consistency in terminology, however, these two terms and one of the symbols have been changed in this text. Moreover, where LaRue uses the letter *O* to designate introductory material, the letter *I* is used in the present volume for the same purpose.

LaRue uses the letter *N* to designate NEW MATERIAL which may occur after the presentation of the first, second, and closing themes. The letter *Q* is used to identify QUESTIONABLE FUNCTIONS—"too ambiguous in character to justify a more precise symbol." LaRue cautions that "one must fight the temptation to use this symbol as a means of sweeping Shape problems under the rug!"[4]

The exposition, development, and recapitulation in sonata-form will be discussed in general terms and then examined more specifically through the first movement of Mozart's *Sonata in D Major*, K. 576. While many aspects of this work conform to the "classical" model, it remains thoroughly unique and never quite predictable.

THE EXPOSITION

The establishment of the tonic key and the first digression occur in the EXPOSITION. In some works, an INTRODUCTION (I) precedes the FIRST THEME (F). A TRANSITION (T) incorporates a modulation to the related key and leads to the SECOND THEME (S). The second theme group may include another transition and/or additional thematic material often designated CLOSING THEME (K). The exposition ends in the related key. The themes themselves (and the transitions which link them) vary in length and character. In general, the first and second themes contrast in style; if the former is lyric, the latter is likely to be more rhythmic and *vice versa*.

Time line models like that in Example 8–3 below are given with the understanding that they represent a general outline of events and the themes that articulate them. In fact, very few sonata movements conform precisely to such a model; the flexibility of the form traditionally has been one of its most attractive aspects.

EXAMPLE 8–3   The Exposition

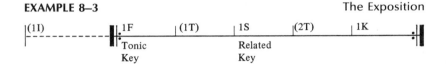

W. A. Mozart, Sonata in D Major, K. 576: Exposition

The first movement of Mozart's *Sonata*, K. 576 opens with an octave arpeggiation of a D major triad. The eight measure parallel period is followed by another in which the right hand is given figuration (Example 8–4).

EXAMPLE 8–4

[4]Jan LaRue, *Guidelines for Style Analysis* (New York: W. W. Norton and Company, 1970), p. 155.

A transition begins in measure 17 with a sixteenth note figure that is essentially an embellishment of the pitch A_5:

The arpeggios return in measure 24 and lead to a strong cadence in the dominant. The rest following the cadence (measure 27) is termed a DOMINANT CAESURA; its function is like punctuation: to help articulate the event that follows (Example 8–5).

EXAMPLE 8–5

The second theme (1S) begins in measure 28 in the dominant; the thematic material is similar to that of the first theme in its ascending triad outline. The six measure phrase is followed by an eight measure contrasting period (based on figural material) and culminates with *another* dominant caesura (Example 8–6).

EXAMPLE 8–6

A second member of the second theme group (2S) appears in measure 42. This theme contrasts with earlier material in several ways: it opens without accompaniment, it is basically stepwise, and it begins with the subdominant chord:

EXAMPLE 8–7

A brief CODETTA (a small coda) consisting of scales over tonic and dominant triad outlines concludes the exposition in the related key. Notice that there is no material in the exposition designated "closing theme;" this aspect of *K. 576* will be discussed later (Example 8–8).

EXAMPLE 8–8

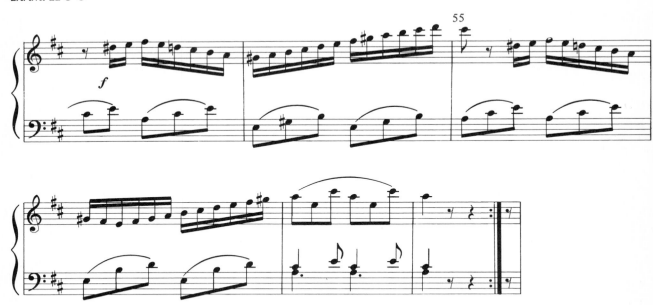

THE DEVELOPMENT

THE DEVELOPMENT SECTION represents the point of greatest digression from the stability of the tonic key and first theme as established in the exposition. The development begins as the exposition ended—in the related key. Various devices such as sequence, imitation, variation, and fragmentation are employed to develop themes or motives in several different keys. In early sonata movements, the development is often episodic; a theme begins, is fragmented in other voices, but never quite completed. In the nineteenth century, however, the development section may include the presentation of completely new themes stated several times in their entirety. The development may feature a relatively thicker and more complex texture designed to heighten the tension.

In terms of length, development sections vary considerably. Those of Haydn and Mozart are often (but not always) relatively brief—sometimes merely a transition to the return of the first theme. In Beethoven and later composers, however, there is often a lengthy and complex "working out" of several themes.

Another common feature of the development section is a decrease in momentum just before the return of the tonic key (the recapitulation). A thinning of texture often coincides with a dominant pedal and like the dominant caesura of the exposition, signals the approach of an important event. The general outline of the development section is shown in Example 8–9.

EXAMPLE 8–9   The Development

| Various Themes/Fragments | ～～～～～～～ | Transition to Recapitulation |
| Related Key⟶Other Related Keys | ～～～～～ | Tonic: V |

Mozart, K. 576: Development

Thematically, the development is limited almost exclusively to the familiar arpeggios of the first theme. The development begins in measure 59 with a sudden shift to A minor, then B♭ major (measure 63), and then G minor (measure 70). Such rapid and often remote modulation is a feature of development sections. In measures 74–75, Mozart employs an enharmonic relationship (E♭ = D♯) to move suddenly back to A minor. A more substantial modulation to B minor occurs beginning in measure 78—again employing an enharmonic relationship and an Italian six in the new key.

After touching on E minor (measure 89), the key of A major reappears in measure 92. Notice the recurrence of the pitch A_3 in measures 92–97. This dominant pedal signals the approach of the recapitulation. The sixteenth notes in measures 97–98 (which outline a dominant seventh chord on accented beats) lead directly to the recapitulation (Example 8–10).

EXAMPLE 8–10

THE RECAPITULATION

The role of the RECAPITULATION is to resolve the tension originally created in the exposition by tonal and thematic digression. This is accomplished not only by a return to the original key, but through a reinterpretation of the *second theme(s)* in the tonic. Thus material that in the exposition had digressed to a related key is now resolved by presenting it in the tonic. The sequence of themes and transitions heard earlier in the exposition is generally (but by no means *always*) followed in the recapitulation.

Especially in the nineteenth century, the recapitulation may end with a significant coda designed to balance the proportions of the movement as a whole. The "classical" recapitulation is shown in Example 8–11.

EXAMPLE 8–11   The Recapitulation

Mozart, *K. 576:* Recapitulation

In the recapitulation, the first period of theme 1F is the same as it was in the exposition. The second period, however, features imitation and an ascending sequence leading eventually to the second theme.

Following the dominant caesura in measure 121, Mozart presents the lyric member of the second theme group (2S) rather than the arpeggiated one (1S) that was heard in the corresponding position in the exposition. Thus while theme 1S represented digression (tension) in the exposition, theme 2S is used to resolve the tension in the recapitulation. Clearly, the return to the *tonic key* is more significant than the recurrence of any particular theme.

In measure 138, Mozart states theme 1S (now in D major) in a clear "closing" role. Notice that where dominant caesuras preceded both 1S and 2S in the exposition, only one appears in the recapitulation (measure 125). The movement concludes with a codetta (Example 8–12).

EXAMPLE 8–12

Looking at the work as a whole, major theme and key areas are diagrammed in Example 8–13.

EXAMPLE 8–13   Mozart, *K. 576:* Time Line Analysis

LATER DEVELOPMENTS

The sonata movements of Beethoven and later nineteenth-century composers generally reflect a concept of larger proportions with freer choices among key relationships. Where more "classical" composers limited themselves to two or three themes, Brahms and Tchaikovsky were as likely to employ many more themes and to use them even in transitional roles. The "four-square" formal construction of Mozart is often replaced in Beethoven and later composers with mere melodic fragments that are expanded and transformed into themes. Some composers, on the other hand, began with complete themes and expanded *them* into even longer formal units.

Romantic composers were fond of alternate key relationships; stating a second theme in the chromatic mediant, for example, was quite common after 1825. Frequent and dramatic changes in tempo, style, and mood pervade the sonata movements of Brahms and his contemporaries.

After a period of neglect following World War I, sonata-form reemerged in the works of composers like Hindemith, Stravinsky, and even Webern. While the traditional divisions of exposition, development and recapitulation are not always immediately clear, the sonata *principle* remains intact.

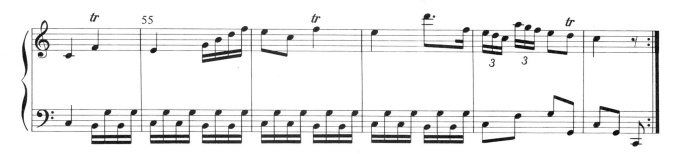

W. A. Mozart, *Sonata in F Major,*
K. 533, Second Movement

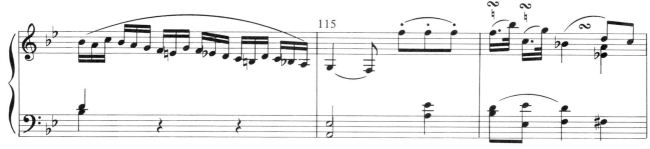

Chapter 9
The Rondo Principle

Based on the alternation of a recurring theme with episodes of contrasting material, the RONDO or REFRAIN PRINCIPLE is one of the oldest and most important in Western music. The poetry of the Medieval Troubadours and Trouvères is often organized around a recurring *couplet*—a refrain which ends each stanza with the same text. Set to music, the *rondeau* represents an early attempt to achieve continuity and balance in a sectional work.

The *rondeau* and other refrain forms continued to be important throughout the Middle Ages and Renaissance. As instrumental music rose in popularity during the seventeenth century, the principle was adopted by the French Clavecinists. The sectional keyboard works of François Couperin (1668–1733) and his contemporaries are often organized through the recurrence of a theme alternated with episodes or *couplets* that contrast in tonality and melodic material. Most often, these *rondeaux* (plural of *rondeau*) are structured in either five or seven parts, each of which is harmonically complete.

Consider the *rondeau* shown in Example 9–1. An eight measure theme (the *rondeau*) alternates with *episodes* of varying length, tonality, and character. Although the theme appears only at the beginning and end of the score, in performance it is heard after *each* couplet.

EXAMPLE 9–1   François Couperin, *Soeur Monique*

In modern terminology, the form of the composition on the previous page is known as a *Seven Part* or *Third Rondo* (A B A C A D A). The *Five Part* or *Second Rondo* has only two episodes (A B A C A).[1] As can be seen in Example 9–1, there is no attempt to form a link between sections; one melody ends, another begins. The more mature "Classical" Rondo, on the other hand, is distinguished by its carefully crafted transitions that minimize the sectional effect and focus attention on the form as a whole.

THE CLASSICAL RONDO

Although most common in the final movement of a sonata, symphony, or concerto, *any* movement of a work may be cast in rondo-form. Both five and seven part rondos are found in the Common Practice Period. The form known as "classical" rondo, however, is in seven parts with the third episode (D) appearing not as new material, but as a tonal reinterpretation of the first episode (B). The structure is a large ternary form (Example 9–2).

EXAMPLE 9–2 "Classical" Rondo-Form

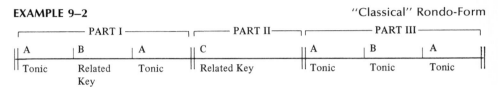

PART I			PART II	PART III		
A	B	A	C	A	B	A
Tonic	Related Key	Tonic	Related Key	Tonic	Tonic	Tonic

Because many of the melodic and tonal principles inherent in rondo-form are the same as those examined earlier in connection with the fugue as well as the sonata and variation principles, the present discussion will be less detailed. The elements of rondo-form will be presented in a general way and then more specifically through the finale of Beethoven's *Sonata in E Major*, Op. 14, No. 1. This seven part classical rondo is concise and clear in form although there are many unique features.

The Rondo Theme

Unlike sonata-form in which key relationships are sometimes of greater importance than themes, the rondo is a form based on *one* theme recurring inevitably in the tonic key. The theme itself is typically periodic and well defined in terms of melody, rhythm, and harmony. Whether a double period or a small binary or ternary form, the rondo theme begins and ends in the tonic. Subsequent theme statements are often varied or abbreviated.

The theme Beethoven composed for the final movement of his *Sonata in E Major* is a six-measure phrase with a two-measure extension (measures 1–8). The phrase is then repeated without the extension (measures 9–14). The sixteenth notes in the second half of the phrase play a major role not only in the transition that follows, but in other sections of the work as well (Example 9–3).

EXAMPLE 9–3

Beethoven, *Sonata in E Major*, Op. 14, No. 1, Third Movement

[1]The First Rondo (A B A) is generally equivalent to a small ternary form.

The Transition

Not all classical rondos have formal transitions between themes and episodes. Depending on the overall proportions, however, several beats or even *several phrases* may provide a smooth link between sections. As in sonata-form, the transitions may be based either on new or old material, but they are generally more figural in character than the rondo-theme. Besides providing continuity, the chief role of the transition is to effect a convincing change of key.

The transition of Beethoven's *Sonata in E Major* (Example 9–4), grows from the scale material associated with the second half of the phrase. The passage begins with imitation and leads smoothly to B major. The dominant caesura in measure 21 has the same role as in sonata-form: to signal the importance of a following event—in this case, the first episode.

EXAMPLE 9–4

The First Episode

The episode provides contrast in tonality and melodic material. The first tonal digression is usually to the dominant or relative major although key relationships in rondo-form are much freer than in sonata-form.

    The melodic material of the first episode is often quite similar to the theme; like the theme, it is usually a complete periodic unit. The first episode of Beethoven's *Sonata in E Major* is a nine measure phrase (4 + 5) which is clearly divided into two subphrases. The contrasts in tonality, harmony, and melodic character, however, make the brief episode structurally significant. The phrase closes with an authentic cadence in B major; the appearance of an A♮ anticipates the return of the rondo theme. The fermatas in measure 30 take the place of a transition (Example 9–5).

EXAMPLE 9–5

The Return of the Rondo Theme

The second statement of the rondo theme may be shorter or varied, but it is always in the tonic key. While the sonata principle rests on tension created by new keys, new themes, and the *expectation* of return to familiar ground, the rondo principle is pretty nearly the opposite: *security* resulting from the inevitability of thematic and tonal recurrence.

The second statement of the rondo theme in Beethoven's *Sonata in E Major* features the same registers, texture, and harmony found in the opening of the movement. The second phrase is now shorter and begins with an abrupt shift to the parallel minor (measure 38). A transition begins in measure 42; a dominant pedal (in G major) anticipates the second episode (Example 9–6).

EXAMPLE 9–6

The Second Episode

Often the longest single section of a classical rondo-form, the second episode is marked by striking contrasts. Key relationships *other* than the dominant or relative major generally prevail. In the eighteenth century, the subdominant or parallel major/minor areas are common; in the nineteenth century, other relationships (a chromatic mediant, for example) are just as frequent. In addition to tonal variety, the second episode may be dominated by contrasts in melodic style, texture, tempo, register, etc.

The second episode of the *E Major Sonata* is 37 measures in length—almost as long as the three previous sections together (46 measures). The key is G major. The choice of a chromatic mediant key relationship is, as we have seen, typical of Beethoven. The melodic material of the second episode is an expansion of the triplet figure that earlier accompanied the rondo theme. The triplets (that are little more than arpeggiated chords) are punctuated dramatically by a strong figure in the bass (measure 55, for example). Beethoven's treatment of the material in this section is highly developmental although clear references to previously stated material are missing (see the discussion of sonata-rondo form, page 218).

Harmony is the most important parameter of the second episode. Beginning in G major, Beethoven touches on several keys (including E minor) before the expected dominant pedal occurs in measure 76. A transition back to the rondo theme begins in the same measure; a chromatic scale spanning three octaves culminates in a fermata (Example 9–7).

EXAMPLE 9–7

The rondo theme returns in the tonic key in measure 84. The second phrase has been eliminated while at the same time, the transition (that earlier led to the first episode) is expanded (Example 9–8).

EXAMPLE 9–8

The Third Episode

While in the five part rondo the second episode is the last, a third digression occurs in the seven part form. As discussed earlier, this section is either new material (Third Rondo) or a reinterpretation of the first episode in the tonic ("classical" rondo). In either case, the length of the third episode is proportional and the transitions (if any) are consistent in style.

Beethoven's tonal innovation is evident in the third episode of the *E Major Sonata*. The material is the same as that of the first episode; it begins in the subdominant and includes a tonicization of F major (the Neapolitan area). As before, a fermata plays a transitional role (Example 9–9).

EXAMPLE 9–9

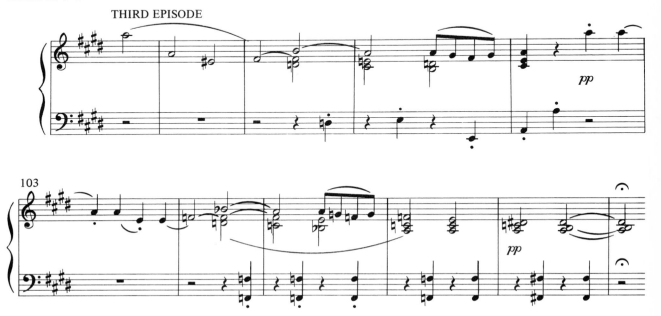

Final Statement and Coda

The final occurrence of the rondo theme is often the shortest. A proportionally substantial coda generally balances the relatively shorter length of the final statement.

Variation is reserved for the final statement of the rondo theme in the *Sonata in E Major*. Syncopation creates a new (and welcome) rhythmic effect and while the first half of the phrase remains fixed in pitch content, the two-against-three creates a fresh setting. In the second half of the phrase, the material in the right hand dissolves into a scale passage as the syncopated version of the theme begins in the left hand. A transition to the coda begins in measure 117 and culminates in the now-familiar fermata (measure 121).

The coda beginning in measure 122 hints at development (in the exploitation of the two-against-three, for example), but quickly disintegrates into scale material preceding the final cadence (Example 9–10).

EXAMPLE 9–10

Beethoven's seven part rondo is typical in thematic structure and form. The overall proportions are clearly ternary with the first and third parts equally balanced in length. The middle part (the second episode) is somewhat shorter. Beethoven is thoroughly consistent in constructing transitions that lead away from the rondo theme, but in employing a fermata to precede it. Although each episode is characterized by distinctive elements in one or more parameters, the style is unified through an economy of melody and clarity of texture. A detailed time line analysis of the work is shown in Example 9–11.

EXAMPLE 9–11   Time Line Analysis

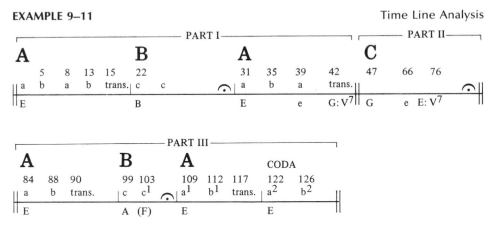

THE SONATA-RONDO

A fusion of sonata and rondo principles is seen in the SONATA-RONDO FORM of the late eighteenth and early nineteenth centuries. The structure is that of a seven part classical rondo. The middle section, however (the second episode) is not new material, but a full-blown development section based on material previously heard. The third part includes a tonal reinterpretation of the first episode to the tonic; this section corresponds to a recapitulation in sonata-form. A typical sonata-rondo is diagrammed in Example 9–12 below.

EXAMPLE 9–12   Sonata-Rondo Form

The sonata-rondo is a hybrid form and while it is common in the works of Beethoven and Mozart (see the third movement of K. 333, for example), its importance in the later nineteenth century is minimal.

SUMMARY

In varied forms, the rondo principle has appeared in compositions from the Middle Ages to the present day. For the finale of a multimovement work, the form is effective since it combines the excitement of contrast with the security of material recurring in a predictable way. Because its role is often to close a major work, the thematic content of a rondo-form is generally less weighty than, for example, that of an opening sonata-form. The character of the form, however, is not inherently "witty" or "gay." Such overgeneralized connotations should be avoided since a study of the literature will reveal rondos of virtually every possible approach.

Chapter 10
The Dissolution of the Common Practice Style

In Chapters 6 and 7, many of the means composers used to produce innovative works within the tonal system were examined; in Chapters 11 to 15 of this volume, totally new materials *outside* the common practice style will be presented. The focus of the present chapter, however, is the somewhat gray area between the expansion of functional tertian harmony and its final decay—a time when rather than using new materials, new uses of *traditional* materials dominated the European musical scene.

MELODY: A RENAISSANCE

Throughout the Common Practice Period, principles of harmonic function governed the constuction of melody. In the late nineteenth century, however, the balance between melodic and harmonic elements sometimes reverts to the pre-tonal era of the Renaissance; harmony often *results* as a by-product of simultaneous melodies. Even in homophonic works, the music is sometimes melodic in concept, and although harmonic elements are present, they may be almost incidental.

The driving force in the opening of Grieg's *Elegie,* for example, is the melody, not the harmony. The melody is constructed of a two measure motive based on a strong descending step progression shown below.

There is an upper harmonic pedal, and when the pitches of the melody are considered along with it, the harmony is tertian; in *concept*, however, the passage is melodic. Upper or lower case letters with appropriate symbols (which represent the quality of the triads without implying any functional relationships) are preferable to Roman numerals as an analytical approach (Example 10–1).

EXAMPLE 10–1

Edvard Grieg, *Elegie*

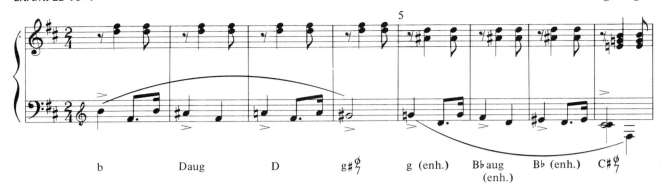

b   Daug   D   g#ø⁷   g (enh.)   B♭aug   B♭ (enh.)   C#ø⁷
(enh.)

There is nothing very unusual about the simple, tonal melody that Hugo Wolf (1860–1903) composed for the *lied* below. The harmony, however, does not imply A minor so clearly. Rather than choosing chord progressions which would reinforce the tonality of the melody, Wolf uses first a descending, then an ascending stepwise bass harmonized in thirds. The concept of the work is again *melodic*; combined with the quarter notes in the soprano, however, the harmonized bass line creates a more or less functional harmony. Notice the use of appoggiaturas in the right hand of the piano; they further obscure the tonality (Example 10–2).

EXAMPLE 10–2

Hugo Wolf, *Spanisches Liederbuch*, No. II

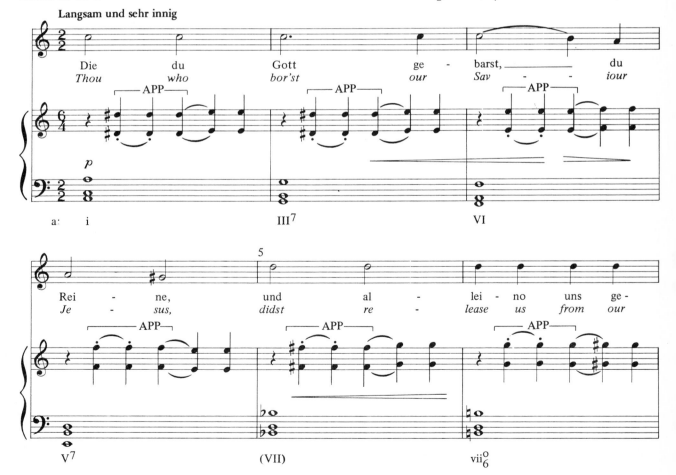

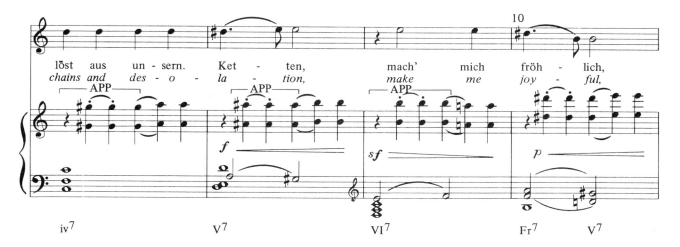

iv⁷ $\quad$ V⁷ $\quad$ VI⁷ $\quad$ Fr⁷ $\quad$ V⁷

Nonharmonic Tones

Passages such as that shown in Example 10–2 abound in the music of the late nineteenth century. The harmony has some tertian basis, but melodic forces contribute to a renovation of the principles. Nonharmonic tones, especially the appoggiatura, play a large part in adding color to traditional harmonies. Conventional resolutions are adhered to (as in Example 10–2), but are often ornamented, delayed, or relatively insignificant in duration. The lengthy appoggiaturas and passing tones, for example, obscure the ordinary harmonic progressions in the Prelude to the first act of Wagner's *Tristan und Isolde* (1865), (Example 10–3).

EXAMPLE 10–3 $\hfill$ Richard Wagner, *Tristan und Isolde*,
Prelude to Act I

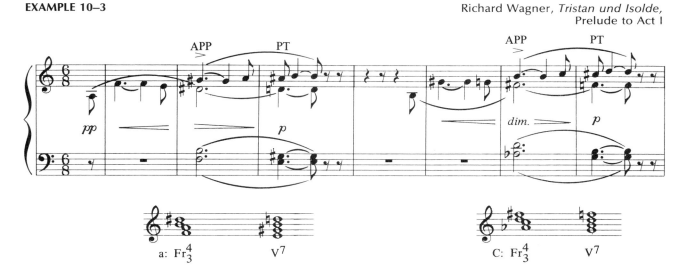

a: Fr_3^4 $\quad$ V⁷ $\qquad\qquad$ C: Fr_3^4 $\quad$ V⁷

Multiple Tonal Axes

The passage above is analyzed first with a progression in A minor, then with the same one in C major. The work does not modulate to C major, but rather moves from a tonal axis on A to an alternate one on C. While the harmonic vocabulary of the late nineteenth century remained tertian, new attitudes toward tonality fostered more flexibility within the system. Some composers adopted an innovative approach in which two or more keys were used not as primary and related secondary area(s), but as MULTIPLE TONAL AXES of more or less *equal* weight. In the *Tristan* Prelude, for example (given more fully in Example 10–4), three keys (A minor, C major, and E major) are used in succession. The progressions around each axis are basically functional, but instead of remaining in one key or modulating to another, Wagner employs the three keys as a *single harmonic resource*. Notice that in the opening passage, there is no tonic chord until measure 20.

The concept of multiple tonal axes represents an important break with the past which set the precedent for later innovations such as polytonality and bitonality (discussed in Chapter 12).

EXAMPLE 10–4

Richard Wagner, *Tristan und Isolde*,
Prelude to Act I

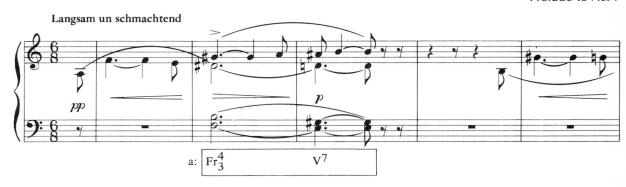

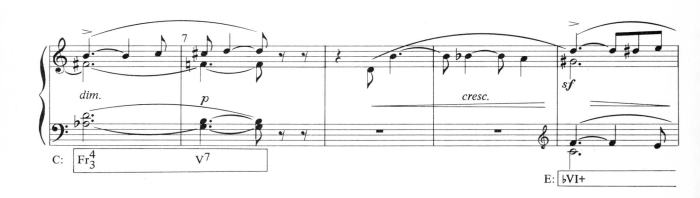

a: V⁹   VI

C: V/V   I⁶₄   V/V   V⁷   I₆

EXTENDED TERTIAN HARMONY: NINTH CHORDS

Like the harmonic seventh which appeared first as a melodic dissonance to be incorporated later as a chord member, the harmonic ninth evolved through melodic motion. While the ninth was present in a number of nonharmonic roles even before 1700 (the 9–8 suspension, for example), the chordal ninth is associated most closely with music of the late nineteenth and early twentieth centuries.

Construction and Resolution

A NINTH CHORD is comprised of a triad with seventh and ninth above the root. The quality of the chord is determined by the qualities of the three component elements: the *triad,* the *seventh,* and the *ninth* (Example 10–5).

EXAMPLE 10–5   Quality in Ninth Chords

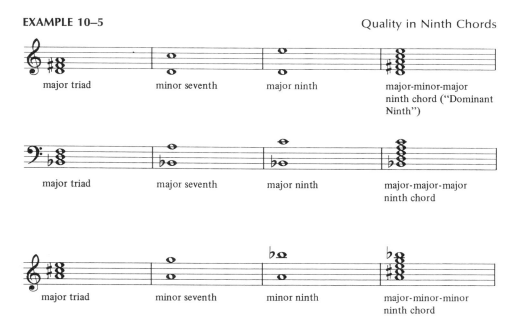

major triad   minor seventh   major ninth   major-minor-major ninth chord ("Dominant Ninth")

major triad   major seventh   major ninth   major-major-major ninth chord

major triad   minor seventh   minor ninth   major-minor-minor ninth chord

The major–minor–major ninth chord is known universally as the "dominant ninth," and is the most common in traditional music. Other qualities of ninth, of course, occur as well (as in Example 10–5 above). In the twentieth century, the theorists and practitioners of jazz have utilized and identified virtually every conceivable type of ninth chord. The symbols they employ, while not entirely applicable to traditional music, are more concise and relevant than many of those adapted from the Roman numeral system (see Appendix A: The Materials of Jazz).

Voice Leading. In four-part harmonizations, the ninth chord appears with omitted fifth; the resolution of both the seventh and ninth is *down by step*. The ninth itself is usually in the soprano (Example 10–6).

EXAMPLE 10–6   Ninth Chords in Four-Part Writing

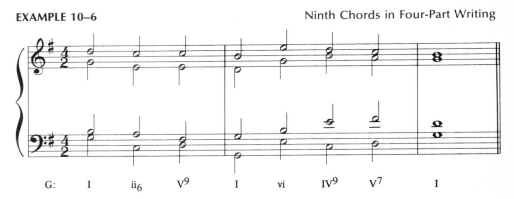

Inversions. Although first inversion is not altogether uncommon, most ninth chords employed in traditional music appear in root position. Except where a chord is formed through contrapuntal motion, second, third, and *fourth* inversions are rare before 1900. In analysis, ninth chords are often identified as V^9, IV^9, or whatever, even if the root is not in the bass.

Use of Ninth Chords

Ninth chords were not new to the nineteenth century; as shown in Example 10–7, composers of the Classical Era employed them occasionally. In the passage below, both the seventh and the ninth are resolved characteristically to pitches in the following arpeggiated chord.

EXAMPLE 10–7   Joseph Haydn, *Sonata in A♭ Major,*
First Movement

Quite often, the preparation and resolution of a chordal ninth so closely resembles that of a nonharmonic figure that analysis is subjective. In such cases, the context of the passage is usually the best guide. The *concept* of the excerpt below is harmonic and the ninths in measures 7 and 9 are appropriately analyzed as chordal (Example 10–8). Still, some would *hear* the E in measure 7 and the D in measure 9 as suspensions over seventh chords.

EXAMPLE 10–8

Reinhold Becker, *Springtime*

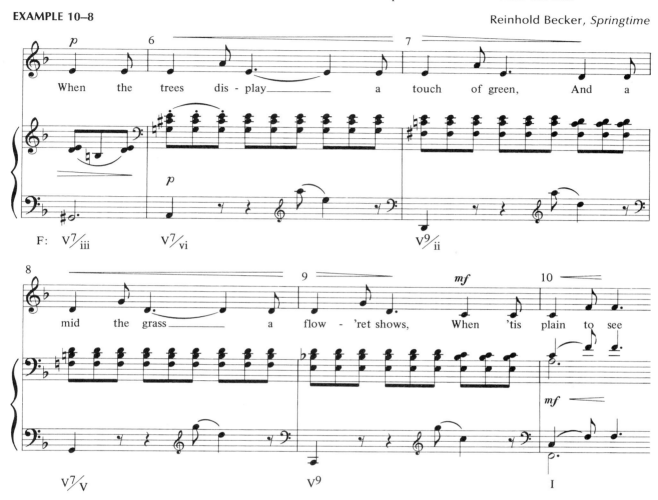

Especially when ninth chords are arpeggiated, the resolution of the ninth proper sometimes gives way to the resolution of another chordal dissonance. In Example 10–9, the ninth, C, moves to the fifth above the bass, and subsequently to the seventh which resolves in typical fashion. The ninth is not left unresolved (as later composers would do), but "reduced" to a seventh which then resolves typically.

EXAMPLE 10–9

Franz Schubert, *Mass No. 6 in E♭ Major, Kyrie*

ALTERED CHORDS OF DOMINANT FUNCTION

The use of borrowed chords, augmented sixth chords, and other chords of subdominant function supplemented the chromatic possibilities of tonal harmony throughout the Common Practice Era. While the use of these materials continued and increased during the late nineteenth century, altered chords of *dominant* function became ever more common.

The Altered Dominant

A dominant triad that is augmented rather than major in quality appears in the music of numerous nineteenth-century composers. In Example 10–10, the raised fifth (D♯) provides a leading tone to the third of the tonic chord and creates a colorful cadential effect.

EXAMPLE 10–10   Benjamin Godard, *Florian's Song*

"First Class" Augmented Sixth Chords

Expanding to the octave, the augmented sixth can emphasize *any* pitch in a diatonic scale. Early nineteenth-century composers employed it to color the dominant; later Romantic composers, however, used augmented sixth chords in dominant roles—to emphasize the tonic. In Example 10–11, the French four–three *replaces* the dominant chord as it resolves directly to tonic.

EXAMPLE 10–11   P. I. Tchaikovsky, *Symphony No. 5 in
E Minor*, Op. 64, Second Movement

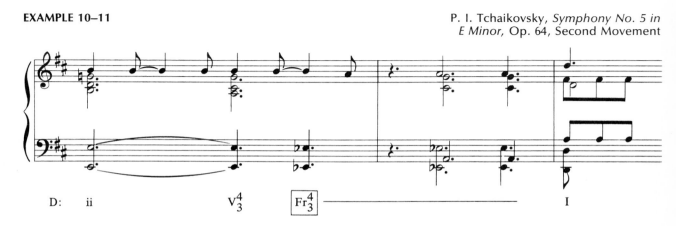

Third Relation

While the perfect fifth dominated the harmonic progressions of the Baroque and Classical periods, root movement by third became increasingly popular in the later nineteenth century. Many composers employed third relation at important cadences either in addition to, or instead of the traditional descending fifth. Notice the chromatic mediant that separates the dominant seventh and tonic chords and provides a striking third relation in Example 10–12.

EXAMPLE 10–12
Franz Liszt, *Wanderers Nachtlied*

NONFUNCTIONAL HARMONY

Motivated by a desire to introduce more color into their compositions, a number of mid- and late nineteenth-century composers began to experiment with harmony that was *nonfunctional*. Since the establishment of tonality results from conscious harmonic choices, a vague tonality occurs when other factors (color, melodic motion, texture, etc.) take precedence over harmonic function. Nineteenth-century composers used a number of techniques and materials that resulted in passages and even entire works which were harmonically nonfunctional.

The Augmented Triad

Rare in the Baroque and Classical Eras, the augmented triad was one of the few really new materials to gain favor in the nineteenth century. Besides appearing in cadential formulas (see Example 10–10), augmented triads occur within the phrase and even in succession. Liszt's work *Nuages Gris*, for instance, illustrates a nineteenth-century *avant-garde* approach (Example 10–13). The composition is based almost entirely on augmented triads. In addition, however, notice the gentle alternation between B♭ and A (in the bass) which Liszt uses to suggest the motion of clouds. Although the work is entirely nonfunctional, the opening triad outlines (heard again between measures 25 and 33) suggest G as a tonal center. The final cadence (which also emphasizes G) results from melodic, rather than harmonic tendencies.

EXAMPLE 10–13

Franz Liszt, *Nuages gris*

Diminished Seventh Chords

In conventional resolutions, chords with strong dominant function define common practice progressions. The diminished triad (with or without seventh) and the major triad (especially with minor seventh) have particularly clear dominant roles. When these roles are abandoned, as in a *series* of major triads or dominant seventh chords, tonal disorientation results. The diminished seventh chord, with its two tritones, has a great tendency to resolve; when a succession of diminished sevenths occurs, tonality is literally suspended. A nonfunctional series of diminished sevenths precedes a (greatly embellished) conventional authentic cadence in Example 10–14.

EXAMPLE 10-14   Franz Liszt, *Etude IV*, "Mazeppa"

Parenthetical Harmony

Because the harmony of the previous example is nonfunctional for the first three measures, Roman numerals are of no practical value; function in D minor appears, however, in the ordinary cadential progression which follows. Brief passages of nonfunctional harmony (like the diminished sevenths which open "Mazeppa") are often described as PARENTHETICAL HARMONY because they temporarily interrupt the movement toward tonic with chords of color rather than function.

A passage similar to the Liszt example is seen in Chopin's *Etude*, Op. 10, No. 1 (Example 10–15). Preceding a tonicization of E major, a parenthetical succession of dominant sevenths obscures the key. Following a tonal progression in C major, another parenthetical passage occurs beginning in measure 70. Notice that the diminished sevenths occur over a dominant pedal—a device often used to maintain a tonal reference within a nonfunctional harmony.

EXAMPLE 10–15

Frédéric Chopin, *Etude*, Op. 10, No. 1

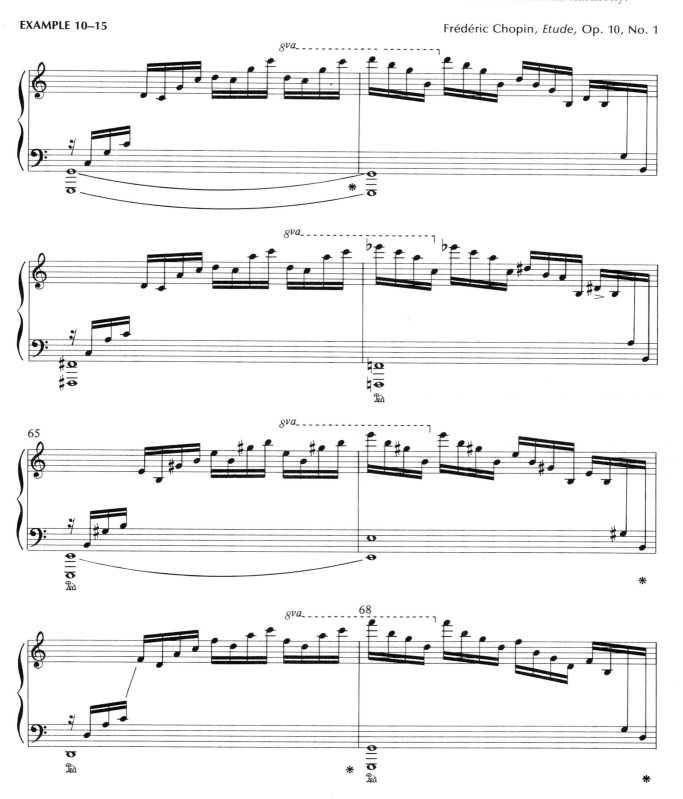

In analysis, parenthetical harmony is identified as one might suspect—with parentheses. If there is a predominant sonority (diminished or dominant sevenths, augmented triads, etc.), this may be indicated within the parentheses.

Tonal Pillars. Strong progressions such as those in measures 68–69 and 76–77 of Example 10–15 are often referred to as TONAL PILLARS—islands of tonal stability amid weak or nonfunctional harmonies. The harmonic reduction below shows both the nonfunctional parenthetical harmony and the tonal pillars that support it (Example 10–16).

EXAMPLE 10–16

Harmonic Reduction, Example 10–15

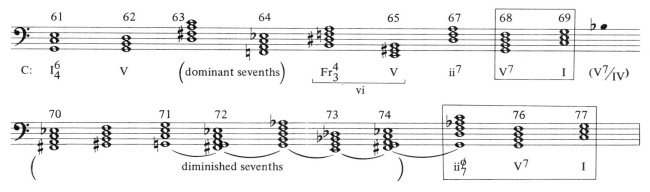

Nonharmonic Tones

In the highly chromatic melody of some nineteenth-century composers, harmonic and nonharmonic roles are sometimes difficult to discern. The harmony in the first few measures of César Franck's *Chorale*, for example, actually looks more functional than it sounds; the meandering chromatic melody partially obscures the E♭ major tonality. A brief passage of nonfunctional diminished sevenths (measures 3 and 4) precedes a strong cadence in the dominant (Example 10–17).

EXAMPLE 10–17

César Franck, *Chorale*

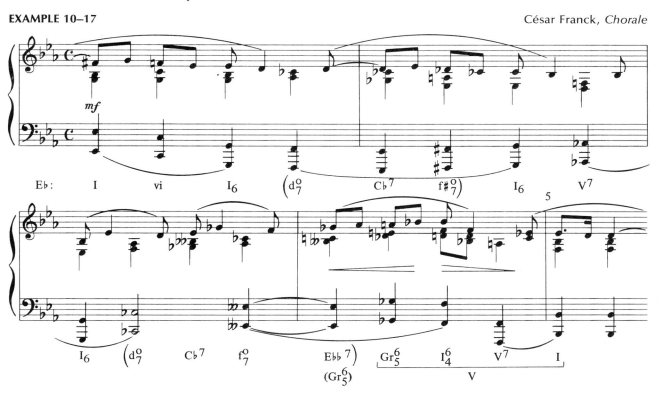

In the harmonic reduction of Example 10–17 shown below, notice the use of various nonharmonic tones in both the functional and parenthetical harmonies (Example 10–18).

EXAMPLE 10–18

Harmonic Reduction, Example 10–17

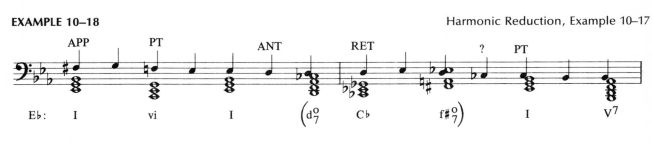

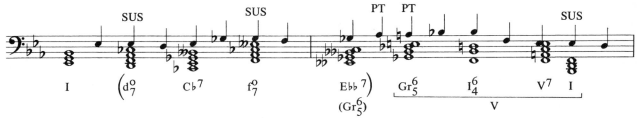

Chordal Mutation

CHORDAL MUTATION is a special type of parenthetical harmony in which a tertian triad (or other sonority) is altered (mutated) by changing one or two pitches—usually up or down by step. Although the new chord may be quite foreign to the first, the common tones permit some sense of organization to be maintained. The resulting harmony is nonfunctional and is usually supported by tonal pillars (Example 10–19).

EXAMPLE 10–19

Chordal Mutation

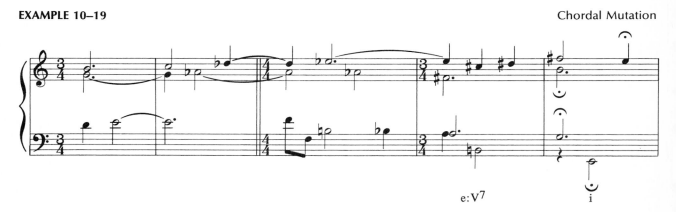

A notable example of chordal mutation occurs in Chopin's *Prelude* Op. 28, No. 4. Throughout the 25 measures, a simple melody is supported by a kaleidoscope of harmonic colors touching on several different keys. To avoid clear function, Chopin uses deceptions (measures 20–21), tonic substitutes (measures 4 and 22), and harmonic dissonance (measures 3, 15, and 16) as well as other alterations. At approximately the mid-point of the work, however, and at the end, the composer provides strong progressions in the tonic key (E minor). Clearly, while typical resolutions are largely avoided, function is never very far away and the two tonal pillars are adequate support for the brief work (Example 10–20). Notice that the first passage of chordal mutation (measures 2–7), though nonfunctional, is organized through root movement by descending third.

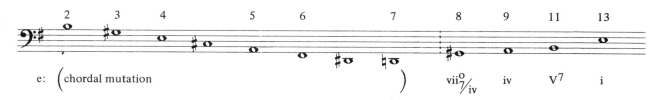

e: (chordal mutation   ) vii°⁷/iv iv V⁷ i

EXAMPLE 10–20   Frédéric Chopin, *Prelude*, Op. 28, No. 4

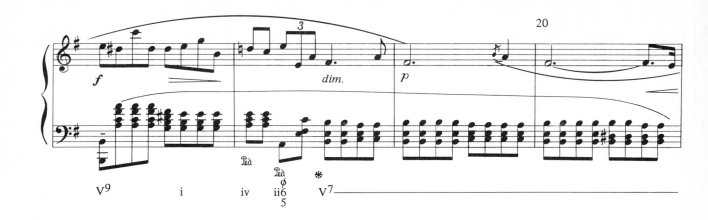

SUMMARY

About the time that Johannes Brahms (1833–1897) was finishing his *Symphony No. 4 in E Minor,* young Claude Debussy was a student at the Paris Conservatory. In the conservative musical climate of the 1880s, Debussy received little encouragement for his innovative ideas. The principles of tonal composition that were conceived before the seventeenth century, codified in the eighteenth century, and brought to full fruition in the nineteenth century were far from obsolete. Although lucrative commissions and important teaching posts invariably went to more traditional composers, Debussy began with the tonal materials described in this chapter and forged a new musical vocabulary in which all parameters share in a delicate balance of subtle shadings. Debussy's music was of tremendous influence on subsequent composers like Stravinsky and Schoenberg—composers who later developed their own distinct and equally revolutionary styles in the twentieth century.

The rise of Nationalism in the late nineteenth century was another factor in the dissolution of common practice music. Composers such as Zoltán Kodály, Béla Bartók, and Modest Mussorgsky turned inward for new resources of melody, harmony, and rhythm. In Russia, Alexander Scriabin (1872–1915) began experiments with the manipulation of musical sets; in America, Charles Ives (1874–1954) appalled audiences with some of the most innovative music written before World War I.

1. Write and resolve the following progressions in four parts.

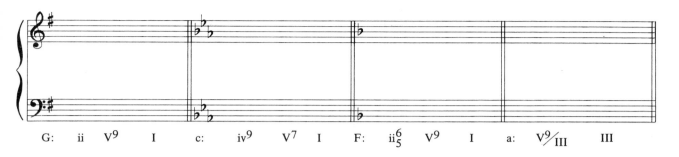

G: ii V⁹ I   c: iv⁹ V⁷ I   F: ii$^6_5$ V⁹ I   a: V⁹/III III

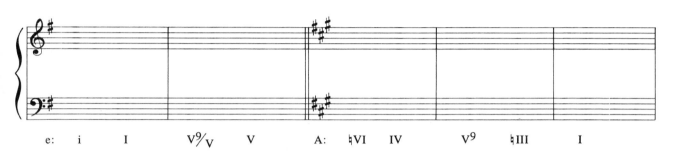

e: i I   V⁹/V V   A: ♮VI IV   V⁹ ♮III I

2. Write cadences in four parts which illustrate the given nineteenth-century technique. Include *three* chords in each progression.

a. Altered Dominant   b. 1st Class Augmented Sixth   c. Third Relation

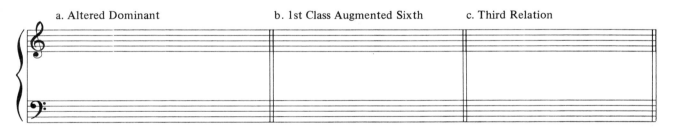

Compose a four-part chorale which employs several ninth chords in traditional resolutions. Begin in E♭ major and modulate through an enharmonic relationship to a foreign key. Provide harmonic analysis.

Given below is the beginning of Hugo Wolf's lied *Sleeping Child*. Study the style of the excerpt given; analyze the harmonic techniques. Complete the composition as a work for clarinet and piano. Recopy the portion given here omitting the text and transposing the voice part for B♭ clarinet. Provide harmonic analysis and be prepared to discuss the techniques and materials you employ.

Write a brief work for string or woodwind quartet (flute, oboe, clarinet, and bassoon) that revolves around three equal tonal axes: B♭ major, D minor, and G major. If you like, choose progressions similar to those in Example 10–4, page 236. Provide analysis.

Provide Roman numeral analysis.

Johannes Brahms, *Vier ernste Gesänge*, No. 4

Reduce the chords to root position and write on the staff provided. Analyze the work from several standpoints: (1) root relationships, (2) nonharmonic tone use, (3) step progressions in the melody, (4) the use of parenthetical harmony, (5) the presence of tonal pillars.

César Franck, *Chorale for Organ No. 2*

Reduce the given composition to root position triads and chords. Study the root relationships, use of chromaticism, and nonharmonic tones. Locate and identify tonal pillars and/or passages of parenthetical harmony. How do pedals clarify the tonality?

Hugo Wolf, *Biterolf*

Kampf - müd' und sonn - ver - brannt, fern an der Hei - den Strand,
Wea - ry, with sword in hand, rest - ing, on hea - then strand,

wald - grü - nes Thü - ring - land, denk' ich an dich.
syl - van Thur - ing - ia - land, I think of thee.

Provide Roman numeral analysis. Discuss the use of chromaticism and nonharmonic tones. Identify borrowed and altered chords. What is the form of the melody? How is it constructed and varied?

Grieg, *Secret*

As directed, compose on or more of the following:

1. A binary composition for flute and piano which employs ninth chords of various types.
2. A composition for piano alone which features chordal mutation with appropriately spaced tonal pillars.
3. A composition for piano or harpsichord using passages of nonfunctional harmony which are based on diminished or augmented sonorities.
4. A chordal work for string quartet in which altered dominants play a prominent role.
5. A composition for clarinet alone based solidly on traditional triads, but highly embellished with chromatic nonharmonic tones.

Chapter 11
Impressionism

Introduction to Chapters 11 to 15: The Twentieth Century

As common practice principles began to be abandoned during the last third of the nineteenth century, composers turned not only to new materials, but to new methods of organization as well. Common practice forms and techniques, after all, had evolved not from a desire to conform, but from the need to *structure*.

Impressionism, a major break with the classical tradition, came in the 1880s and created melodic and harmonic innovations destined to link the nineteenth and twentieth centuries. Between the World Wars, two major trends flourished in music. Movements like Expressionism and Primitivism, based on expanded tertian materials, represent the final transformation of traditional Western music. The other movement, in its rejection of tonality as the primary organizational principle, fostered the first truly "new" music of the twentieth century—Serialism. As the second half of the century began, these two trends developed alongside still newer movements: electronic music, indeterminacy, computer music, and a host of more obscure trends yet too young to be evaluated definitively.

The style of music known as IMPRESSIONISM originated from movements in art and literature; it represents a decisive break with traditional musical concepts. In the 1870s, a group of French *avant-garde* painters broke away from the traditional idealized and sculpturesque style to concentrate on color, atmosphere, and spontaneity. The Impressionists painted not the heroic, but the commonplace. In paintings like Monet's *Impression: Sunrise* (from which the movement took its name), artists tried to capture a subject from everyday life as it existed under momentary light and atmospheric conditions. A somewhat later movement known as NEO-IMPRESSIONISM (represented principally by the works of George Seurat) features a more scientific approach in which a canvas is dotted with pure (unmixed) colors that when viewed from a distance, blend into various shadings and shapes.

In French literature, the movement known as SYMBOLISM evolved along parallel lines at about the same time. The guiding spirit of literary symbolism was an earlier figure, Charles Baudelaire (1821–1867). Baudelaire's poetry (*Les Fleurs du Mal*, for example) centers on new and shocking themes:

death, despair, evil, and above all, human weakness. Influenced greatly by Baudelaire, later symbolists such as Stephan Mallarmé and Maurice Maeterlinck stressed the mystic, the supernatural, and the psychological.

Impressionism in Music

The champion of musical Impressionism and Symbolism is Claude Debussy (1862–1918); many, in fact, consider him *the* representative of these movements. Debussy's influence on later composers such as Stravinsky and Schoenberg was so great that he must be considered the most important link between the Romantic Era and the twentieth century.

Trained in the usual manner at the Paris Conservatory, Debussy rejected traditional concepts very early and set out to explore new musical resources. The style he developed is so distinctive that later composers completely avoided some of his materials for fear of being labeled "an Impressionist." Debussy's style is improvisatory but not random; his music is well planned and carefully balanced in every detail.

The "typical" Impressionist work is not a vast catalogue of strikingly new materials. On the contrary, while some new elements are usually present, the vocabulary is quite similar to that of Brahms and Liszt. Alongside some very important new techniques and materials, new *concepts* of melody, harmony, rhythm, and form account for most differences between late Romantic and Impressionist music.

MELODY

Many Impressionist compositions are based entirely on major or minor scales. In addition to these traditional resources, however, exotic scales constitute a prime element in the melodic vocabulary. While reviving some old forms such as the pentatonic scale and the Church Modes, Debussy and his contemporaries experimented with chromatic, whole tone, and synthetic scales as well.

The Whole Tone Scale

Debussy did not "invent" the whole tone scale, but he was one of the first to employ it extensively. Of all Impressionist characteristics, this scale is perhaps best known to the average listener. Debussy was attracted to the whole tone scale for precisely the same reason that Bach, Haydn, or Brahms would have rejected it: its tonal ambiguity. There is no leading tone and the resulting harmony is comprised entirely of augmented triads.

The use of whole tone and other exotic scales posed new and interesting problems for the Impressionists. Tension and relaxation, for example, traditionally balanced through melodic and harmonic tendencies, had to be approached through other means (rhythm, texture, or orchestration, to name but three).

Debussy's use of a whole tone melody is seen in Example 11–1. There is no tonal orientation in the scale itself; accents of various types give the phrase direction and balance.

EXAMPLE 11–1
Claude Debussy, "Voiles" from Preludes,
Volume I

The Pentatonic Scale

The revival of the pentatonic scale occurred in the late nineteenth century amid an awakening of interest in non-Western music. Like the whole tone scale, the pentatonic has no half steps; it combines tonal ambiguity with exoticism. In the example below, Debussy uses a pentatonic scale as the basis of both melody and harmony (Example 11–2).

EXAMPLE 11–2   Claude Debussy, "Pagodes" from *Estampes*

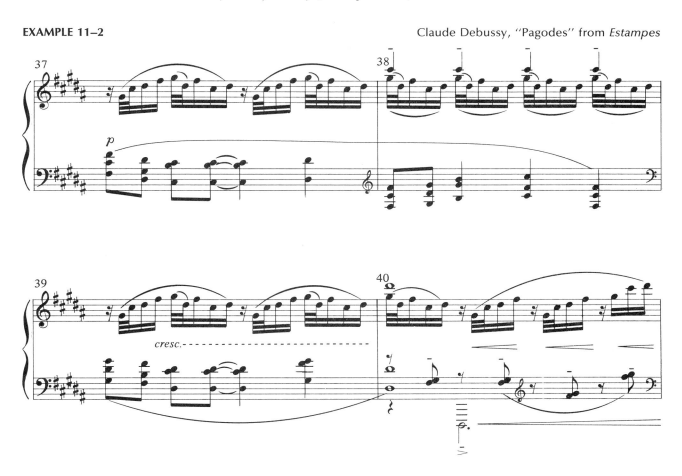

The Church Modes

Searching for new melodic materials, Debussy, Ravel, and others rediscovered the Church Modes. In addition to a melodic style quite close to Gregorian chant in its elegant simplicity, the use of modal scales gives Impressionist music a vaguely antique atmosphere. A striking use of the Phrygian mode, for example, is seen in the opening of Debussy's *Quartet* (Example 11–3).

EXAMPLE 11–3   Claude Debussy, *Quartet*, First Movement

In Debussy's monumental orchestral work *La Mer*, a number of modes are employed. The passage below, for example, is Lydian (Example 11–4).

EXAMPLE 11–4   Claude Debussy, *La Mer*, Second Movement

Synthetic Scales

Debussy's affinity for unique melodic materials includes some he invented himself. The following passage, for example, is neither Lydian nor Mixolydian, but a combination of the characteristics of both modes (Example 11–5).

EXAMPLE 11–5   Claude Debussy, *La Mer*, First Movement

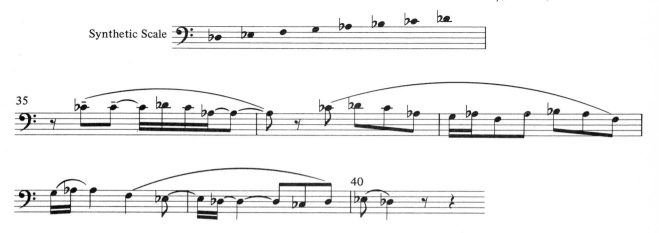

A variety of old and new scale forms provided the melodic material for Impressionist works; used harmonically, the same materials produced even more innovative results.

HARMONY: NEW CONCEPTS

The salient element of Impressionist harmony is the CHORD—not the progression. To Debussy, the chord was an abstract entity to be exploited for the sake of its color.

Debussy was among the first major composers to make non-functional harmony an important stylistic element. The philosophical principles that had ruled music since before the time of Bach were now abandoned in favor of a single guideline: chord movement is governed by *color*, not function. Yet because a random use of color in Impressionist music is no more appropriate than random triads in traditional harmony, Debussy and his contemporaries developed a number of techniques to achieve continuity and balance.

PLANING

Since the Middle Ages, theorists have consistently recommended the use of contrary motion as a means of achieving maximum part independence; parallel fifths and octaves were especially restricted. But Debussy always *liked* parallel motion—particularly parallel perfect intervals. Unbound by convention, he originated a style of harmony known today as PLANING, where chords move in parallel motion with a melody. Similar in concept to the *fauxbourdon* of the fifteenth century, planing effects a fusion of melody and harmony into a single parameter.

Because their use produces quite different harmonic results, a distinction between three types of planing is helpful: *chord-type, diatonic,* and *mixed.* All three types of planing result in harmony that is nonfunctional.

Chord-Type Planing

A "thickening" of a melodic line with chords of *constant* quality is known as CHORD-TYPE PLANING. In Example 11–6 below, the chords in measures 1 and 2 are all minor; in measures 5 and 6 they are added tone chords (see page 273). Notice the parallel tritones in the bass; they create a whole tone effect.

EXAMPLE 11–6   Claude Debussy, *Pelléas and Mélisande,* Act III, Scene II

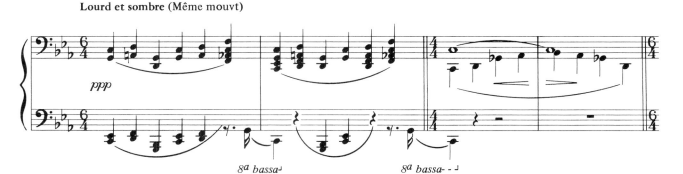

Diatonic Planing

Parallel harmony involving different chord qualities within a single scale system is known as DIATONIC PLANING. In the nonfunctional passage below, second inversion triads move in parallel motion with the contour of the melody (measure 33). Because the chords all belong to E♭ minor, the planing is classified as diatonic.

EXAMPLE 11–7

Claude Debussy, "La Fille aux cheveux de lin" from *Preludes*, Volume I

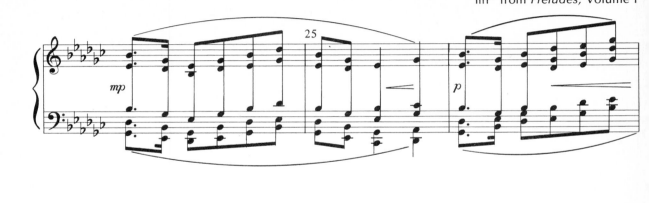

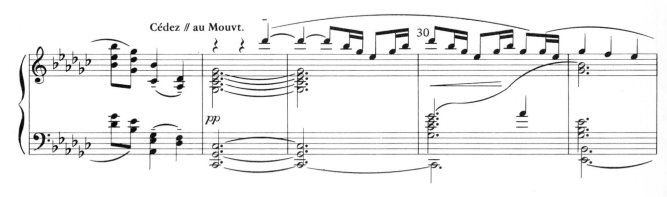

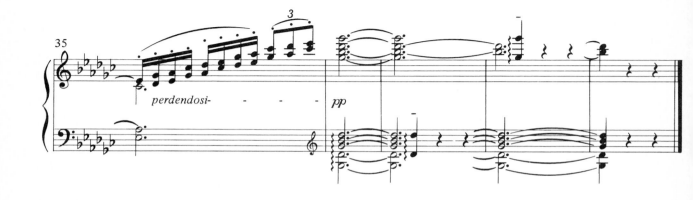

Mixed Planing

The parallel movement of chords of different qualities and outside any single scale or mode is known as MIXED PLANING. In Example 11–8 below, some chords are major, others minor. Notice that while the pitches conform to no one scale system, the tonally ambiguous passage is anchored by an ostinato pedal. This device is common in Impressionist music as a means of suggesting a tonality within nonfunctional harmony.

EXAMPLE 11–8

Claude Debussy, "La Puerta del vino" from *Preludes,* Volume II

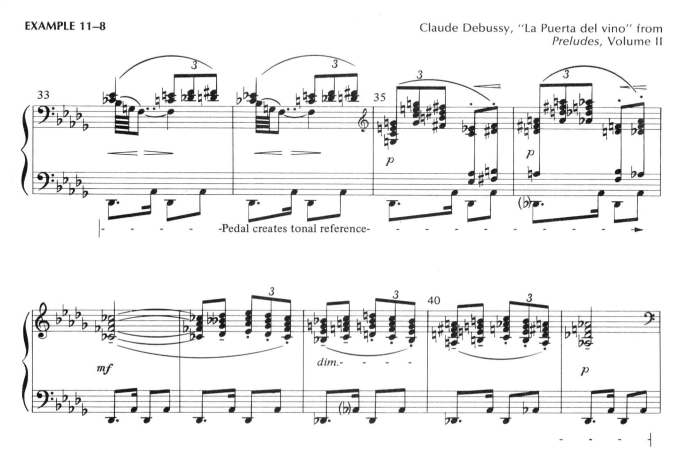

PANDIATONICISM

PANDIATONICISM is a special type of nonfunctional harmony within a single scale system, but *without* conventional tendencies of resolution. In effect, any tone within the scale system can occur after or simultaneously with any other tone. Most often, passages that are pandiatonic are linear in origin. Like the masses and motets of the fourteenth and fifteenth centuries, the harmony results from converging melodic lines. Missing in the Impressionist music, however, is the traditional concept of dissonance and its resolution.

The opening of the *Quartet* by Maurice Ravel (1875–1937) is pandiatonic within an F major scale system. Although the harmony is nonfunctional, a number of melodic techniques contribute to the establishment of F as the tonal center. The triad and chord outlines, for example, and the harmonized F major scale in the second violin and cello add to the tonal orientation. Beginning in measure 5, the instruments reverse their direction and descend—this time pandiatonic in F natural minor (Example 11–9).

EXAMPLE 11–9

Maurice Ravel, *Quartet,* First Movement

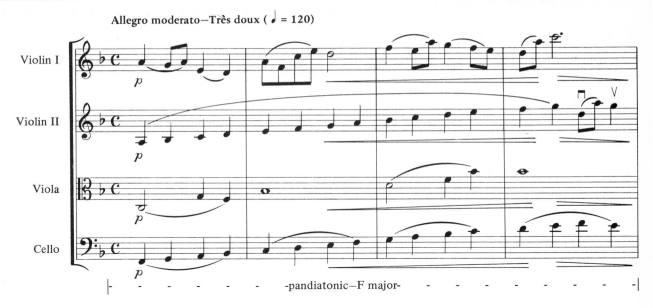

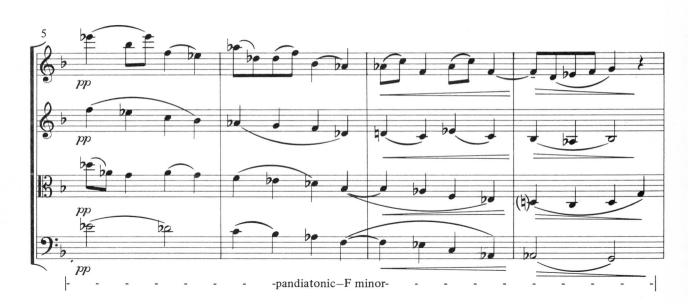

OTHER NEW HARMONIC RESOURCES

Whole Tone Harmony

The whole tone scale produces a nonfunctional harmony comprised of augmented triads. Because each triad is of the same quality, none has a tendency to resolve and none assumes any more importance than another. Notice that in the example below, double sharps are avoided through enharmonic spellings.

Because the effect of whole tone harmony is so distinctive, composers rarely employ it for more than a few measures at a time. A notable exception is Debussy's "Voiles" from *Preludes*, Volume I (Example 11–10).

EXAMPLE 11–10

Claude Debussy, "Voiles" from *Preludes*, Volume I

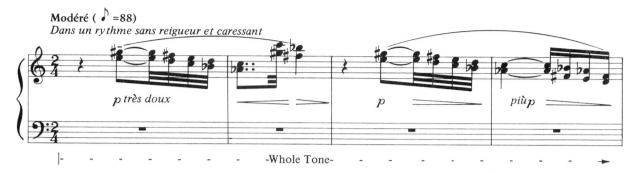

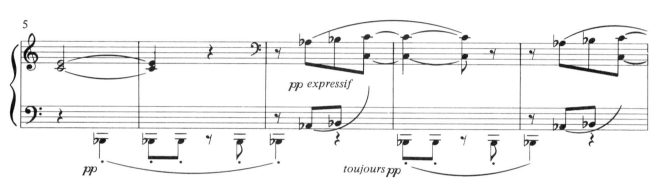

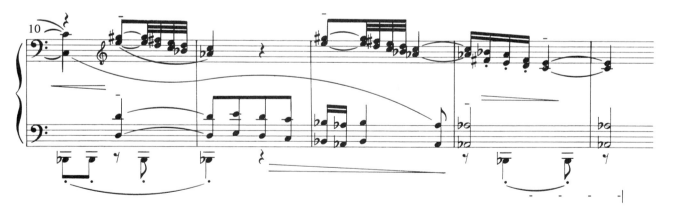

Quartal Harmony

In addition to new harmonic materials already mentioned, a number of composers began to experiment with QUARTAL HARMONY—chords based not on the third, but the fourth.

Quartal harmony is both relatively dissonant and nonfunctional; the Impressionists used it mainly for color in works that were basically tertian. Debussy employs chord-type planing of quartal sonorities in the middle section of the "Sarabande" from *Pour le piano* (Example 11–11).

EXAMPLE 11–11

Claude Debussy, "Sarabande" from *Pour le Piano*

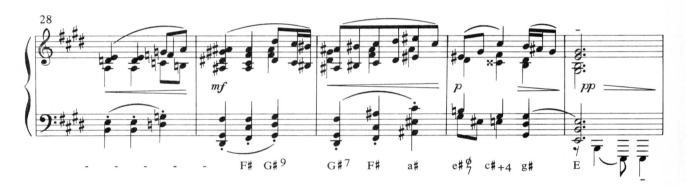

Later composers used the fourth as the basis of a new concept of harmony; this phenomenon will be discussed in Chapter 12.

TRADITIONAL HARMONIC MATERIALS

While passages of functional harmony abound in Impressionist music, composers often employed conventional progressions colored through the use of dissonance, exceptional cadences, third or tritone relation, and other means as well.

Seventh and Ninth Chords

One of the most distinctive elements in the Impressionist vocabulary is *Extended Tertian Harmony*—SEVENTH and NINTH CHORDS. These chords are frequent in traditional harmony, of course, but while common practice composers carefully prepared and resolved the dissonance(s), the Impressionists used seventh and ninth chords exactly like they used simple triads—for color and effect. In the passage below, notice the use of seventh chords of various qualities; many of them are third-related. Notice too the modal cadence to D♯ in measure 7 (Example 11–12).

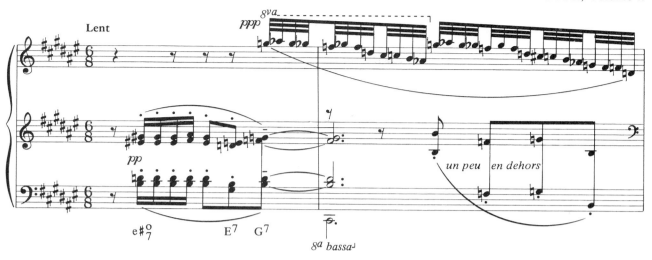

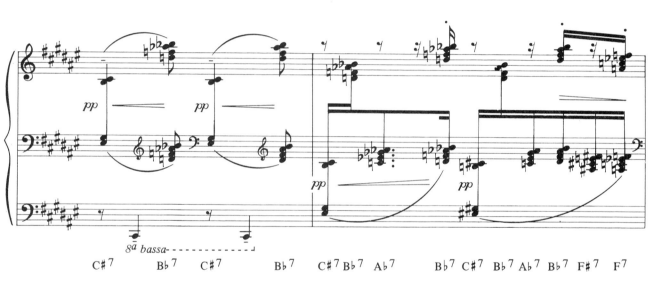

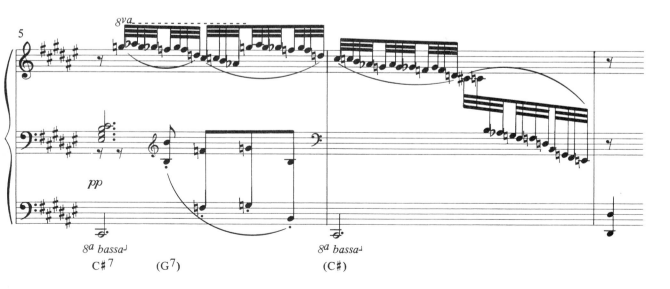

While the Impressionists employed ninth chords in series, they were also used to add color to conventional cadences. In the passage below, nonharmonic tones and a chordal ninth are employed in a traditional authentic cadence (Example 11–13).[1]

EXAMPLE 11–13   Claude Debussy, *First Arabesque*

Third and Tritone Relation

Common throughout the nineteenth century, third relation is especially prevalent in Impressionist works; many examples have been cited previously. Neither was the tritone root relationship new with Debussy. Carefully prepared and resolved, the Neapolitan six–dominant progression is a regular feature of Baroque and Classical music. In the hands of late nineteenth-century composers such as Modest Mussorgsky (1839–1881), however, the tritone relation is used to create an effect. In his *Boris Godunov*, Mussorgsky creates an atmosphere of excitement through an alternation of dominant seventh chords on A♭ and D (Example 11–14).[2]

EXAMPLE 11–14   Modest Mussorgsky, *Boris Godunov*,
Act I, Scene II

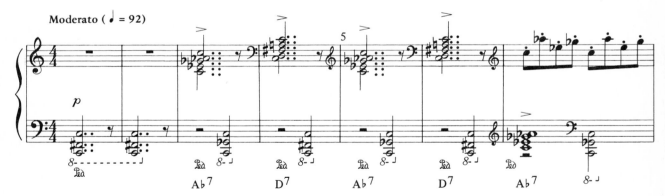

[1]Some theorists would consider the fourth beat of measure 45 an *eleventh* chord (B–D♯–F♯–A–C♯–E). Chords higher than the ninth, however, are more a feature of music after 1920 than they are of Impressionist music. The E♮ in measure 45 *sounds* like an anticipation and there is no real reason to identify it as a chord tone. Moreover, the seventh and ninth resolve by step in traditional fashion; the "eleventh" does not.

[2]Although not an Impressionist, Mussorgsky anticipated a number of Impressionist techniques.

Added Tone Harmony

Another technique employed by late nineteenth-century composers to breathe new life into old materials is ADDED TONE HARMONY—an alteration of conventional tertian chords through the addition of one or more dissonant pitches. A simple triad, for example, retains its functional tendencies, yet becomes a completely new sonority through the addition of a second, fourth, or sixth above the bass.

In his suite *Pour le Piano*, Debussy employs chord-type planing using triads with added sixth (Example 11–15).

EXAMPLE 11–15
Claude Debussy, "Sarabande" from
Pour le piano

FORM, RHYTHM, AND ORCHESTRATION

In addition to new concepts of melody and harmony, Debussy's approach to form was innovative as well. From the beginning, he rejected the sonata and rondo—the traditional "grand forms;" instead of inventing new ones, he *instinctively* created a unique shape for each work.

Phrase Structure

The term "mosaic" is often used to describe Debussy's melodic style. Melodies are short, cell-like fragments (rarely as long as four measures) that are repeated, varied, transposed, and transformed. The effect is never one of planned symmetry, but of spontaneity.

The movement "The Little Shepherd" from Debussy's keyboard suite *The Children's Corner* is illustrative of his formal approach. The work is based on four melodic fragments:

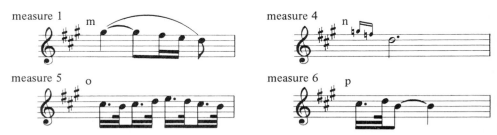

The first two motives *(m* and *n)* begin and end the first phrase respectively. Motive *n* serves as a cadential embellishment (Example 11–16).

EXAMPLE 11–16

Claude Debussy, "The Little Shepherd" from *The Children's Corner*

The third and fourth motives *(o* and *p)* are heard in the next phrase (Example 11–17).

EXAMPLE 11–17

A second statement of motive *o* is more extended; a strong cadence in A major (introduced by motive *m*) concludes the phrase (Example 11–18).

EXAMPLE 11–18

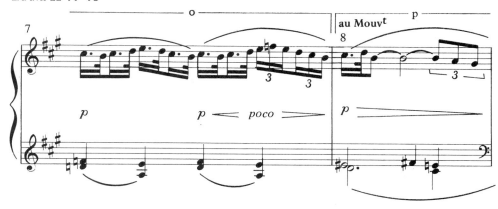

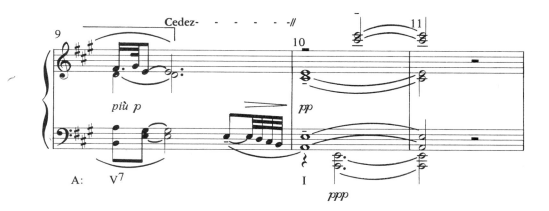

As the work continues, motives are transformed through a number of traditional techniques: compression, expansion, inversion, and so on. The melodic material is always fresh, yet always clearly derived from the first two phrases (Example 11–19).

EXAMPLE 11–19

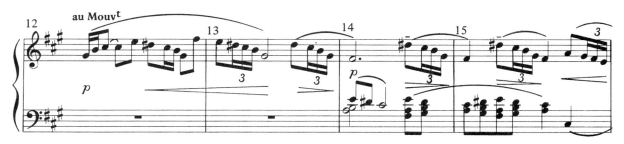

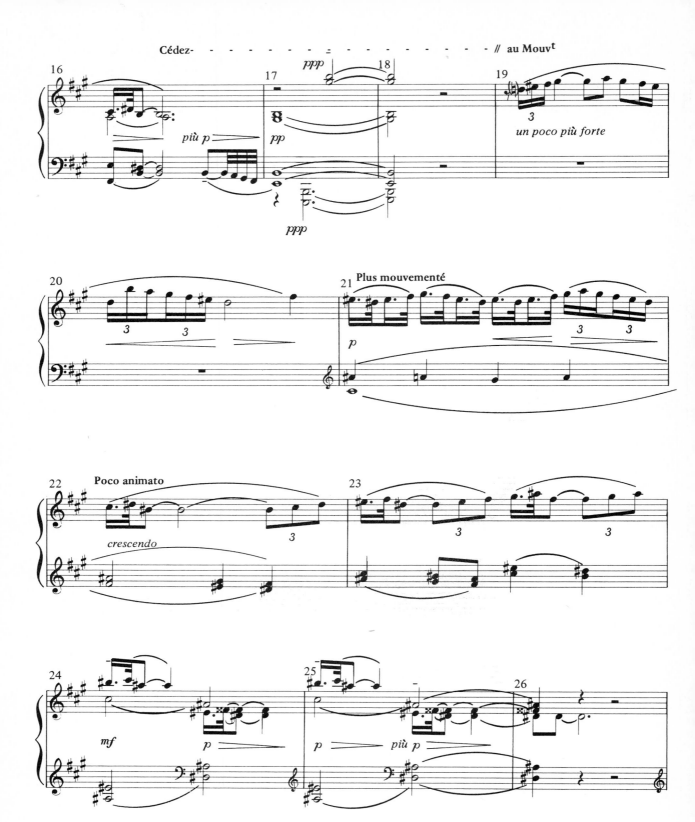

A complete return of measures 7–11 occurs beginning in measure 27. This "recapitulation" serves to round out the work and balance the more lengthy middle section (Example 11–20).

EXAMPLE 11–20

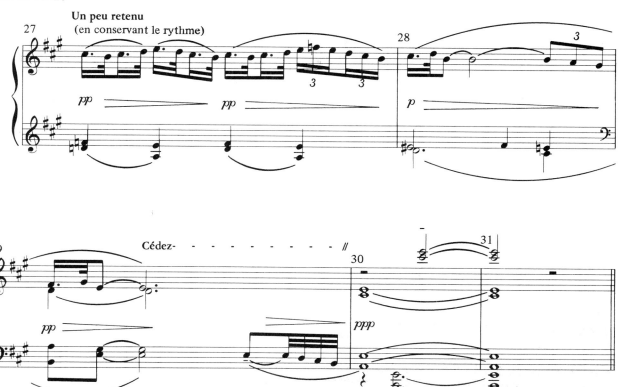

Formally, "The Little Shepherd" is in three parts. The middle section emphasizes both the dominant, E (measures 12–18), and the remote key of G♯ (measures 21–26).[3] As is often the case in Impressionist music, a single pitch serves as the link in a modulation. Held over from the chord in measure 26, the D♯ falls to D♮ as the dotted figure and the key of A major return.

RHYTHM

Debussy's use of rhythm is among the most forward-looking elements of his style; his innovations caused immediate and long lasting influence on the next generation of composers. Through a subtle, flexible rhythm, Debussy achieved his goal of an improvisational effect. The barline is never sacred and although he employs changing meters far less often than others (Ravel, for example), there is nothing about Debussy's rhythm that sounds predetermined.

Many Impressionist works are virtual catalogues of rhythmic effects. Hemiola is common as is two-against-three (sesquialtera), syncopation, and polyrhythm. The passage below from *La Mer* is typical (Example 11–21).

---

[3]In contemporary music which often includes the use of *both* major and minor modes, one speaks simply of "G♯" rather than "G♯ major" or "G♯ minor."

EXAMPLE 11–21

EXAMPLE 11–22

Claude Debussy, *La Mer*, First Movement

Debussy and other Impressionist composers used rhythm to add the animation, the sparkle to a passage of nonfunctional harmony. In another example from *La Mer*, each of five different parts is articulated by a different rhythm (Example 11–22).

In some Impressionist works, rhythm rises above its traditional role of creating momentum and continuity to become *structural*—an equal partner with melody, harmony, and form. Such a concept of rhythm foreshadows monumental twentieth-century works such as Stravinksy's *Le Sacre du printemps*.

ORCHESTRATION

The parameter of orchestration has previously not been discussed in detail because while the orchestras of Bach, Mozart, and Brahms were all different, and while they contributed to the overall stylistic effect, instrumentation was much less important than melody, harmony, form, or rhythm. In Debussy's approach to orchestration, however, one sees most clearly the association between musical and graphic Impressionists. The orchestra is used to produce an *atmosphere* that is punctuated by independent lines. Debussy dots the page with instrumental color exactly like Renoir and Degas used dots of bright colors blended into a particular effect. This practice of using "points" of musical color is known as *pointillism* and is an important element in the styles of several twentieth-century composers.

Although the Impressionist orchestra is typically large, the size is not for the purpose of producing great volume. On the contrary, even in major orchestral works, instruments are used a few at a time; the result is the texture of a chamber work with all the color of the Romantic orchestra.

An excerpt from Debussy's *Prélude à l'aprés-midi d'un faune* (1894) appears on pages 289–292 in full score. Study this passage and observe the subtle shadings of orchestral color. The flute dominates, but is supported by a delicate atmosphere punctuated by wind and harp commentary.

THE ANALYSIS OF CONTEMPORARY MUSIC: CHORD CHEMISTRY

Because we are (unfortunately) conditioned to hearing and performing mainly music from the Common Practice Era, the analysis of music outside that period is often problematic. Except to tell us that the music is nonfunctional, Roman numerals are of little practical value. Prose descriptions of the music may be valuable for research or teaching, but are less helpful in a performing score. In recent years, several theorists have proposed analytical systems for dealing with the complex harmony of contemporary music. One of these approaches, particularly valuable in the study of Impressionist music, is the so-called "Chemistry" analysis devised by Howard Hanson.[4]

Among other topics, Hanson's book *The Harmonic Materials of Modern Music* includes a system of harmonic analysis based on a study of the component intervals (the "chemistry") of chords. Chemistry analysis entails not only calculating the quality of intervals above the bass, but of *all* intervals sounding within the chord. Intervals are classified in one of six categories according to their relative stability (Example 11–23).

---

[4]"Cnemistry" analysis is based on the same concepts and accomplishes much the same purposes as the procedure often described as the computation of *Interval Vector*.

Category	Analytical Symbol	Intervals
PERFECT	P	Perfect Fifth/Perfect Fourth
MAJOR	M	Major Third/Minor Sixth
MINOR	N	Minor Third/Major Sixth
SECOND	S	Major Second/Minor Seventh
DISSONANCE	D	Minor Second/Major Seventh
TRITONE	T	Augmented Fourth/Diminished Fifth

Intervals that are not included in the categories above are respelled enharmonically. A diminished seventh, for example, would be classified as *N*—a major sixth; an augmented third would be *P*—a perfect fourth.

The process of chemistry analysis begins with measuring and recording intervals above the bass. Octave duplications are discounted; to avoid errors, it is best to rewrite the chord with octaves eliminated and with all of the pitches contained within a *single* octave. Thus for analytical purposes, a chord should be reduced to its raw material:

becomes

Intervals are calculated and recorded above the bass; this done, the next lowest pitch is then considered the bass and intervals are reckoned above it. The process is repeated until all but the highest pitch has served as the bass (Example 11–24).

EXAMPLE 11–24   Calculation of Chord Chemistry

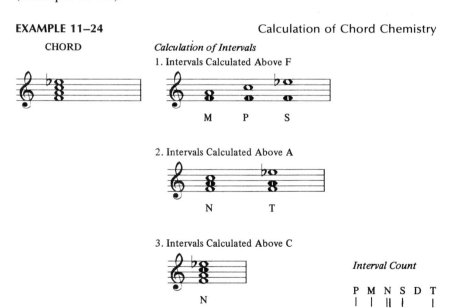

The data from the chemistry analysis are expressed using (in order) the letters PMNSDT as appropriate. Where two or more intervals of the same type are present (the two "Ns" in the chord above, for example), this information is expressed as an exponent. The complete symbol for the chord shown above is PMN²ST. Complex, nontertian chords are analyzed using the same process (Example 11–25).

EXAMPLE 11–25

EXAMPLE 11–25   Nontertian Chords—Interval Content

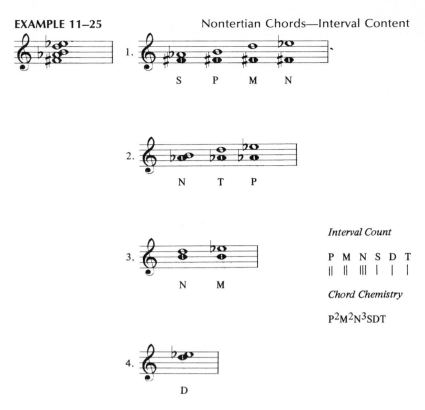

The value of Chord Chemistry Analysis is not in a chord-by-chord approach as with Roman numerals, but in comparing the interval content at specific points in a composition—harmonic pillars, important melodic ideas, ostinatos, etc. Compare, for example, the chemistries of the three chords shown in Example 11–26. The first is an inverted major triad; the second is a more complex chord based on minor thirds and tritones; the third, a whole tone sonority. From the analytical symbols, the chemistry of each chord and the differences between them in terms of dissonance and relative stability are clear. Not only are the intervals contained in each chord important, the interval categories *lacking* may give valuable information concerning the harmonic and/or melodic structure.

EXAMPLE 11–26   Comparative Chemistry Analysis

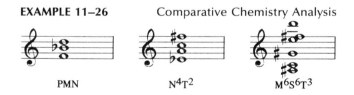

SUMMARY

The use in analysis of Chord Chemistry instead of Roman numerals accents the differences between Impressionist and common practice music: the former relies on separate intervals and chords; the latter is based on progressions of pitches and triads. Although Impressionism in music as in painting continued to be important well into the twentieth century, its primary function was as a link between the old and the new. Just as the innovations of Monet and Gauguin combined with other influences to produce Cubism in the early twentieth century, the new ideas of Debussy were joined with those of a few other composers to bridge the gap between the traditional and the revolutionary.

1. Provide Chord Chemistry Analysis for the following chords and scales.

2. Compose a whole tone melody for violin of 10–15 measures. Select one or more techniques to insure that E is heard as a tonal reference point. The melody may deviate from the basic material as appropriate. Avoid periodic formal structure.

3. Repeat the exercise on the previous page using a synthetic scale of your own invention. Write the melody for cello and create an emphasis on the pitch F♯. Explore the various triad outlines available in your scale.

scale: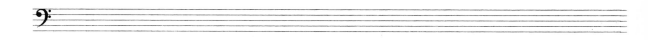

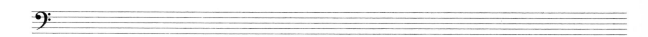

4. Using the composition below as a guide, write a waltz in Impressionist style. Choose one or two techniques and restructure the work around them. Change *any* parameter you wish. Consider a modal or pentatonic melody, harmonic planing, and perhaps an ostinato bass. Use a separate sheet for your composition and provide an analysis.

Schubert

The Kyrie *Cunctipotens* below is in Mode I (Dorian). Using the chant as a stylistic and melodic guide, compose a piece for solo flute, violin, or oboe that is based on Dorian mode and that preserves the rhythmic flow of the chant while employing traditional melodic and metric notation. Embellish the melody as appropriate.

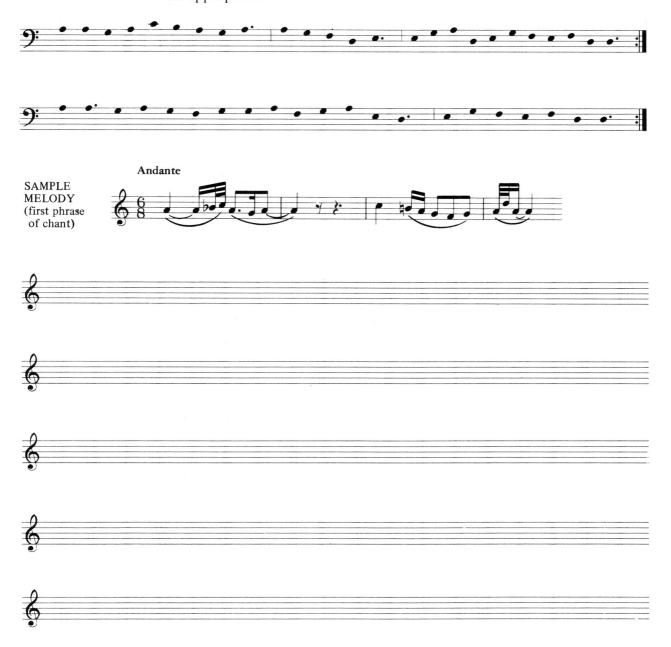

SAMPLE
MELODY
(first phrase
of chant)

1. Harmonize the following phrase using in turn chord-type, diatonic, and mixed planing. Insure that the phrase ends with a cadential effect with E as the center. The harmony of each version need not be limited to planing although this should be the predominant technique.

a. Chord-Type Planing

Ravel

b. Diatonic Planing

c. Mixed Planing

Recopy the eight measures of Ravel's *Quartet* (Example 11–9). Compose at least two additional phrases which are stylistically similar and which continue the pandiatonic harmony. Make certain that F remains the tonal center. Use other Impressionist techniques if you wish, but retain the same style.

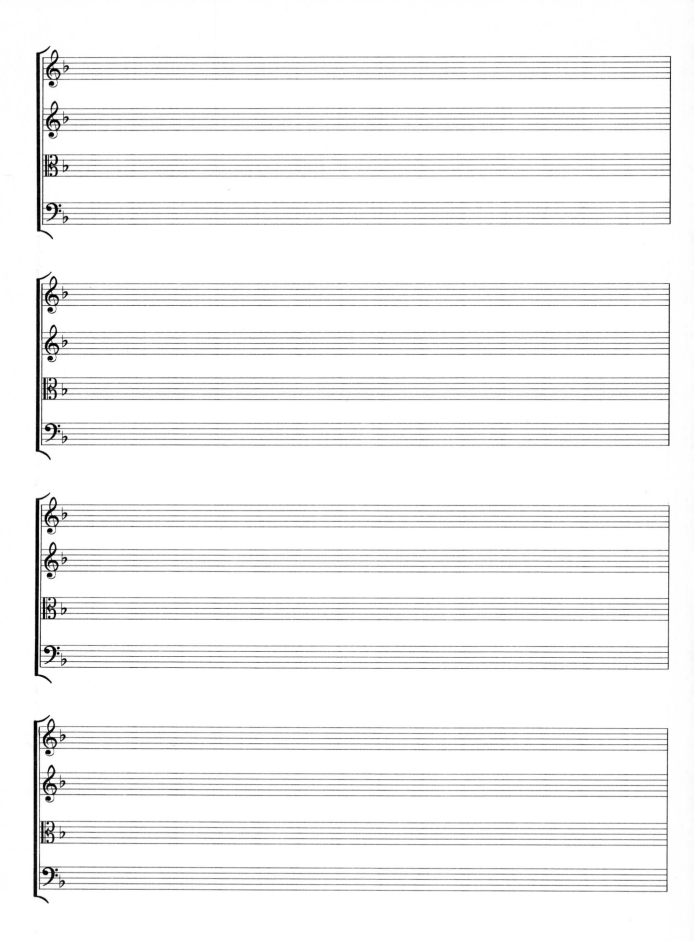

Provide analysis as directed.

Claude Debussy, *Prélude à l'aprés-midi d'un faune*

SUGGESTIONS FOR ADDITIONAL PROJECTS

1. Write a composition for piano that employs added tones to conventional functional progressions. Other techniques may be used as well, but remember that too many different materials result in disorientation.

2. Compose a passage for woodwind quintet (flute, oboe, clarinet, French Horn, and bassoon) that is based primarily on quartal chords but which includes strong tonal cadences.

3. Set the following poem in an Impressionist style. Pay careful attention to the natural spoken accents and inflections. Avoid a repetitive metric pattern. Avoid as well a periodic phrase structure.

Roads

I cannot stand and look upon a road
    with cool, unfettered eyes.
It is at once a calling and a goad
    and all in spite of me, my heart replies.
For there is something in my feet that aches
    to touch the road that leads to any land.
And there is something in my soul that makes
    my every ache a mandate and command.
And all the roads I go will never drown
    this call in me, for well I know
I cannot be content to rest or lay me down
    while there is yet another road to go.

SUGGESTED LISTENING

Claude Debussy, *Prélude à l'aprés-midi d'un faune* (1894)

        String Quartet (1893)

        Deux arabasques (1888)

Frederick Delius, *On Hearing the First Cuckoo in Spring* (1912)

Charles T. Griffes, *The White Peacock* (1915)

Maurice Ravel, *String Quartet* (1902)

        Jeux d'eau (1901)

        Shéhérazade (1903)

The analysis below illustrates how important structural features may be identified on a performing score. On the following pages, continue the analysis in a similar style.

Claude Debussy, ''Sarabande'' from *Pour le piano*

Claude Debussy ''Sarabande'' from *Pour le piano* (continued)

Chapter 12
New Concepts and Materials

The early twentieth century was a time of many new movements. Just as a reaction against the lush romanticism of Wagner and Franck led Debussy to consider new resources, many composers responded negatively to Impressionism. *Primitivism,* associated chiefly with Stravinsky and Bartók, was a reaction against Impressionist ambiguity and understatement. Works in this vein often feature driving rhythms and harsh dissonance. Especially in the music of Arnold Schoenberg, *Expressionism* resulted from a deeply introspective viewpoint; musically, it was manifested in still greater harmonic dissonance and angular melody. Finally, after the ravages of World War I, *Neoclassicism* brought a return not only to smaller ensembles and traditional forms, but to classical concepts of symmetry.

Alongside the several "isms" of the twentieth century, a number of composers worked more or less independently and were more influential on succeeding generations than they were on their own. Alexander Scriabin (1872–1915), for example, was among those who laid the groundwork for the Serial Technique. Charles Ives (1874–1954), fifty years ahead of his time, experimented with microtones and anticipated many later developments such as polytonality and atonality. Erik Satie (1866–1925) questioned the very purpose of music and its existence "for art's sake."

Few composers before 1925 completely rejected either tonality or traditional aesthetic values. On the contrary, their music was a natural evolution of nineteenth-century Romanticism tempered by Impressionist color. Free to select their own methods and materials, most composers relied on established techniques such as chromaticism, planing, and rhythmic irregularity. At the same time, however, a number of new concepts offered an entirely new musical vocabulary; these concepts are the focus of the present chapter.

NEW CONCEPTS IN MELODY

Melodic Style

The traditional distinction between vocal and instrumental melodic styles becomes blurred in some music of the early twentieth century. In the keyboard and orchestral works of Prokofiev, Shostakovitch, and others, melodies are comprised of wide leaps, angular turns, and unanticipated tonal shifts. Similar characteristics are evident in the vocal writing of other composers who, seeking an expressive style, made severe demands on performers. The melodic style of the work below, for example, is disjunct; without the text, one might assume that the intended medium were violin or clarinet—not soprano voice (Example 12–1).

EXAMPLE 12–1   Hugo Wolf, *Singt mein Schatz wie ein Fink*

The Melodic Cell

Many composers in the early twentieth century viewed the *interval* as a melodic entity much as Debussy had liberated the chord from its traditional role in the progression. With a technique similar to Debussy's mosaic phrase structure, composers often crafted themes from a melodic cell (or motive), then expanded, compressed, transposed or transformed them to form a complete phrase. In the passage below from *Density 21.5* (for solo flute)[1] by Edgar Varèse (1883–1965), notice the development of the opening three-note cell to create constantly new, yet related material (Example 12–2). Observe too, the important ascending step progression that provides direction and momentum to the phrase.

[1]In a sense, Varèse's *Density 21.5* is an *atonal* composition because no single tonal center is built and maintained in the traditional manner. The question of tonality/atonality, however, is far from clear cut. As will be discussed in Chapter 13, a work is atonal when no sense of tonality exists *or* when a brief tonal center or centers occur through nontraditional means. The first five measures of *Density 21.5* center on F♯; this area, however, is created primarily through agogic and metric accents—not through conventional melodic and harmonic tendencies. Students must be prepared to deal with music which fits neither the tonal nor the atonal category with precision.

EXAMPLE 12–2

Edgar Varèse, *Density 21.5*

Stravinsky adopted a similar melodic style, but rather than actually transforming a melodic cell, he more often simply added to it so that the *same* pattern is constantly repeated with additions. This process is often termed "Additive" melody. In Example 12–3, a single rhythmic idea generates a passage of seventeen measures.

EXAMPLE 12–3

Igor Stravinsky, *Petroushka*

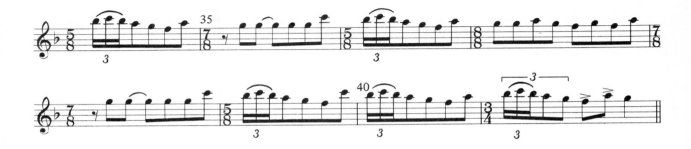

NEW CONCEPTS IN HARMONY

Most composers of the early twentieth century remained loyal both to tonal and tertian principles. The striking new sounds they produced resulted in large part from a new attitude toward dissonance.

DISSONANCE

Although the practice of leaving dissonances unresolved was established in the late nineteenth century, many twentieth-century composers rejected the relatively "soft" dissonances of the Impressionists (ninth chords, triads with added sixth, and so forth) and employed harsh, clashing sonorities. Not only are dissonances often left unresolved, they are scored and/or doubled in a manner which heightens the dissonant effect. In many works, traditional concepts of tension and relaxation cannot be equated with consonance and dissonance. The new role of dissonance was not "to afford elegance" in a consonant resolution (as Zarlino proclaimed in the sixteenth century), but as a tonal resource equal in expressive potential to consonance.

Typical use of dissonance is seen in the piano arrangement of Stravinsky's *Le Sacre* shown in Example 12–4. Along with the simple, additive melody in the upper part, there is a meandering line of eighth notes harmonized with mixed planing. Where Debussy might have used a unison pedal to support the upper voices, however, Stravinsky employs yet another series of triads. Together, the three parts have a predominance of minor seconds; the effect is tonal, but dissonant.

EXAMPLE 12–4   Igor Stravinsky, *Le Sacre du printemps*, Part II

TONALITY

While much of the music written before World War II is tonal, tonality is not established as predictably as it is in Brahms or Mahler, for example. Many twentieth-century works are tonal without including a single functional progression; tonality is established through more subtle techniques. The term FREE TONALITY is frequently used to describe the process of creating a tonal reference point through nontraditional means.

The Ostinato

Inherited from the Impressionists, the ostinato became an important means of suggesting tonality in a nontraditional way. In Example 12–5, although the scale system of the lower voice is neither major nor minor, and the ostinato in the upper voice is likewise ambiguous, the repetition of the pitch G and the agogic accent on the pitch C provide a stable sense of tonality. Notice the contrapuntal motion between the two voices at the cadences in measures 5 and 9.

EXAMPLE 12–5   Béla Bartók, *Bagatelle III*

MODULATION

As concepts of tonality changed during the early twentieth century, so inevitably did those of modulation. Where Mozart or Brahms used carefully crafted transitions to link major tonal areas, composers like Prokofiev and Shostakovitch were as likely to introduce abrupt key changes, even within a phrase.

The finale of Prokofiev's *Sonata No. 6* centers on A and has a Lydian inflection. The sudden introduction of B♭ and G♭ (measures 5–6) precedes an E♭ melodic minor scale in measure 7. The return of the original tonality is accomplished through a functional progression: IV–V$_4^6$–i (Example 12–6).

EXAMPLE 12–6

Sergei Prokofiev, *Sonata No. 6*, Op. 82,
Fourth Movement

Vivace

The C Major Prelude from Shostakovitch's *Twenty-Four Preludes and Fugues* reflects a typical twentieth-century attitude toward key. There is no question that the tonal center is C, but the composer appears to use whatever chromatic materials he wishes as a supplement. Some of the chords are both dissonant and quite remote (measure 12, for example). The striking effect of such unexpected dissonant and chromatic shifts is often termed "wrong note harmony" and is associated with Shostakovitch, Prokofiev, and other contemporary Russian composers (Example 12–7).

EXAMPLE 12–7

Dimitri Shostakovitch, *Prelude No. 1* from *24 Preludes and Fugues*, Op. 84

Melodic motion in one or more voices may effect a link between keys. Bartók, for example, moves from an area centered on B to one on A♭ primarily through a descending bass (measures 4–7). Notice that the cadence in measures 6–7 is authentic in the new key (Example 12–8).

EXAMPLE 12–8   Béla Bartók, *Bagatelle VI*

New Version © Copyright 1950 by Boosey & Hawkes, Inc. Reprinted by permission.

BIMODALITY

The passage in the example above illustrates BIMODALITY—the use of *both* major and minor modal degrees within a given tonality. Notice that in the tonal area on B (measures 1–5), both D and D♯ are present consistently; in the cadence on A♭, both C and C♭ appear. Bimodality is an important element in the styles of several twentieth-century figures including Stravinsky and Schoenberg.

POLYCHORDS

When two or more chords, *each having a different root* are combined to form a larger sonority, the structure is known as a POLYCHORD. While a conventional ninth or even seventh chord might be thought of as having two overlapping triadic elements, a true polychord is characterized by the contrast of the two elements.

Ninth, eleventh, and thirteenth chords are common in music of the twenieth century; these chords, however, are *heard* as the extension of thirds above a single root.

Polychords generally feature the *contrast* of the two elements. The chords below are less likely to be heard as extended tertian structures because the upper chord belongs to a different scale system than the lower.

Some composers employ polychords solely for their dissonant effect. Stravinsky, for example, uses an E♭⁷/F♭ polychord in the horns and strings to create a raw, primitive atmosphere (Example 12–9).

EXAMPLE 12–9

Igor Stravinsky, *Le Sacre du printemps*

Prevalent especially after World War I is a new concept of harmony based on the polychord. The passage below from William Schuman's *Three Score Set* is comprised entirely of polychords. The dissonances are generally not as harsh as those in the Stravinsky example, but the effect is striking nevertheless. Notice the use of inversions and the variety of chord qualities. These factors, as well as the relationship between the two roots of each chord, are important areas for analysis (Example 12–10).

EXAMPLE 12–10

William Schuman, *Three Score Set*

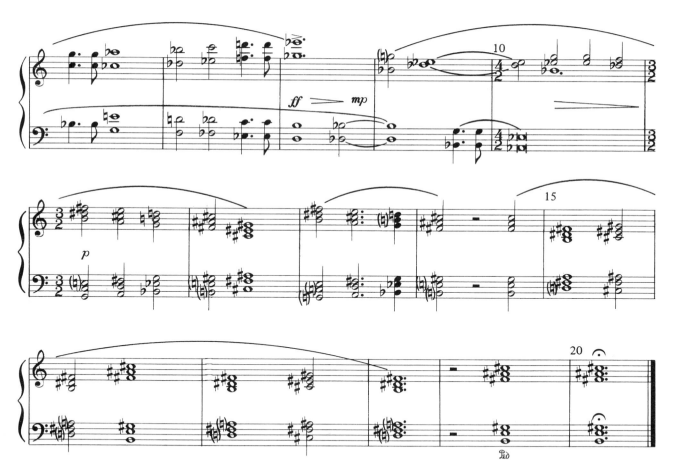

POLYTONALITY

A harmonic technique associated especially with some French composers of the 1920s and 1930s *(Les Six)* is POLYTONALITY—the simultaneous establishment of two or more different tonal centers. Tonal areas may be created either through conventional functional progressions or with more modern techniques.

Some composers employ different key signatures for each voice. In the work below, Bartók uses four sharps in the upper staff, four flats in the lower (Example 12–11).

EXAMPLE 12–11   Béla Bartók, *Bagatelle I*

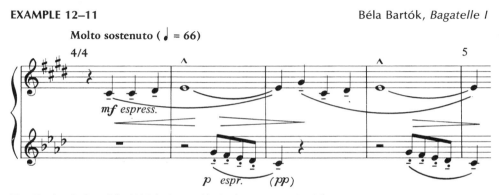

Among twentieth-century composers who often dispensed with key signatures altogether is Darius Milhaud (1892–1974). In the second movement of his *Saudades do Brazil*, the upper voice is in F♯ minor while the lower is in F minor (Example 12–12).

EXAMPLE 12–12

Darius Milhaud, *Saudades do Brazil*
(Botafogo)

Reprinted by permission of Editions Max Eschig, Paris, owners of the copyright.

Simultaneity

In his *Fourth Symphony* (Example 12–13), Charles Ives creates a complex mixture of independent voices that is both polytonal and polyrhythmic.[2] The concept of SIMULTANEITY—the combination of simple elements into a more complex texture—is important in the music of Ives and other twentieth-century composers as well.

---

[2]POLYRHYTHM is distinguished from polymeter by the fact that in the former there is only one notated meter, while in the latter, the music is actually written in two or more different meters.

EXAMPLE 12–13

Charles Ives, *Symphony No. 4* Second Movement

New Concepts and Materials   **311**

NONTERTIAN HARMONY

Many of the same composers who expanded tertian principles to include polytonality were also those who experimented with and refined nontertian harmony. Discussed briefly in Chapter 11, Quartal Harmony appeared in the late nineteenth century. Harmony based on the second developed somewhat later but is of equal importance in contemporary music.

QUARTAL HARMONY

Associated with several major twentieth-century figures, quartal harmony is most often based on three- or four-note sonorities:

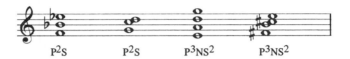

$$P^2S \qquad P^2S \qquad P^3NS^2 \qquad P^3NS^2$$

A larger number of perfect fourths or the use of fourths that are not perfect creates a more dissonant and less stable chord:

$$P^2M^3NS^2DT$$

The compositional problems associated with whole tone harmonies are encountered also with quartal structures: their sound is so distinctive that continued use may result in fatigue. Accordingly, most composers use quartal harmony with discretion. *Every* chord is rarely quartal; tertian and other types of nontertian chords provide variety. The excerpt below is typical; the quartal chords used to harmonize the descending scale passages are tempered by a tertian pedal (Example 12–14).

EXAMPLE 12–14   Roy Harris, "Bells" from *Little Suite*

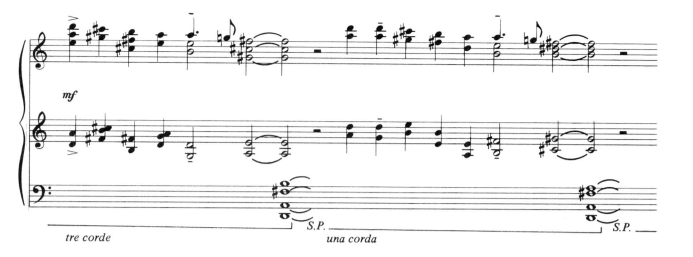

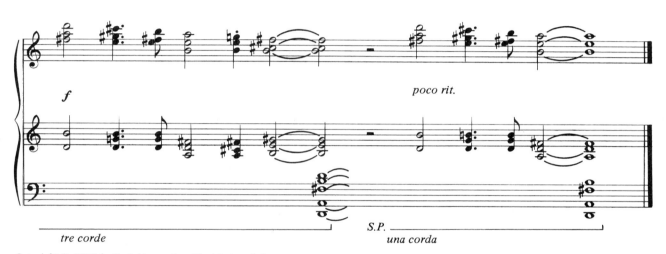

An *a cappella* choral work featuring a mixture of quartal and tertian chords is shown in Example 12–15. Both of the two major cadences are on E; notice that in the first, Hindemith omits the third (measure 11).

EXAMPLE 12–15   Paul Hindemith, *A Swan* from *Six Chansons*

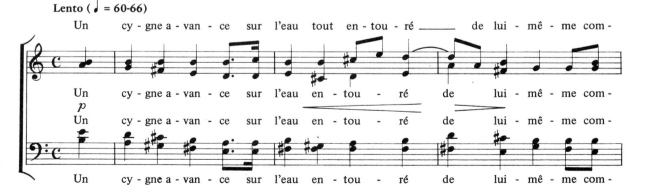

à cet ê - tre a - jou-te la trem-blan-te i - ma - ge de bon - heur et de dou - te.

SECUNDAL HARMONY

Chords based on seconds have the same dual role in twentieth-century harmony as do chords based on fourths: they provide effect within a tertian system; when used consistently, they create a new concept of harmony. Individual chords in seconds are termed CLUSTERS; the harmonic concept is known as SECUNDAL.

Clusters

A number of twentieth-century composers were attracted to clusters as a means of enlivening tertian harmony. A cluster may include from three to as many as twelve or more different pitches; typical examples are shown below.

NSD M^2S^3T $P^2MN^2S^2D^2T$

A distinctive use of clusters is seen in the introduction to the Polka from Shostakovitch's ballet *The Golden Age* (Example 12–16). The four-note cluster has the effect of a half cadence—anticipating the coming theme. Notice the unusual notation necessary to indicate both F_4 and $F\sharp_4$ in the same chord (measure 3).

EXAMPLE 12–16   Dimitri Shostakovitch, "Polka" from *The Golden Age*

A more complex use of clusters is seen in Ives' song *Lincoln, the Great Commoner* (Example 12–17). Amid tertian and nontertian chords, Ives uses six-note clusters to suggest the effect of an earthquake's "wrenching the rafters."

EXAMPLE 12–17   Charles Ives, *Lincoln, the Great Commoner.*

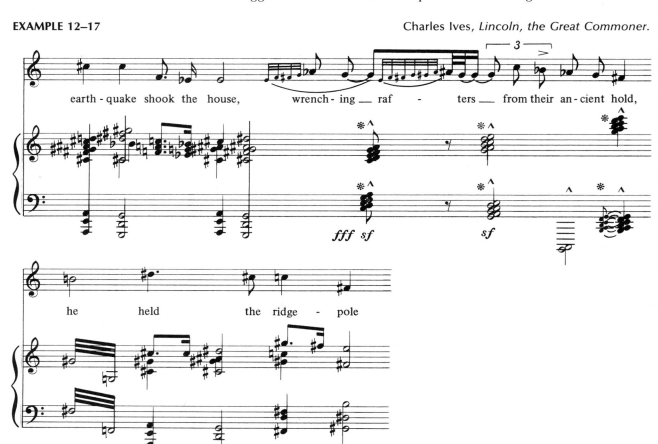

Secundal Harmony

When clusters dominate a composition, the harmony is secundal. In Example 12–18, clusters are to be played with the entire forearm. The notation Cowell employs has become standard; the sharp sign at the top of each symbol indicates a cluster played on the black keys. The simple, naive melody in the upper voice is clearly F♯ Mixolydian.

EXAMPLE 12–18

THE ANALYSIS OF CONTEMPORARY MUSIC: HARMONIC FLUCTUATION

Paul Hindemith's theories of melodic structure were discussed briefly in Chapter 13 of Volume I. Series Two, it will be remembered, is a measure of interval strength ranging from the most stable (the perfect fifth) to the least stable (the tritone). The root or predominating pitch of each interval is shown in Example 12–19 by a whole note.

EXAMPLE 12–19

Series Two
root
indeterminate

Determination of Chord Root

Hindemith's Series Two is useful in determining the root of either a simple or complex chord. The root of the chord is determined by finding the strongest or "best" interval; the root of that interval (according to Series Two) is taken as the root of the entire structure.

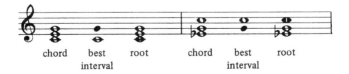

chord   best   root   chord   best   root
interval   interval

The procedure outlined above provides the same information concerning root-bass relationship as does conventional Roman numeral analysis. Hindemith's system, however, is especially valuable in the analysis of complex tertian and nontertian sonorities. Where two or more "best" intervals of the same type and quality are present (two perfect fifths, for example), the *lower* of the two roots is considered the root of the chord. As with Hanson's Chord Chemistry Analysis, all intervals other than the tritone are reinterpreted enharmonically as either perfect, major, or minor in quality.

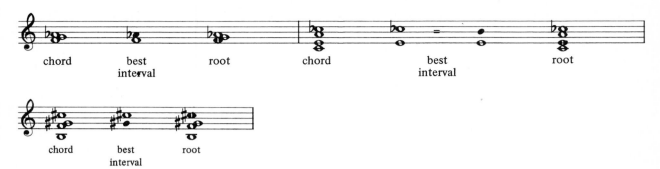

chord   best   root   chord   best   root
      interval   interval

chord   best   root
      interval

Harmonic Fluctuation

According to Hindemith, harmonic tension results from inversion, dissonance, the presence of a tritone, or a combination of these three elements. The "up and down" change in stability and tension in a chord progression Hindemith terms HARMONIC FLUCTUATION.[3] In formulating a theory of contemporary harmony (for both analysis and composition) he classifies chords according to their relative tension; *Group A* includes chords without a tritone, chords in *Group B* contain one or more tritones. Within these two categories, Roman and Arabic numerals are used to designate various degrees of tension and instability. Study the complete system shown in Example 12–20.

EXAMPLE 12–20   Table of Chord Groups

A. CHORDS WITHOUT TRITONE   **B. CHORDS WITH ONE OR MORE TRITONE**

I. Without Second or Seventh   II. Without Minor Second or Major Seventh
1. Root and Bass Identical   1. With Minor Seventh Only;
                                  Root and Bass Identical

2. Root Above Bass   2a. With Major Second or Minor Seventh;
                                  Root and Bass Identical

                                 2b. Root Above Bass

                                 2c. More Than One Tritone

[3]Paul Hindemith, *The Craft of Musical Composition*, Vol. I, (New York: Associated Music Publishers, Inc., 1945), p. 116.

A. CHORDS WITHOUT TRITONE	B. CHORDS WITH ONE OR MORE TRITONE
III. With Second, Seventh, or Both	IV. With Minor Second, Major Seventh, or Both; One or More Tritones
1. Root and Bass Identical	1. Root and Bass Identical

| 2. Root Above Bass | 2. Root Above Bass |

| V. Indeterminate | VI. Indeterminate |

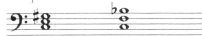

While the analysis of harmonic fluctuation is tedious, it is valuable in a chord-by-chord study of representative passages. For each of the excerpts in Example 12–21, two or more analyses are given. Study the music and determine which system is most valuable for each passage. What, for example, are the shortcomings of each method? The advantages?

EXAMPLE 12–21   Comparative Analysis

A. J.S. Bach

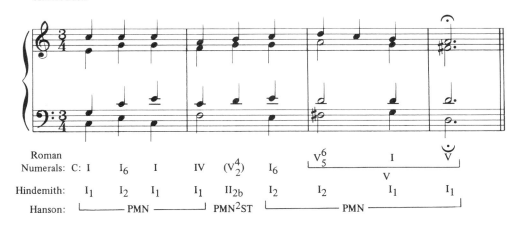

Roman Numerals:	C: I	I₆	I	IV	(V₂⁴)	I₆	V₅⁶	I	V
Hindemith:	I₁	I₂	I₁	I₁	II₂b	I₂	I₂	I₁	I₁
Hanson:	PMN			PMN²ST	PMN				

B. Chopin

Roman Numerals:	e:	i		V⁷			(	chordal mutation			)
Hindemith:		I₂	III₂	III₂	II₂b	VI	II₂c	II₂b	II₂a	II₁	III₁	VI
Hanson:		PMN	P²M²ND	P³NS²	PMN²ST	N⁴T²	M²S²T²	PMN²ST	PMN²ST	PMN²ST	P²MN²S	N⁴T²

New Concepts and Materials **319**

C. Hindemith

| Hindemith: | III$_2$ | | III$_2$ | III$_2$ | III$_2$ | III$_1$ | III$_2$ | III$_2$ | III$_1$ | III$_1$ | | III$_2$ |
| Hanson: | P^{2}S | | P^{2}MNS^2 | P^{3}NS^2 | P^{2}S | P^{3}NS^2 | P^{2}MNS^2 | P^{2}S | P^{3}NS^2 | P^{2}M^{2}ND | | P^{2}MNS^2 |

The analysis of harmonic fluctuation is only one facet of Hindemith's approach to harmonic analysis. Students are urged to obtain a copy of *The Craft of Musical Composition* (Volume I) and study the method in more detail.

NEW CONCEPTS IN RHYTHM

On May 29, 1913, Stravinsky's new ballet *Le Sacre du printemps* premiered in Paris. Audience reaction was not only critical, but violent. In addition to other innovations, *Le Sacre* ushered in a new era in rhythm. Although conventionally notated, there are passages in which all traces of beat and meter are missing, yet in which the rhythm drives forward with such momentum that it virtually assumes control of the work's structure. In *Le Sacre,* rhythm becomes a structural element equal in importance to melody, harmony, and form. In the passage below (Example 12–22), notice the constant sixteenth note micro structure, the total lack of metric regularity, and the use of accents to further complicate and vary the effect.

EXAMPLE 12–22

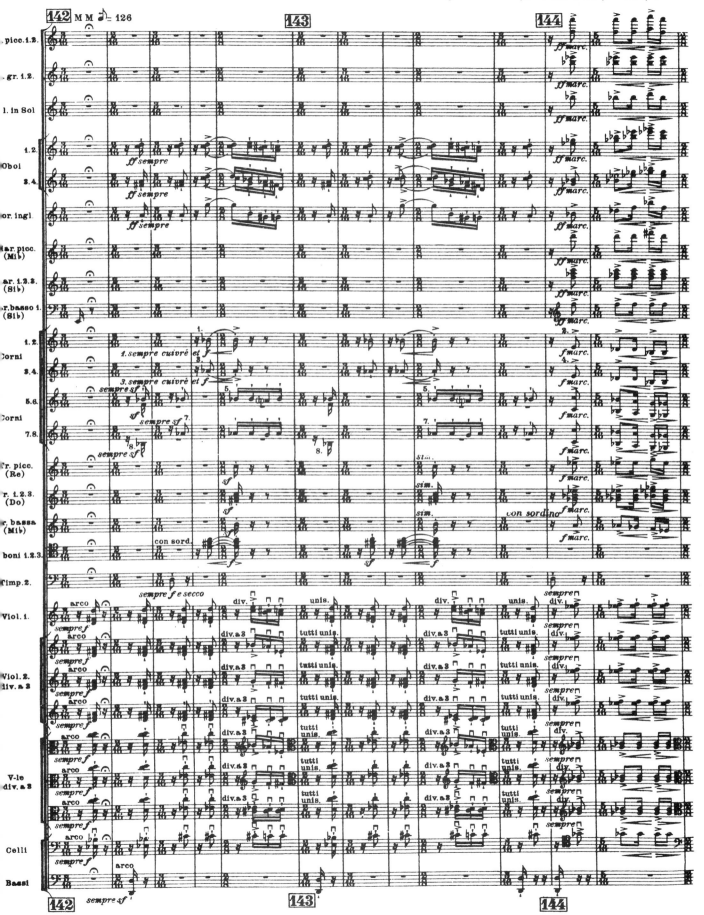

Among composers to make formal presentation of new systems of rhythmic notation is Henry Cowell. In his book *New Musical Resources* (1919), Cowell outlines a rhythmic system which includes new symbols for third, fifth, seventh, ninth, and other nontraditional fractional parts of a beat. A composition employing this new notation is shown in Example 12–23.

EXAMPLE 12–23   Henry Cowell, *Fabric*

NEW CONCEPTS IN FORM

While some composers searched for new means of expression in melody, harmony, and rhythm, others returned not only to the forms of earlier eras, but to the styles and concepts as well. The most prominent of these movements, NEOCLASSICISM, is associated with composers such as Stravinsky, Hindemith, and Prokofiev.

NEOCLASSICISM

Neoclassicism is characterized by a return to Baroque and Classical forms: the fugue, sonata, continuous and sectional variations, the dance suite. Within these and other forms, classical concepts of balance and symmetry, textural clarity, and economy of resources returned as well. Naturally, composers retained many contemporary idioms in their Neoclassical works. Until one looks closely at the harmony, however, the first theme of Stravinsky's *Symphony in C* might be mistaken for Mozart (Example 12–24).

EXAMPLE 12–24

Igor Stravinsky, *Symphony in C,*
First Movement

Paul Hindemith is sometimes described as being Neobaroque in his ornate and highly contrapuntal approach. The fugue shown below is clearly contemporary, yet the traditional fugal procedure (including the tonic–dominant first entry pair) is retained (Example 12–25).

EXAMPLE 12–25

Paul Hindemith, *Fugue in A♭* from
Ludus Tonalis

ARCH FORM

Of the few really new forms to emerge in the early twentieth century, Arch Form, associated principally with Bartók, is probably the most important. ARCH FORM is characterized by a symmetry in themes and/or key schemes in the pattern shown below. Many of Bartók's compositions employ an arch form; the third movement of *Music for Strings, Percussion, and Celesta* is notable among them.

INNOVATIONS IN TIMBRE

A quest for new timbres resulted in some of the most original music of the early twentieth century. Many composers experimented with obtaining unique sounds from conventional instruments. The bassoon solo that opens *Le Sacre*, for example, was in an uncomfortably high register for performers of that day (Example 12–26).

EXAMPLE 12–26   Igor Stravinsky, *Le Sacre du printemps*

Harmonics, innovative articulations, and extremes in register added greatly to the inventory of timbres. The piano was not exempt; Cowell's *The Banshee* calls for the performer to touch the strings of the piano in various ways. As explained in an accompanying table, the letters designate different ways of touching the strings (with the flesh of the finger or fingernail) or movement on them (sweeping from high to low, low to high, etc., Example 12–27).

EXAMPLE 12–27

Henry Cowell, *The Banshee*

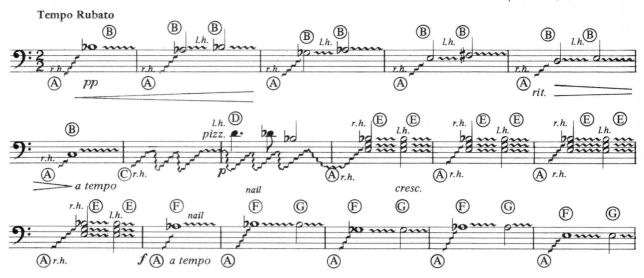

SPRECHSTIMME

Although the concept originated in an opera by Engelbert Humperdinck (1854–1921), Schoenberg was among those responsible for popularizing SPRECHSTIMME—a method of vocal performance in which the singer approximates the notated pitch. Sprechstimme is indicated by an "x" on the note stem; the performer adds a rising or falling inflection in pitch depending on the direction of the melodic line (Example 12–28).

EXAMPLE 12–28

Arnold Schoenberg, *Pierrot Lunaire Rote Messe*

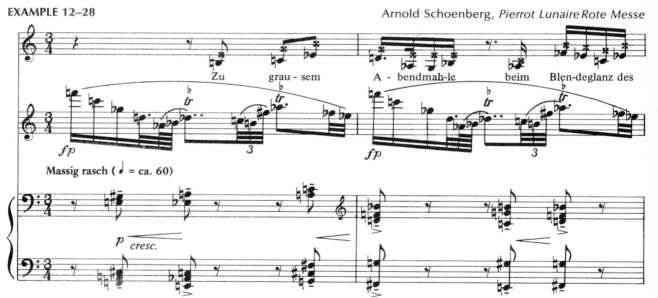

KLANGFARBENMELODIE

Early in the twentieth century, a new concept emerged in which a "melody" resulted not from different pitches, but from the same pitch with varying timbres. Known as KLANGFARBENMELODIE (Tone Color Melody), this concept is evident in a number of works by Schoenberg and his pupil Anton Webern (1883–1945). In the orchestral passage below, pitches change infrequently while timbres are constantly varied (Example 12–29).

New Concepts and Materials **327**

SUMMARY

The preceding discussion of twentieth-century concepts has centered on developments before World War II and in particular, those that originated from late nineteenth-century materials. Modes, synthetic scales, and innovations in style dominated melody. A new concept of dissonance led to startling changes in harmony: clusters, polychords, bimodality, and the like. Although their music was often considered bizarre by audiences accustomed to Strauss and Mahler, many composers forged ahead with even more radical sounds and concepts.

In addition to the new techniques covered in this chapter, two concepts emerged in the first quarter of the new century which are of such importance that an entire chapter will be devoted to each. *Atonality,* with its array of new sounds and organizational problems is discussed in Chapter 13. *Serial Composition,* a systematized atonality, is the subject of Chapter 14.

SUGGESTED COMPOSITION PROJECTS

1. Compose a minuet for string quartet that employs typical minuet rhythmic and formal structure, but features either quartal or secundal harmony (as directed). If you wish, the harmony may be varied to include tertian chords and perhaps unison or solo passages as well.

2. Write a fanfare for trumpet that centers on F and includes either hemiola or simple syncopation. Next, write an accompaniment for piano composed primarily of large clusters. Use the fist, hand, or forearm to vary the effect. Be conscious of the upper and lower pitches of each cluster. For variety, some of the clusters might be arpeggiated.

3. Write a composition for an available instrumental ensemble that illustrates a Neoclassical approach. The work need not be lengthy, but should clearly create a "classical" atmosphere while employing contemporary melodic, rhythmic, and/or harmonic techniques.

Use the given melodic cells to produce a complete phrase or period. Employ a variety of approaches including transformation and the "additive" process associated with Stravinsky. Use either a major or minor tonality as suggested by the key signature. Feel free to vary the meter signature.

1. Write a brief composition for cello and piano that illustrates the establishment of an E (major and/or minor) tonality through harmonic ostinato. Employ the melodic and rhythmic techniques of your choice.

2. On a separate piece of paper, expand the melody below into a complete two-phrase period. In the first phrase, establish a G tonality through the repetition of key pitches. Before or during the second phrase, modulate to a contrasting key.

3. Using the Bartók work on page 309 (Example 12–11) as a model, compose a polytonal work for violin and clarinet. Structure the upper voice in B major (and/or minor) and the lower voice in a contrasting key. Use key signatures. Be conscious of planning cadences and phrase structure. The score should be a *concert score* but be careful not to exceed the ranges of the two instruments. The composition should be about one minute in length.

Write a phrase for flute and piano which illustrates the use of relatively dissonant polychords used to highlight a basically functional, E♭ major tertian harmony. Use melodic, rhythmic, and formal techniques of your choice.

Using the Table of Chord Groups (Example 12–19) as a guide, identify the following chords according to their relative stability. Darken the pitch that is the root of each sonority.

As directed, provide analysis for the following excerpts:

Prokofiev, *Sarcasms*, Op. 17, No. 3

Honegger, *Symphony No. 5*

Hindemith, *Ludus Tonalis*

Provide analysis as directed.

Barber, *Church Bell at Night* from
Hermit Songs Op. 29, No. 2

Ives, *Religion*

New Concepts and Materials   **337**

SUGGESTED LISTENING

Béla Bartók, *Allegro Barbaro* (1911)
  String Quartet No. 3 (1927)

Paul Hindemith, *Mathis der Mahler* (1938)
  Ludus Tonalis (1943)

Arthur Honegger, *Pacific 231*

Charles Ives, *Sonata No. 2* (Concord, Mass. 1840–1860) (1909–15)
  Symphony No. 4 (1910–16)

Darius Milhaud, *La Création du Monde* (1923)

Serge Prokofiev, *Classical Symphony* (1917)

Eric Satie, *Parade* (1917)

Arnold Schoenberg, *Gurrelieder* (1900)

Dmitri Shostakovitch, *Symphony No. 5* (1937)

Igor Stravinsky, *The Firebird* (1911)
  Le Sacre du printemps (1913)
  L'Histoire du soldat (1918)

Chapter 13
Atonality

The practice of establishing tonality through a dominant-tonic relationship is the essence of traditional Western music. Not only do composers like Mozart and Brahms establish or imply many keys within a work, there is generally one overall tonal center to which the other keys are related. The tonal center is constantly reinforced by its own dominant-tonic relationship and by those of the related keys.

As discussed earlier in this volume, the tendency to define key lessened in the mid–nineteenth century. In Chopin, for example, progressions often abandon their functional roles to such an extent that lengthy passages are tonally obscure. In Wagner, especially in *Tristan*, the harmony is so chromatic and ambiguous that although careful analysis reveals the presence of one or more tonal axes (see Chapter 10), an overall tonal center is not always obvious to the listener. Debussy, of course, established a new harmonic style based not on function, but color. These and other developments preceded the music we know today as atonal.

Atonality: Two Definitions

ATONALITY is often defined as the absence of a tonal center. A number of composers, however, have taken exception to such a negatively phrased definition. Schoenberg, for example, contends that the process is not one *lacking* anything, but one in which all twelve tones are treated with equal importance. He proposed the term PANTONAL to designate this technique.

Since brief tonal references may emerge by chance (or subconscious choice) even when the composer's stated aim is to avoid them, a broader definition of atonality includes not only works in which there is no perceptible tonal center, but those in which tonality may be established through nontraditional means. Such compositions have been discussed in Chapters 11 and 12; they are not atonal in the sense that *no* tonality exists, but in that generally no tonal center is established through functional harmonic progressions.

Problems of Organization

Throughout the history of Western music (excluding only some of the most *avant-garde* trends), the effectiveness of a composition has depended upon building and maintaining relationships in several parameters. The establishment of these relationships has been, perhaps, more often by instinct than design. The articulation of tonal areas by different themes, for example, just "sounded right" to early eighteenth-century composers; decades later, sonata-form was defined and formally proposed.

Likewise, in atonal music, the search for alternate means of organization led early twentieth-century composers to exploit instinctively relationships involving new melodic and harmonic concepts. They chose combinations of pitches which caused the music to "hold together" even without the melodic and harmonic tendencies associated with tonality. Only in the 1960s and 70s have these new relationships been documented and systematized.

RELATIONSHIPS IN ATONAL MUSIC

In the many individual solutions to problems of organization in atonal music, four relationships have appeared consistently throughout the twentieth century: *Transposition, Inversion, Inclusion,* and *Complementation.* These four relationships form the core of contemporary atonal theory. Before viewing their roles in analysis and composition, however, it is necessary to establish a convenient means of studying them singly and in combination. This is accomplished through elementary set theory.

The Set

One of the most crucial (and for some troubling) concepts associated with atonal music is that of the set. Most simply, a SET is a collection of items. Any number of items may form a set, but the order of those items as well as any duplication(s) among them is *disregarded.* To illustrate these concepts, consider the following set of three shapes which we will designate "Set 1."

If the order of the shapes is changed and/or if any of them is repeated, the collection of items is still Set 1.

If *new* shapes are present, however, or if any of the original ones are *omitted,* the collection is not Set 1, but is some other set.

The C major triad represents another set—a set of notes. Regardless of the order, and despite any doubling, the pitches C,E,G constitute the same set.

If notes are added or omitted, a new set is formed.

TRANSPOSITION

Students are familiar with the term *transposition* from its association with tonal music. In the present context, however, TRANSPOSITION refers to the manipulation of a pitch formation (motive, chord, and so on) in the most general sense. A three note set (D,E,F) for example, is transposed by moving each pitch up or down by the same interval.

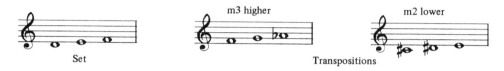

Ordered and Unordered Transposition

The previous examples are ordered transpositions. An ORDERED TRANSPOSITION is one in which the original order is maintained. If the order is different, the transposition is UNORDERED.

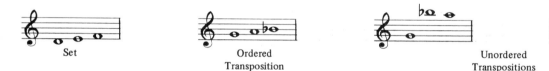

"Indistinct" Transposition

Transposition sometimes produces pitches equivalent to those of the original set. Transposed down a major third, for example, the set C,E,G♯ is duplicated (C and E literally, G♯ enharmonically at the octave). Such transpositions in which no new pitches appear are termed INDISTINCT because they are not distinct from the original.

The following set is used to illustrate the various relationships discussed in this chapter:

Both the original and transposed versions of the set are seen in Example 13–1.

EXAMPLE 13–1   Set Transposition

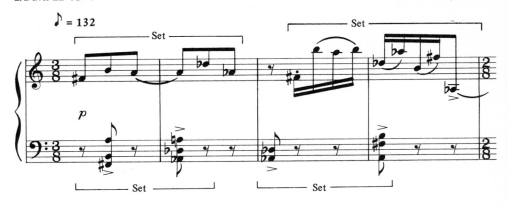

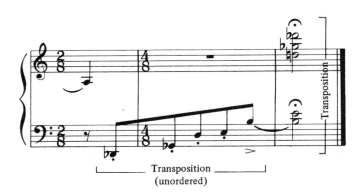

Transposition _____
(unordered)

In atonal composition, set transposition provides momentum as melodic and harmonic units are moved up or down. Another means of providing movement is through set inversion.

INVERSION

INVERSION is the process of taking a set and producing its mirror image by using the original intervals in the opposite direction.[1]

In a harmonic context, inversion is illustrated below.

Inversion is a mutual relationship; each triad above is the inversion of the other. In particular, notice that the major triad is the inversion of the minor and *vice versa*.

[1]To distinguish mirror inversion from other types of inversion (the inversion of an interval or triad, for example), Howard Hanson proposes the term INVOLUTION for the former. The term, however, has not become standard and it will not be used in this text.

Ordered and Unordered Inversion

As in transposition, sets may be arranged in an ordered or an unordered way. The examples above are ordered inversions; an unordered inversion of the same set is shown below.

Set   Unordered
             Inversion

Transposed Inversion

Even if an inversion (whether ordered or unordered) is transposed, it retains the relationship with the original set.

Set   Inversion   Transposed Inversions

"Indistinct" Inversion

An INDISTINCT INVERSION is one which is identical in pitch content to the original set or one of its transpositions. Inverted, the set C,D,E becomes C,B♭,A♭. In a different order, however, this same inverted set is available by transposing the original up a minor sixth.

Set   Indistinct   Transposition
             Inversion

The example above illustrates the fact that inversion does not always produce new material. Sets that are symmetrical in intervallic structure, like that below, exhibit this characteristic.

Set   Indistinct   Transposition
             Inversion

The use of set inversion is shown in the passage below (Example 13–2). The original set is the same one used in Example 13–1.

EXAMPLE 13–2   Set Inversion

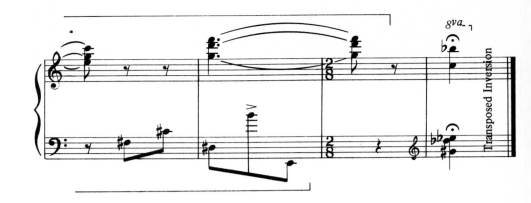

INCLUSION

When one set contains another, the relationship is known as INCLUSION. If Set 1, for example, is part of Set 2, they are related by inclusion.

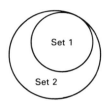

Musically, inclusion may be illustrated by supposing that Set 1 comprises the pitches C,D,E,F and that Set 2 comprises the pitches C,D,E,F,G,A,B,C. The tetrachord (Set 1) is part of the C major scale (Set 2) and related to it by inclusion.

In a similar manner, the two chords below are related by inclusion.

Nonliteral Inclusion

The set F♯,G♯,A♯ is not included in a C major scale. In a nonliteral sense, however, it *is* related by inclusion to a C major scale because it is a transposition of a third set, C,D,E—a set which is included.

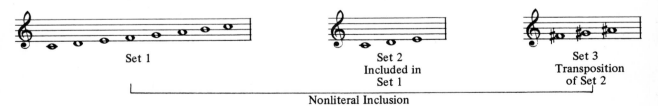

Because order is not a factor considered in the definition of a set, order is not a factor in determining relationships among sets. Other arrangements of the pitches F♯,G♯,A♯ are still related to the C major scale through nonliteral inclusion.

Set 1

Sets Related by Nonliteral Inclusion

In the same way, the two sets below are related through nonliteral inclusion.

Set 1

Set 2

Although not literally included in Set 1, Set 2 is an inversion of G,B,D—a third set which *is* included in Set 1.

Set 1

Set 2
Included in Set 1

Set 3
Inversion of Set 2

Related through Nonliteral Inclusion

The inclusion relation is prominent in Example 13–3 below. In addition to the original set (from Example 13–1), new sets are formed both by using segments of the original set and by adding pitches to it. The following relationships are seen in the example below:

Set A   Included in Original Set
Set B   Contains Original Set
Set C   Transposition of Set A
Set D   Transposition of Set B
Set E   Contains Original Set
Set F   Included in Original Set

EXAMPLE 13–3

Set Inclusion

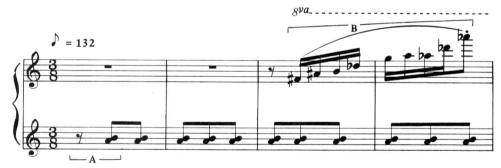

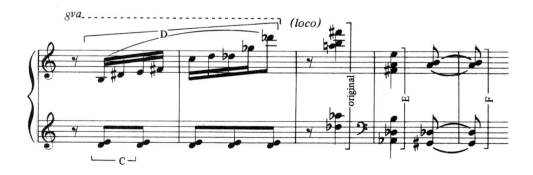

COMPLEMENT

The COMPLEMENT of a given set of notes is another set made up of all the notes not in the first (given) set. The complement of a C major scale, for example, is a set containing the five black notes "left over." Interestingly, these complementary pitches form a pentatonic scale. Like mirror inversion, complement is a mutual relationship; each set below is the complement of the other.

In a harmonic context, the complement relationship may be illustrated, for example, by a hexachord (Set 1) which is complemented by another (Set 2); the two sets have no pitches in common.

Nonliteral Complement

By definition, a set and its complement have no notes in common. In a literal sense, therefore, the pentatonic scale C,D,E,G,A is not the complement of a C major scale. Taken nonliterally, however, the relationship is "complementary" since C,D,E,G,A is a transposition of G♭,A♭,B♭,D♭,E♭—the set that forms the literal complement of a C major scale.

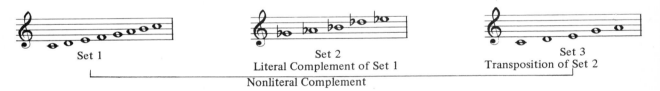

In Example 13–4 below, the right hand is given an ostinato based on the original set while in the left hand, the literal complement unfolds.

EXAMPLE 13–4   The Complement Relation

SUMMARY

One set may be related to others in four important ways.

1. Transposition (ordered or unordered)

2. Inversion (ordered, unordered, or transposed)

3. Inclusion (literal or nonliteral)

4. Complement (literal or nonliteral)

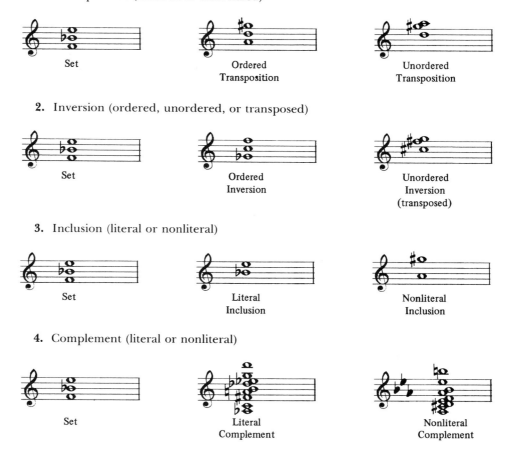

CHORD CHEMISTRY

Another relationship which may be significant in atonal music concerns CHORD CHEMISTRY—the interval content. Not only do atonal composers employ chords that are identical in interval content, they frequently compose music that tends toward one or two of the six interval categories (PMNSDT). A whole tone sonority, for example, is heavy with intervals in the categories MST; predominantly quartal harmonies have more perfect intervals and major seconds than they do intervals of other types.

Neither transposition nor inversion changes the interval content of a set. Each of the sets below is different in pitch content, yet each has the same interval content.

PN²SDT
Set

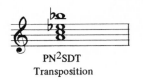

PN²SDT
Transposition

PN²SDT
Inversion

Nonequivalent Sets with Identical Chemistries

Any two sets related by transposition or inversion have the same chemistry. In certain cases, however, a pair of sets not standing in these relationships (that is, NONEQUIVALENT SETS) will also have the same chemistry. The set C,E,G,F♯, for example, has the chemistry PMNSDT; another set, C,C♯,E,F♯ has the identical chemistry, but is related to the first by neither transposition nor inversion.

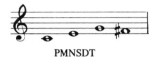

PMNSDT

PMNSDT

The two sets below also exhibit this sort of relationship. They have identical chemistries, yet they are not otherwise related by transposition or inversion (they do happen to be complementary, but this relationship is not always found in such cases).

P³M²N⁴S²D²T²

P³M²N⁴S²D²T²

The chemistry of sets is important because those with identical or nearly identical chemistries will be similar in "flavor" and harmonic tension. Sets with quite different chemistries likely will be perceived as contrasting.

The following analysis of *The Cage* by Charles Ives shows how the relationships between sets can be traced and studied in atonal music.

ANALYSIS: *THE CAGE,* BY CHARLES IVES

Charles Ives (1874–1954) wrote 114 Songs (mostly before 1920) and both published and distributed this collection at his own expense. Much like Bartók's *Mikrokosmos,* Ives' songs represent a catalogue of *avant-garde* techniques and show him as a composer far ahead of his own time.

The Cage (1906) is both unmeasured and atonal. Ives employs a variety of harmonic and melodic materials, yet maintains a remarkable degree of structural consistency. The voice part will be considered first, the piano part next, and the composite structure of the two parts after that.

The Voice Part

The single stanza of text which Ives wrote for *The Cage* is divided into five segments. For analytical purposes, these will be identified with the letter "V" (for voice) and an appropriate Arabic numeral to designate order.

The first vocal segment (V1) extends from the first word "A" to the word "cage;" it is based on a whole tone pentachord:

V1

A leop-ard went a-round his cage

Beginning with the word "from" and extending through "stopped," the second segment is a transposition of V1 a minor third higher. The two segments have no pitches in common. The designation $V1_2$ indicates the second occurrence of segment V1.

$V1_2$

from one side back to the oth - er side; he stopped

Segment V2 begins on the word "only" and concludes with "meat." Because the melodic material is a complete whole tone scale, segment V2 is related by inclusion both to V1 (literal) and $V1_2$ (nonliteral).

V2

on - ly when the keep - er came a - round with meat;

The next segment (V3) is based on a hexachord comprised of a whole tone pentachord with an added half step:

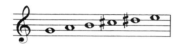

Beginning on the word "A," segment V3 concludes with the word "wonder." The relationship between it and other segments is close; in a nonliteral sense, V3 includes both V1 and $V1_2$.

V3

A boy who had been there three hours be - gan to won - der,

An exact return of segment V1 on the words "Is life anything like that?" completes the five–part structure of the voice part.

"Is life an - y - thing like that?"

Obviously, the prevailing melodic material of the voice part is the whole tone scale; less obvious but revealed through analysis are the close relationships among the five segments (Example 13–5).

EXAMPLE 13–5   Relationships in Voice Part

Segment	Construction	Relationship to V1
V1	Whole Tone Pentachord	—
$V1_2$	Whole Tone Pentachord	Transposition
V2	Whole Tone Scale	Inclusion (literal)
V3	Hexachord—Whole Tone Pentachord plus Half Step	Inclusion (nonliteral)
V1	Whole Tone Pentachord	Repetition

The Piano Part

The predominant sonority of the piano part is quartal. The repeated introduction is comprised of five-note quartal chords that culminate in an interesting sonority which in its chemistry suggests both the MST intervals of the voice part and the PMNS intervals prevalent elsewhere in the piano part.

$P^3M^4N^3S^2D^3$

evenly and mechanically,
no ritard., decresc., accel., etc.

(repeat 2 or 3 times)

After the double bar, the opening quartal chords return, this time a perfect fourth higher. The sonority that concluded the introduction is transposed as well, but because the previous chord is held over into it, a new, seven-note chord appears on the word "side." This more complex sonority includes both the quartal chord and the transposition of the chord which ends the vamp.

$P^5M^4N^4S^4D^3T$

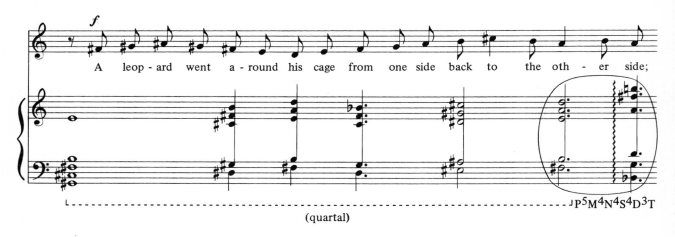

A leop - ard went a - round his cage from one side back to the oth - er side;

(quartal) $P^5M^4N^4S^4D^3T$

Beginning on the word "only," quartal chords (ordered transpositions of those heard earlier) return and are followed by chords in fifths (see Example 13–6).

On the word "wonder," a chord appears which is the literal complement of the vocal segment V1.

VI

"Wonder" Chord

Other observations can be made about the "wonder" chord and its relationship to the voice part. It includes segment V1₂ (literally) and V3 (nonliterally): the chord includes segment V3 both in transposition (E♭,F,G,A,B,C) and inversion (C,D♭,E♭,F,G,A). Clearly the "wonder" chord has a major role in linking the voice and piano parts.

Composite Structure

When the voice and piano parts are taken together, recurring segments are seen in the composite structure. One of these segments, a projection of perfect fifths, is heard ten times in the brief work (sometimes transposed).

$P^4MN^2S^3$

The first occurrence of this sonority includes the third piano chord (after the double bar) plus the voice part on the words "his cage" (Example 13–6).

Other composite structures can be isolated and traced throughout *The Cage*. While Ives was probably not aware of this organization, it is interesting and instructive to realize that it exists nevertheless.

EXAMPLE 13–6   Charles Ives, *The Cage*

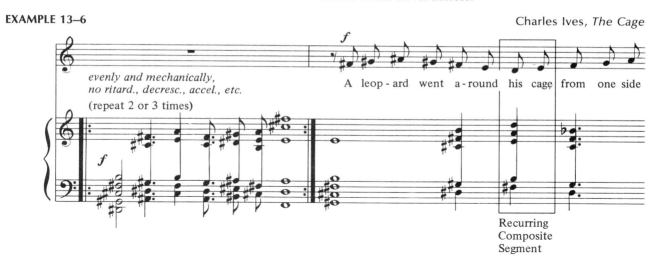

A boy who had been there three hours be-gan to won-der, "Is life an-y-thing like that?"

The Cage is atonal, but not random. The melody is consistently whole tone, the accompaniment predominantly quartal; together, the parts are organized through recurring segments of various qualities. In addition, transposition, inclusion, and the complement relation play major structural roles; the inversion relationship is only marginally present.

Many relationships are present in *The Cage,* but students must realize that they are now prepared not only to find and classify such relationships, but to recognize their paucity or absence as well. Consciously or not, Ives chose to feature certain melodic and harmonic patterns. Other composers, either consciously or subconsciously, *avoid* building such relationships. Although the analysis of these latter works may deal more with the structural roles of form, rhythm, or timbre, the relative lack of common melodic and harmonic relationships is significant.

For each set given, construct the appropriate related set. In some cases, there are several correct answers.

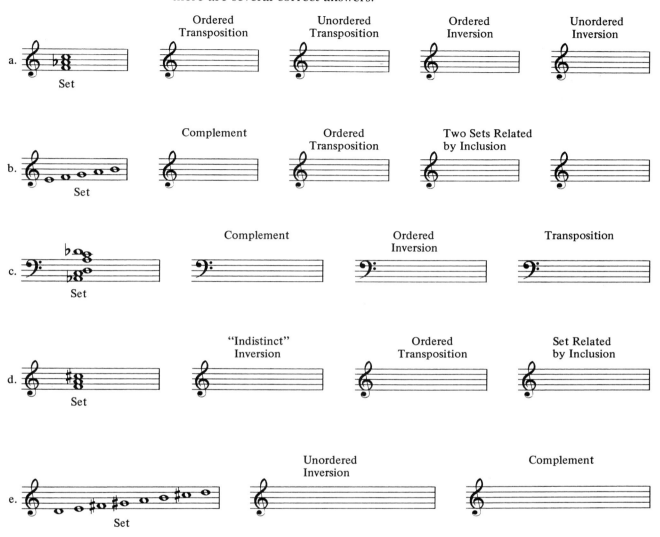

Determine the relationship(s) between the given set and those that follow it. If none of the four standard relationships exists, write "none."

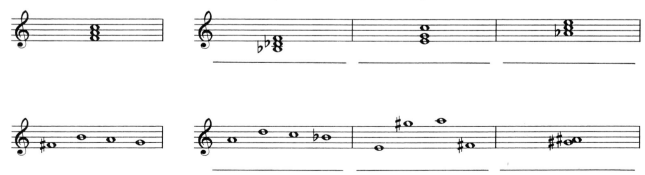

Using techniques of set transformation, continue the string trio below. Structure the work as a small ternary form with the middle section comprised of repeated block chords. If you wish, indicate *pizzicato* in one or more sections of the work. Write the abbreviation *pizz* above the part or parts in question. When regular bowing is resumed, use the word *arco*. Label all set transformations.

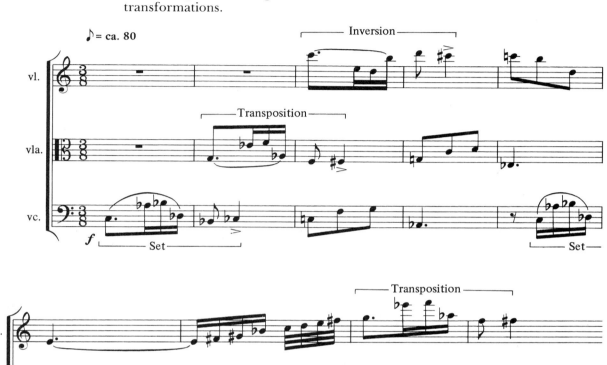

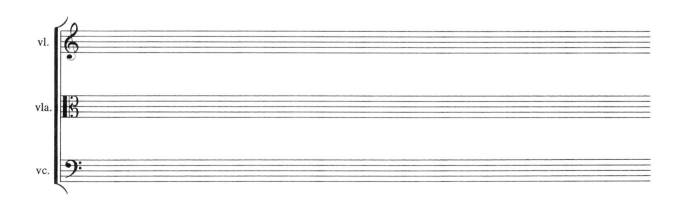

Compose an atonal work for trombone (or cello) and piano. The work may resemble Ives' *The Cage* in structure and style, or it may be completely different. Remember the need for contrast and variety as well as structure and unity. Label transformations of the melodic set.

Michael Hunt, *Mysterious*

Kendall Stallings, *To the New O'Connell's.*
Text by Jon Dressel

soul to frig-id, so-ber sleep will up and join us as we

keep warm faith with this great green en-deav-or_____ hoist the I-rish

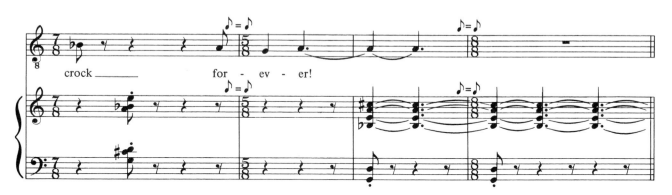

crock_____ for-ev-er!

Used by permission of Kendall Stallings and Jon Dressel.

Sehr langsam

SUGGESTED LISTENING

Alban Berg, *Wozzeck* (1920)

Arnold Schoenberg, *Five Pieces for Orchestra,* Op. 16 (1909)
Pierrot Lunaire (1912)

Edgard Varèse, *Density 21.5* (1937)
Octandre (1924)

Anton Webern, *Six Pieces for Orchestra,* Op. 6 (1913)

Chapter 14
Serial Technique

Although a number of earlier composers conducted experiments with similar systems of organization, Arnold Schoenberg is credited with having conceived and developed the basic principles of the serial technique. As discussed briefly in Chapter 12, much of Schoenberg's early music (works like *Erwartung* and *Pierrot Lunaire*) is associated with Expressionism; the disjunct melodies and jarring dissonance represent both a natural outgrowth of late Romantic chromaticism and the antithesis of Impressionist delicacy. Between 1913 and 1923, however, Schoenberg produced no new works as he devised and refined the various principles of a new approach to atonal composition. One of the first works based entirely on the serial method is the fifth of the *Five Pieces for Piano*, Op. 23 (1923). In the years before World War II, only a handful of composers embraced serial composition; since 1945, however, the method has become one of the most (if not *the* most) influential developments in the twentieth century.

THE TWELVE TONE METHOD

SERIALISM is a method of composition in which traditional common practice principles are abandoned and replaced with new concepts which lend a high degree of organization to music typically atonal and dissonant. Serialism is not a style of composition, but a method. One has only to compare serial works by Berg, Babbitt, Stravinsky, and Copland (to name but four) to appreciate that in actual practice, vastly different compositional styles result from the use of the same abstract method.

The Tone Row

A basic concept of serialism is the TONE ROW—a set of pitches arranged in a fixed order. The most common tone row is an ordering of twelve different pitch classes; this sort of tone row is fundamental to the twelve tone method.

Pitch Class

A PITCH CLASS is a category comprising one of the pitches of a chromatic scale together with all of its enharmonic and octave duplications. Each pitch of a chromatic scale is in a different pitch class. Pitches that are enharmonic equivalents are in the same pitch class.

Twelve Different
Pitch Classes

All Pitches in the
Same Pitch Class

In the melody below, although there are nine different pitches used, there are only four different pitch classes represented (Example 14–1).

EXAMPLE 14–1

The Twelve Tone Row

The TWELVE TONE ROW is made up of twelve different pitch classes. The particular note name one uses to represent a pitch class is unimportant, but a given pitch class may not appear more than once in the same row (both B♯ and C, for example, may not appear). On the other hand, the pitches C, C♯ and C♭ are all in different pitch classes; *all three* could be used in the same twelve tone row.

Rows in the abstract are usually written within a single octave (as scales are), but in actual practice—in composing a melody, for instance—a composer makes octave choices that permit the desired melodic contour to emerge.

COMPOSITIONAL APPLICATIONS

Construction of the Row

The tone row is an abstract entity devised by the composer, yet rather than choosing pitches at random, many composers impart a good deal of structure to the row itself. Alban Berg's row for the *Violin Concerto,* for example, is constructed of superimposed major and minor triads with a whole tone series at the end.

For his *String Quartet,* Op. 28, Anton Webern composed a row based on three tetrachords. The first is a transposition of the pitches B♭ A C B♮; in German, the letter "H" is used for B♮ and the letter "B" for B♭—thus the tetrachord is based on the name "BACH." The other two tetrachords are related to the first; the second is an inversion; the third, a transposition.

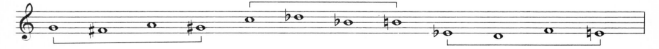

Harmonic and Melodic Application of the Row

The row may appear melodically or harmonically. In Alban Berg's *Lyric Suite,* the first violin states the pitches of the row in order from 1 to 12 (Example 14–2).

EXAMPLE 14–2

Alban Berg, *Lyric Suite*

The following twelve tone row is the basis of the composition by Hanns Jelinek .

Notice that this row is based primarily on perfect intervals and that it contains *no* half steps. In terms of interval content, compare Jelinek's row to those of Berg (Example 14–2), Schoenberg (Example 14–4), and Webern (page *377*). The construction of the row itself is but one of many factors in the twelve tone method that is controlled entirely by the composer.

The first statement of the row in Jelinek's *Fluently* is identified in Example 14–3; trace the use of the row in the remainder of the work.

EXAMPLE 14–3

Hanns Jelinek, "Fluently" from *Six Short Character Sketches*, Op. 15, No. 2

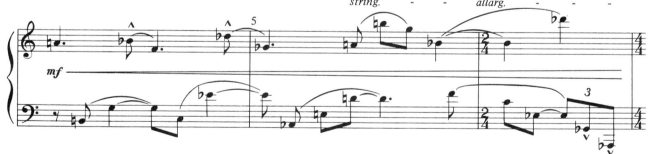

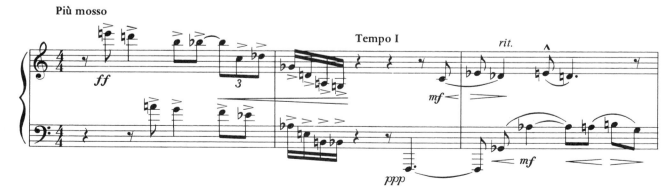

The tone row Schoenberg composed for his *Klavierstück* (Op. 33a) is first heard not in linear fashion, but as a series of three tetrachords (Example 14–4). The segmentation of the row into trichords, tetrachords, hexachords, or whatever, is a regular feature of serial composition.

EXAMPLE 14–4   Arnold Schoenberg, *Klavierstück*, Op. 33a

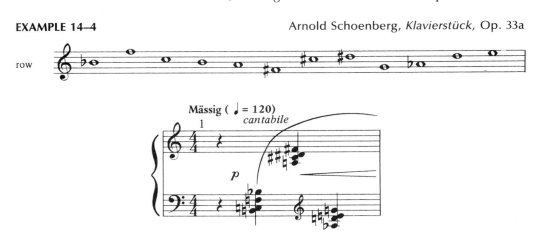

TRANSFORMATIONS OF THE ROW

While the various octave placements that are available allow the composer some freedom in his use of the row, the possibilities remain rather limited. To provide additional variety, a number of other techniques are available and their use has become standard. These techniques will be discussed and illustrated using the row Milton Babbitt (b. 1916) composed for his *Duet* (given in full on page 381).

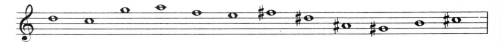

Transposition

A familiar technique used to provide alternate versions of an original row is ordered TRANSPOSITION. The original row (the abstract material) is termed the PRIME FORM; in composition and analysis it is designated P_0. A transposition of P_0 a half step higher is designated P_1. Subscript numerals indicate the interval of transposition in successive ascending half steps (Example 14–5).

EXAMPLE 14–5

Transposition of the Prime Form[1]

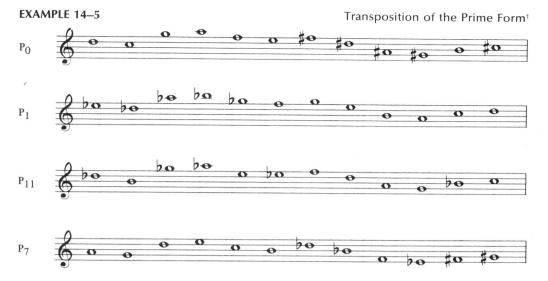

A transposed version of the original row offers the composer more flexibility as there are now eleven additional row forms to choose from. In addition to transposition, three other transformations are standard: *Retrograde, Inversion,* and *Retrograde Inversion.*

Retrograde

The RETROGRADE form results from stating the prime form (P_0) backward.

The retrograde form shown above is literal. As with the prime form, however, there are eleven transposed retrograde forms. Each transposition of the retrograde is the literal retrograde of one of the transposed prime forms (Example 14–6).

EXAMPLE 14–6

Retrograde Forms

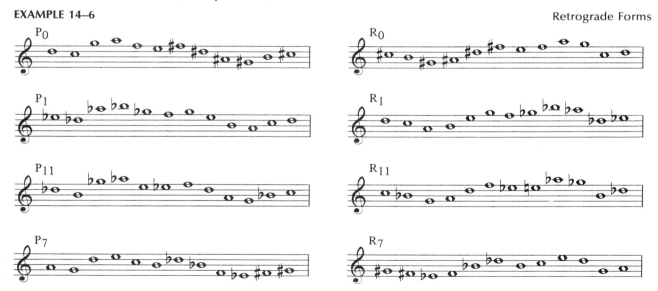

[1]In serial composition, if no accidental appears beside a pitch, that pitch is understood to be natural. Still, many composers place a flat, sharp, or natural sign beside *every* pitch to insure accuracy.

Inversion

Another common transformation of the row is its mirror INVERSION. Beginning with the first pitch of P_0, the inversion is determined by reversing the direction of intervals in the prime form.

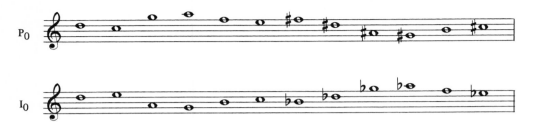

The row form designated I_0 begins with the same pitch as P_0; transposed versions are also available (Example 14–7).

EXAMPLE 14–7   Inverted Forms

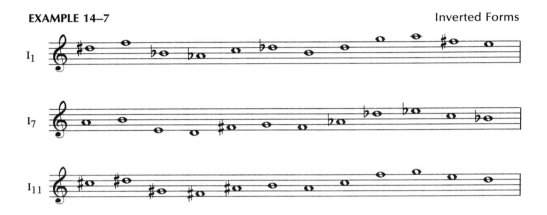

Retrograde Inversion

The RETROGRADE INVERSION of the original row results from the inversion's being stated backward.

Like the prime, retrograde, and inverted forms, the retrograde inversion is subject to eleven transpositions. Two are shown in Example 14–8 below.

EXAMPLE 14–8   Retrograde Inverted Forms

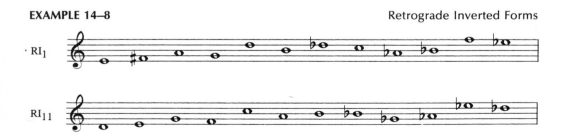

When the four forms of the row and their various transpositions are considered, there are 48 different versions—all intervallically tied to the original (P_0).[2]

THE MATRIX

The forty-eight row forms can be conveniently displayed by constructing a MATRIX. Because octave placement is not a consideration in determining row forms, the matrix is constructed using letter names rather than actually notating pitches on a staff. There are three steps in the process of constructing a matrix.

1. Write the pitches of the original row from left to right using letter names. This provides not only the prime form (left to right), but the retrograde as well (right to left).

$P_0 \rightarrow$ D   C   G   A   F   E   F♯   D♯   A♯   G♯   B   C♯ $\leftarrow R_0$

2. Determine the inverted form and write it from top to bottom using the same letter name to represent both the first pitch of P_0 and the first pitch of I_0. The retrograde inversion is read from bottom to top.

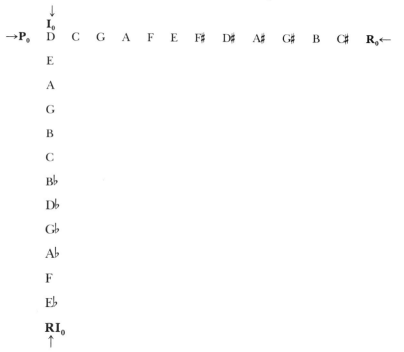

3. Transpose the prime form to begin successively with the pitches of the inversion. The sequence of transpositions will not fall in order down the page (P_1, P_2, etc.) but will depend upon the order of pitches in the inversion. When transpositions of the prime form have been completed, the transpositions of the inversion are available as well and should be identified by number. Obviously, the transpositions of the prime and inverted forms yield those of the retrograde and retrograde inversion as well (Example 14–9).

---

[2]Some rows have fewer than forty-eight different forms. If the second hexachord of a given row, for example, is a retrograde of the first, there will be only twenty-four different forms. The row for Webern's *Symphony*, Op. 21 (discussed on page 377) is such a row.

EXAMPLE 14–9   Matrix, *Duet* by Milton Babbitt

	I₀	I₁₀	I₅	I₇	I₃	I₂	I₄	I₁	I₈	I₆	I₉	I₁₁	
P₀	D	C	G	A	F	E	F♯	D♯	A♯	G♯	B	C♯	**R₀**
P₂	E	D	A	B	G	F♯	G♯	F	C	B♭	D♭	E♭	**R₂**
P₇	A	G	D	E	C	B	D♭	B♭	F	E♭	F♯	G♯	**R₇**
P₅	G	F	C	D	B♭	A	B	A♭	E♭	D♭	E	G♭	**R₅**
P₉	B	A	E	F♯	D	C♯	D♯	C	G	F	A♭	B♭	**R₉**
P₁₀	C	B♭	F	G	E♭	D	E	D♭	A♭	G♭	A	B	**R₁₀**
P₈	B♭	A♭	E♭	F	D♭	C	D	B	F♯	E	G	A	**R₈**
P₁₁	D♭	B	G♭	A♭	E	E♭	F	D	A	G	B♭	C	**R₁₁**
P₄	G♭	E	B	D♭	A	A♭	B♭	G	D	C	E♭	F	**R₄**
P₆	A♭	G♭	D♭	E♭	B	B♭	C	A	E	D	F	G	**R₆**
P₃	F	E♭	B♭	C	A♭	G	A	F♯	D♭	B	D	E	**R₃**
P₁	E♭	D♭	A♭	B♭	G♭	F	G	E	B	A	C	D	**R₁**
	RI₀	RI₁₀	RI₅	RI₇	RI₃	RI₂	RI₄	RI₁	RI₈	RI₆	RI₉	RI₁₁	

Notice that when the matrix is constructed correctly, the first pitch of P₀ appears diagonally across the page from left to right. If this phenomenon does not occur, an error has been made.

FREE USE OF THE ROW

Composers are not always strict in their use of the row. The final pitch (or pitches) of one form, for example, may be elided with the beginning of another. Opportunities for combining row forms that overlap can be determined from examining the matrix. Notice that in the Babbitt row (Example 14–9) the final two pitches of P₀ and the first two pitches of RI₈ are the same. These two forms can be combined linearly in two different ways:

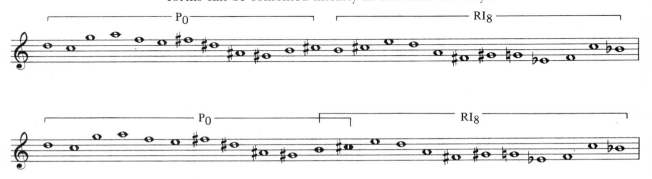

Sometimes composers alternate harmonic and melodic applications of the serial method. Complicating this process even further is the fact that some

composers take pitches out of order. Two or three pitches, for example, are sometimes used as an unordered melodic cell.

Alban Berg (1885–1935), a pupil of Schoenberg, is known for his free use of the serial method and in particular, for his fondness of melodic cells that may create a fleeting tonal reference. The passage from his *Lyric Suite* (Example 14–10) is typical.

EXAMPLE 14–10

Alban Berg, *Lyric Suite*

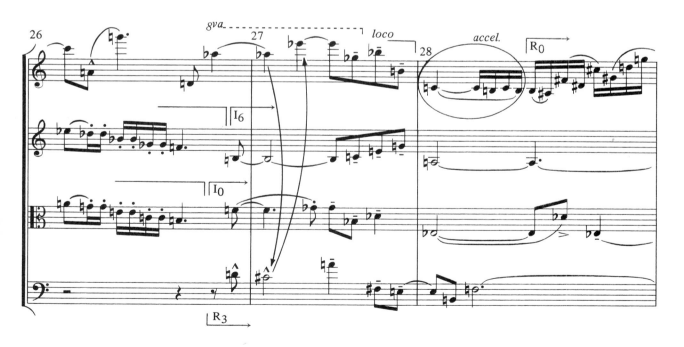

The row form R_0 is begun in the second violin in measure 22 (not shown) but moves to the viola in measure 23 as the second violin begins a new row form—I_6. Notice that while the pitch A is omitted from I_6, it occurs at the appropriate point nevertheless as it is sustained in the viola. In measure 27, the pitch C♯ is omitted from the prime form in the first violin but is present in the cello (R_3). Observe also that several row forms are elided: P_0–I_6 (measure 24, again in measure 25) and R_0–I_0 (measure 29).

Several times in this brief excerpt, Berg treats two pitches as an ordered melodic cell (circled on the score). Also of interest is the unordered use of the first and second hexachords of P_0 as scale passages (measures 33–34). Finally, observe that while Berg's treatment of row forms is basically linear, in measure 33, RI_0 is distributed among three instruments harmonically.

The symbol H⌐ seen in the passage above stands for the designation *Hauptstimme* (principal voice); it is used in conjunction with the symbol N⌐ which designates the *Nebenstimme*, or secondary voice. Serial composers—especially the "Viennese Classicists" (Schoenberg, Webern, and Berg)—often used these markings on the score so that performers would be aware when they had principal and secondary roles respectively.

Rows with Fewer and More than Twelve Tones

While the twelve tone row is by far the most common, smaller and larger series have been devised by some composers. Stravinsky, for example, uses the following five tone row in his *In Memoriam Dylan Thomas:*

Rows with more than twelve tones are uncommon; a notable example, however, is the thirteen tone row Luciano Berio (b. 1925) composed for *Nones* (1954):

Unlike twelve tone rows, those with thirteen or more tones always involve pitch duplication (in Twelve Tone Equal Temperament).

COMBINATORIALITY

While the transformations of the original row are based on maintaining a set *order* of pitches, other aspects of serial composition depend on *content*. Combinatoriality is such a phenomenon. Central to the understanding of combinatoriality is the concept of hexachordal *aggregates*.

Aggregates

Given two different forms of the same row, if the first hexachord of one form has no notes in common with the first hexachord of the other form, then the two hexachords taken together are said to form an AGGREGATE. Between them, the two hexachords contain all twelve pitch classes. Obviously, if all of this is true for the paired first hexachords, it is true of the paired second hexachords as well.

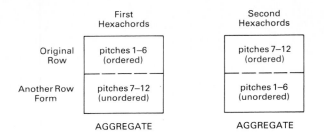

In Example 14–11 below, the first six pitches of P_0 taken together with the first six pitches of R_0 form an aggregate; all twelve pitch classes are present. The same is true for the second hexachords of the two row forms.

EXAMPLE 14–11   Aggregates

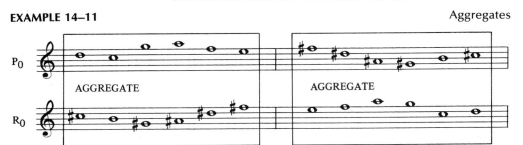

Any row in which two row forms may be combined to form hexachordal aggregates is COMBINATORIAL. In determining combinatoriality, there are four possible types of relationship:

PRIME	PRIME	PRIME	PRIME
combined with	combined with	combined with	combined with
RETROGRADE	PRIME	INVERSION	RETROGRADE INVERSION

The combinatorial relationship between the prime and its retrograde (Example 14–11, above) might be termed "quarter-combinatoriality" (for reasons which will become apparent); this relationship exists with *every* prime-retrograde row pair (P_0–R_0, P_7–R_7, and so on). Other combinatorial relationships, however, may or may not be present in a given row.

Semi-Combinatoriality

A row is SEMI-COMBINATORIAL if in addition to the aggregates of the prime-retrograde pairing, there are aggregates produced between the prime and *any* one other row form: prime-transposition of prime, prime-inversion (or transposed inversion), prime-retrograde inversion (or transposed retrograde inversion).

The row below from Schoenberg's *Klavierstück* (Op. 33a) is semi-combinatorial. A combination of P_0 and I_5 produces all twelve pitch classes in the first hexachords; likewise, the second hexachords have no pitches in common and form an aggregate (Example 14–12).

EXAMPLE 14–12   Semi-Combinatoriality

The principle of combinatoriality permits a composer to select row forms so that between melody and accompaniment there are no pitches duplicated. The P_0–I_5 semi-combinatorial relationship is a particular favorite of Schoenberg's. Notice his free use of these two row forms in Example 14–13.

EXAMPLE 14–13

Arnold Schoenberg, *Klavierstück*, Op 33a

Secondary Rows. Another feature of combinatoriality is based on a linear use of the two different row forms. If a row form is followed by the *retrograde* of its combinatorial partner, a *new* twelve tone row is formed between the second hexachord of the first row form and the first hexachord of the second row form. New rows thus produced are termed SECONDARY ROWS (Example 14–14).[3]

EXAMPLE 14–14

Secondary Row

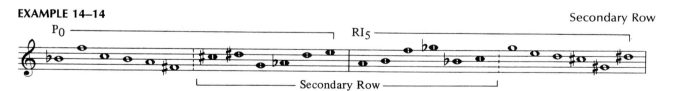

All-Combinatoriality

When a row is ALL-COMBINATORIAL, its prime may be combined to form an aggregate with at least one transposition of its retrograde inversion, also with at least one transposition of the prime itself, *and* with at least one trans-

[3]This is the same phenomenon Babbitt terms "Secondary *Sets*." For a thorough discussion of this and other aspects of serial composition, see *Serial Composition and Atonality* (4th edition) by George Perle.

position of the inverted form. These relationships exist in an all-combinatorial row in addition to the prime-retrograde pairing which is *always* available. Remember, in discussing combinatorial relationships, we are talking about *content* and not order.

The row Babbitt composed for his *Duet* is all-combinatorial; in addition to the P_0-R_0 combination, aggregates are produced by combining P_0 with I_{11}, P_0 with RI_5, and P_0 with P_6. The type of very helpful diagram shown in Example 14–15 originated with George Perle.

EXAMPLE 14–15   All-Combinatoriality

Pitch Content of Inner Columns

Pitch Content of Outer Columns

ANALYSIS: *SYMPHONY, OP. 21*, BY ANTON WEBERN

Webern composed his two movement *Symphony* in 1928; it is his first major work in the twelve tone method. Although there are no real liberties taken within the "classical" system, Webern's manipulation of the row illustrates the use of serialism as a creative, rather than a purely mechanical process. The work is scored for nine instruments although no more than four play at any one time. Like many of Webern's compositions, the *Symphony* is brief; together, the two movements last scarcely ten minutes.

The row itself is highly structured; it is comprised of two hexachords, the second of which is a retrograde of the first. The two hexachords have no tones in common, of course, but each presents melodically the same collection of interval types.

N   D   D   M   D   (T)   D   M   D   D   N

Webern uses the row in a strict, linear fashion; pitches are passed from one instrument to another with constant variations in timbre and register. This technique, it will be remembered, is known as *pointillism*.

In the first movement of his *Symphony*, Webern chooses row forms and employs them so that the predominant sonority is the minor second. While this interval is notable in the row itself, Webern's choices of row forms and harmonic alignment contribute to this particular harmonic effect. The process reflected in these choices is *composition*—the creation of music rather than a sterile application of the serial method.

The prime form begins in the second horn (pitches 1–4), is passed to the clarinet in measure 6 (pitches 5–8), and concludes in the cello (pitches 9–12). Simultaneously, however, three other row forms (I_8, I_0, and P_4) unfold in a similar manner. Together, these four different parts form a double canon in contrary motion.

The full score of Webern's *Symphony* begins on page 383. Use the matrix on page 378 to study the row forms identified and to trace others in the remainder of the movement. Remember, however, that tracing row forms is not the only important element in the analysis of serial music. Many other factors should be considered: How strictly is the method employed? Is any one row form associated with a particular voice, instrument, or register? When row forms appear simultaneously, are combinatorial or other relationships present?

In addition to the characteristics of the row and its manipulation, an analysis should take into consideration factors like timbre (especially in a work like Webern's *Symphony*), rhythm, texture, and form. Serial composers often choose traditional forms and formal techniques; the first movement of the *Symphony*, for example, is canonic; the second is a set of variations.

A final consideration in the analysis of a twelve tone work is the composer's attitude toward the serial method itself. Many works, like Webern's *Symphony*, are rather strict in their adherence to the basic principles of serial composition. Other composers, as we have seen, exercise a great deal of flexibility. When pitches occur out of sequence, when one row form is abruptly broken off in favor of another, there is usually a reason—a musical one. A thorough analysis should not only determine where digressions occur, but the relative impact that they have on the work.

SUMMARY

In 1932–1933, Anton Webern gave a series of eight lectures which were later published under the title *The Path to the New Music*. Willi Reich, editor of the publication, comments on Webern's purpose:

> It is very characteristic that Webern should have called both cycles [series of lectures] "paths." He, who was always "under way," wanted to show others the way too. First, he wanted to show what had at various times over the centuries been "new" in music, meaning that it had never been said before.[4]

---

[4]Anton Webern, *The Path to the New Music*, ed. by Willi Reich, (Bryn Mawr, Penn.: Theodore Presser Company, 1963), p. 7.

The music of Schoenberg, Webern, and Berg *was* new, and like two earlier "new musics" (the fourteenth-century *Ars Nova* and the *Nuove Musiche* of the Florentine Camerata), serialism was (and in some quarters continues to be) attacked as being contrary to nearly every principle by which music previously had been judged. No less important is the fact that *time* has proven Schoenberg's new music, like that of the fourteenth and seventeenth centuries, to have been a historical turning point of monumental proportions. Nearly every major composer since 1945 has embraced the serial method at some point in his or her career; these composers have been influential on succeeding generations. They have taught their own students (the composers of the 1960s, 70s, and 80s) that the triad is perhaps not the only legitimate harmonic material, and that the minor second may not be quite as "harsh" as their teachers may have led them to believe. The result has been change—change not only in melodic and harmonic materials, but in the very concept of *music*.

Anton Webern, *Symphony,* Op. 21, First Movement (Matrix)

	I_0	I_9	I_{10}	I_{11}	I_7	I_8	I_2	I_1	I_5	I_4	I_3	I_6	
P_0	A	F♯	G	A♭	E	F	B	B♭	D	C♯	C	E♭	R_0
P_3	C	A	B♭	B	G	G♯	D	C♯	F	E	D♯	F♯	R_3
P_2	B	G♯	A	B♭	G♭	G	C♯	C	E	E♭	D	F	R_2
P_1	B♭	G	G♯	A	F	F♯	C	B	E♭	D	C♯	E	R_1
P_5	D	B	C	C♯	A	B♭	E	E♭	G	F♯	F	G♯	R_5
P_4	C♯	B♭	B	C	A♭	A	E♭	D	F♯	F	E	G	R_4
P_{10}	G	E	F	G♭	D	E♭	A	A♭	C	B	B♭	D♭	R_{10}
P_{11}	G♯	F	F♯	G	D♯	E	B♭	A	C♯	C	B	D	R_{11}
P_7	E	C♯	D	D♯	B	C	F♯	F	A	G♯	G	A♯	R_7
P_8	F	D	D♯	E	C	C♯	G	F♯	B♭	A	G♯	B	R_8
P_9	F♯	D♯	E	F	C♯	D	G♯	G	B	B♭	A	C	R_9
P_6	D♯	C	C♯	D	A♯	B	F	E	G♯	G	F♯	A	R_6
	RI_0	RI_9	RI_{10}	RI_{11}	RI_7	RI_8	RI_2	RI_1	RI_5	RI_4	RI_3	RI_6	

Construct a row based on the technique of your choice and use it as the basis of a composition for brass quartet. Use as many different forms of the row as you like. Plan the composition carefully as to style, rhythmic structure, form, and so on. Include a summary of your intended structure and trace the use of different row forms on the score itself. Show all instruments *in concert pitch* (remember, however, that *parts* for trumpet and horn must be transposed).

Provide an analysis of the following composition.

Milton Babbitt, *Duet*

Anton Webern, *Symphony*, Op. 21, First Movement

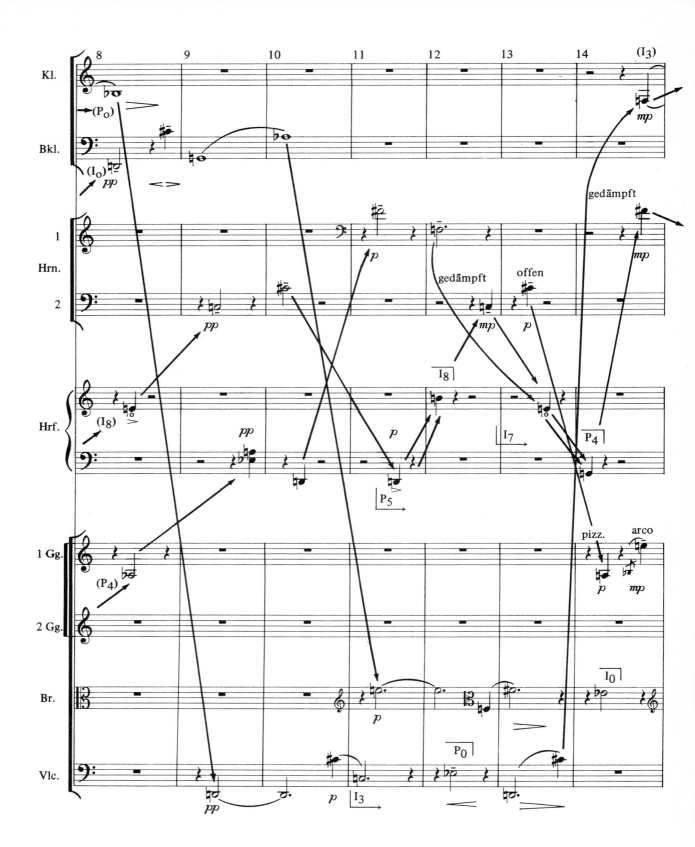

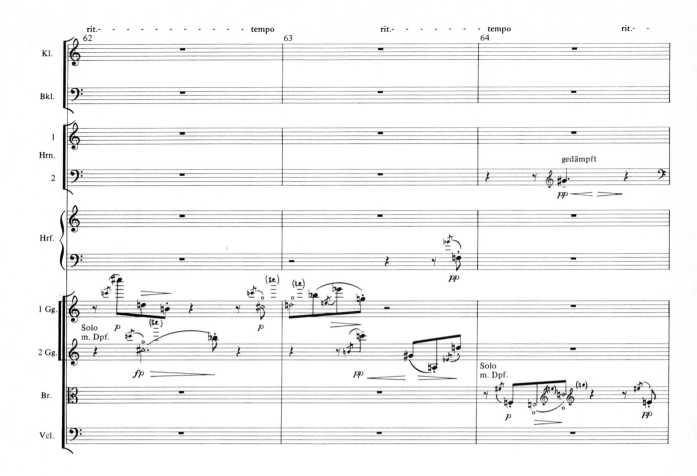

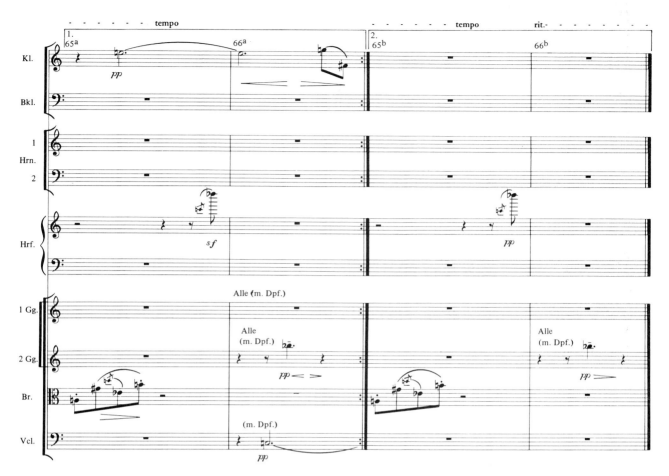

SUGGESTED LISTENING

Alban Berg, *Concerto for Violin* (1935)

Luciano Berio, *Nones* (1954)

Luigi Dallapiccola, *Il Prigioniero* (1949)

Arnold Schoenberg, *Two Piano Pieces,* Op. 33a and 33b (1927, 1932)
   Piano Concerto (1942)

Igor Stravinsky, *In Memoriam Dylan Thomas* (1954)
   Requiem Canticles (1967)

Anton Webern, *Variations for Piano,* Op. 27 (1936)
   Cantata, Op. 29 (1939)

Chapter 15
Music Since 1945

The most universal characteristic of music composed since 1945 may be simply its diversity. Composers today are experimenting with a whole new world of instruments capable of making traditional and quasi-traditional sounds. In addition, the recording industry has greatly increased our awareness of non-Western music. At present, we are in a period of exploration—a time when the very concept of music itself is being challenged.

Since the end of World War II, three major influences have appeared in Western music: *Electronic Music, Indeterminacy,* and *Extended Serialization.* In different ways, each of these three movements has freed composers from the past and given them the opportunity to explore in depth all of the parameters of sound.

ELECTRONIC MUSIC

The first major event in the development of electronic music occurred in 1948 at the ORTF (Office de Radio-Television Français) in Paris. There the French engineer Pierre Schaeffer composed a series of études using recordings of acoustic sounds. The electronic rearrangement of these sounds Schaeffer called MUSIQUE CONCRÈTE; music in which all sounds are produced electronically is known as MUSIQUE ÉLECTRONIQUE. While Schaeffer's initial experiments were with disc recordings, the use of magnetic tape offers the composer of today considerably more flexibility.

During the 1950s, the techniques of composing with a tape recorder became quite sophisticated. Multiple layers of sounds were produced on single channels; by cutting the tape and splicing the sounds back together in various arrangements, composers produced original electronic music.

The first electronic music synthesizers were developed in the late 1950s. The principle of voltage controlled synthesis enables the composer to control every parameter of electronically produced sound by regulating the voltage that passes through the synthesizer. In the 1960s, synthesizers were popularized by the success of recordings like *Switched-on Bach* (Walter Carlos). Today, practically every popular music group employs at least one synthesizer.

COMPOSITIONAL TECHNIQUES

Working independently and in "schools," composers have developed a number of common techniques for manipulating sounds in electronic compositions.

Speed Change

Simply by increasing or decreasing the speed of the playback, composers can alter pitch and duration. If C_4 were recorded for four seconds and then played back twice as fast, not only would the duration then be two seconds, the pitch would be C_5.

Reverse Playback

REVERSE PLAYBACK refers to the technique of turning the tape upside down and playing it forward.[1] The most interesting result of reverse playback is a reversal of the normal attack and decay characteristics of a sound.

Overdubbing

OVERDUBBING is the combination of two or more sounds on a single recorded channel. This technique permits composers to control the texture of an electronic composition.

Tape Echo

TAPE ECHO is produced by recording a single sound on one channel and then re-recording the same sound while playing back the first. The gap between the re-recording and the playback (along with the speed of the tape) determines the distance between sound and its echo.

Tape Looping

TAPE LOOPS are used to create an ostinato effect in an electronic work. The sounds a composer chooses for the ostinato are recorded on a single piece of tape which is spliced together as a loop. The loop can be played indefinitely and re-recorded while other sounds are added.

In addition to the techniques described above, composers use devices such as reverberation units and phase shifters to alter recorded sounds. Synthesizers have dramatically increased the possibilities for electronic sound modulation with devices such as sequencers and filters. Synthesizers are also utilized for sound sources to create microtonal music.

THE ANALYSIS OF ELECTRONIC MUSIC

The analysis of electronic music presents a unique challenge. Although the principles of formal design are often similar to those employed in previous centuries, there is usually no visual score; the analysis of electronic music centers on the *listening* process. While composers like György Ligeti have produced "listening scores" (See Example 15–1), most electronic music exists solely on tape or disc.

Observation

Several listenings will be required to analyze an electronic work. The first playing should be used to make several observations about the composition.

---

[1] Reverse playback is not possible on quarter-track tape recorders.

EXAMPLE 15–1

György Ligeti, *Artikulation* ("listening score")

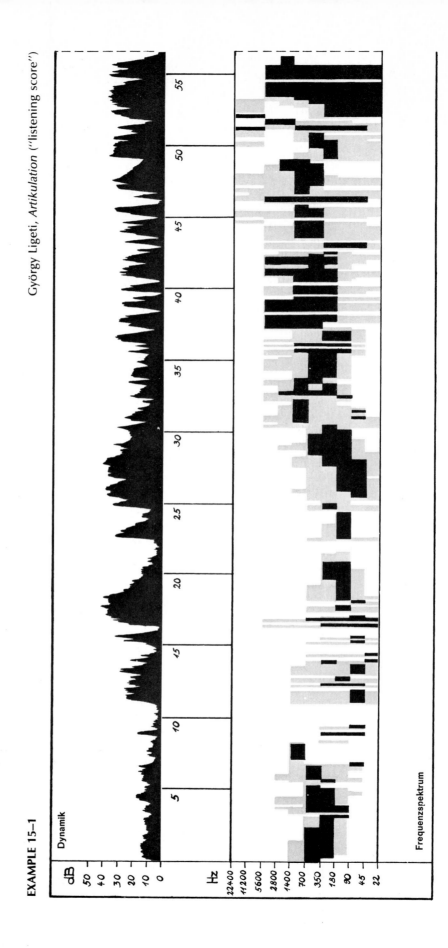

1. Are sounds produced electronically or acoustically?
2. Does the piece involve any live performance?
3. What is the total length of the piece?
4. What contrasts are present? Dynamic? Texture? Frequency?

Analysis

The second and subsequent listenings should be used to gather more specific information about the materials and structure of the composition. To this end, a graph of the work is of considerable value. While the listening score for *Artikulation* (Example 15–1) shows dynamics, frequencies, and durations with precision, a much more general representation of the work's structure is valuable for study purposes. Having previously determined the length of the work, time relationships may be shown on a horizontal axis divided into an appropriate number of sections. Densities can be shown by drawing blocks, wedges, lines, dots, circles—whatever seems appropriate to represent the general outlines of the work. Dynamics may be indicated with the traditional symbols. Frequency should be shown in a very general way: a gradually ascending or descending tendency, for example, or perhaps a period of stasis. A sample listening score for a three minute work is shown in Example 15–2. Naturally, the symbols chosen by individual students to represent the same sounds will vary greatly. Whether or not the "score" actually represents the music is less important than the development of an organized method of critical listening.

EXAMPLE 15–2   Listening Score

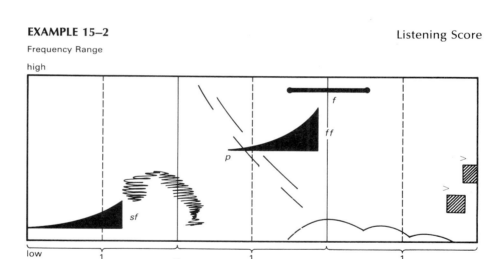

Conclusions

Having listened to the work several times and gathered some specific data about its structure, some of the following questions might be answered:

1. Does the piece follow a traditional musical form (binary, ternary, theme and variations, etc.)?
2. Is the work improvisatory? If so, how would you describe the formal structure?
3. What parameters give the clearest sense of form?
4. Where do patterns of tension and release occur? By what means are they created?

Throughout the history of music there have been various attempts to introduce random or accidental processes into musical compositions. As early as the eighteenth century, William Hayes discussed the possibilities of "chance" music.[2] Not long after that, Mozart composed a string quartet (k.294d) in which specifically composed musical phrases could be arranged by the performers according to a roll of the dice. In a more general sense, the art of improvisation (whether it be Baroque variations on a ground bass or modern jazz) is an indeterminate process.

John Cage (b.1912) is often credited with having been the first composer to promote seriously the use of chance operations during the act of composing and/or performing. Some of his compositions (*Music of Changes,* for example) are designed through a highly organized use of chance operations often based on the sixty-four hexagrams found in the *I Ching*—the Chinese book of Changes. Other compositions by Cage are almost entirely random; his *4' 33",* for example, stipulates only the duration of the piece.

There are essentially only two categories of indeterminacy: *Composer Indeterminacy* and *Performer Indeterminacy.* Some compositions fall into both categories.

COMPOSER INDETERMINACY

When the composer makes random decisions during the compositional process the technique is known as COMPOSER INDETERMINACY. The score can be either traditionally notated with no options for the performer (who may be unaware that the work is indeterminate) or notated in such a way that the performer is also involved in the random process.

PERFORMER INDETERMINACY

There are several ways in which the composer may involve the performer in chance operations during the performance; three of the most important are *Indeterminate Notation, Mobile Structures,* and *Frame Notation.*

Indeterminate Notation

In their own way, indeterminately notated scores have become a type of *Augenmusik*—music for the eyes. The composer provides the performer with a graphic score and with a set of instructions concerning the general framework of the composition. In many cases, the performer is free to make decisions about the interpretation of the symbols; in other works, the composer's directions are more specific. Three different indeterminate scores are shown in Examples 15–3, 15–4, and 15–5. While the Ligeti and Feldman scores have relatively specific instructions, the Berberian is open to a much freer interpretation; the graphics' location on the page gives only a general notion of range.

[2]Hayes' book, titled *The Art of Composing Music by a Method Entirely New, Suited to the Meanest Capacity,* was published in 1751.

EXAMPLE 15-3

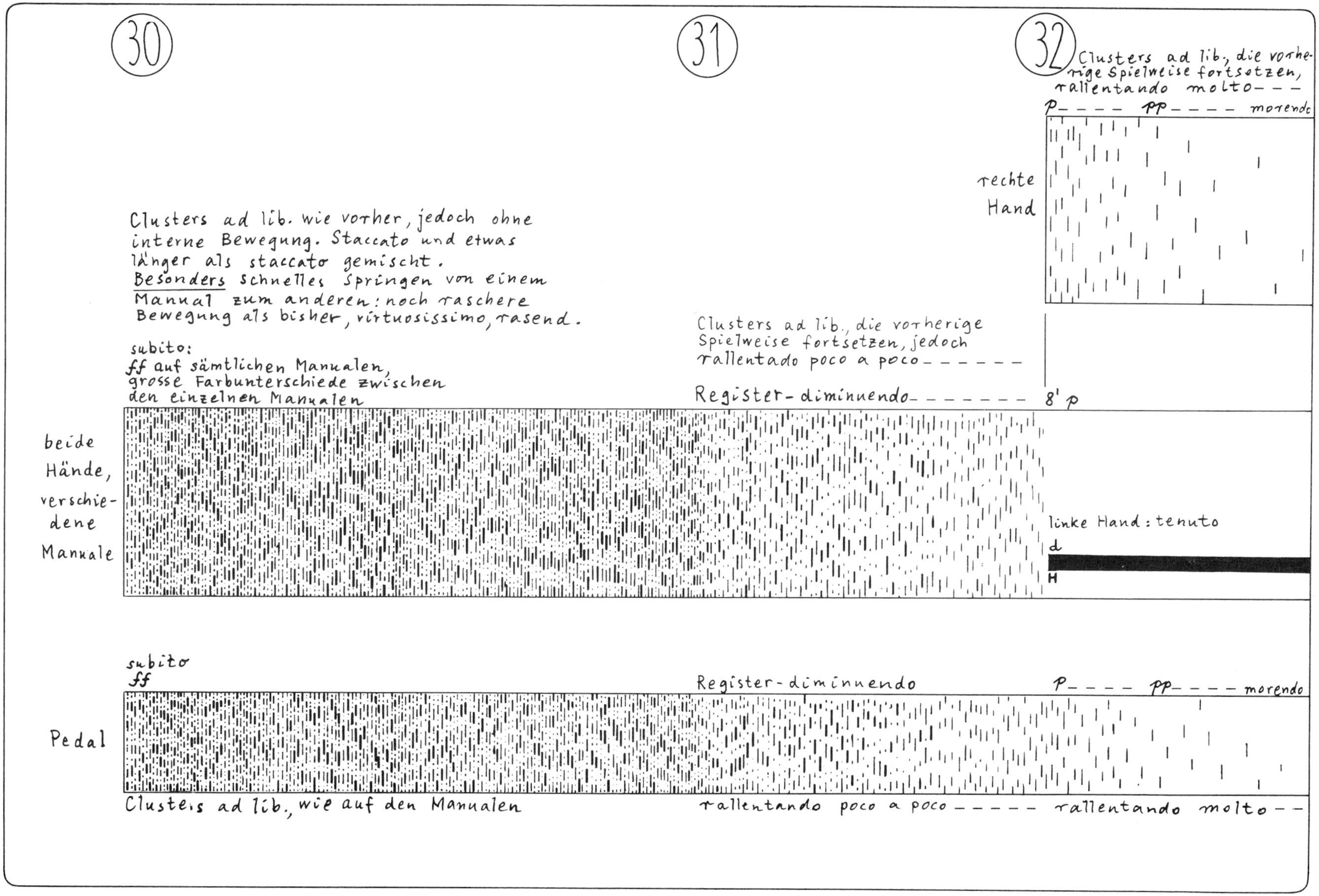

③⓪

③①

③②

Clusters ad lib. wie vorher, jedoch ohne
interne Bewegung. Staccato und etwas
länger als staccato gemischt.
Besonders schnelles Springen von einem
Manual zum anderen: noch raschere
Bewegung als bisher, virtuosissimo, rasend.

subito:
ff auf sämtlichen Manualen,
grosse Farbunterschiede zwischen
den einzelnen Manualen

beide
Hände,
verschie-
dene
Manuale

Clusters ad lib., die vorherige
Spielweise fortsetzen, jedoch
rallentando poco a poco – – – – –

Register–diminuendo – – – – – – –

8' p

linke Hand: tenuto

d

H

Clusters ad lib., die vorherige Spielweise fortsetzen,
rallentando molto – – –

p – – – pp – – – morendo

rechte
Hand

subito
ff

Register–diminuendo – – – –

p – – – pp – – – morendo

Clusters ad lib., wie auf den Manualen

rallentando poco a poco – – – – – rallentando molto – –

Pedal

EXAMPLE 15–4

Cathy Berberian, *Stripsody*

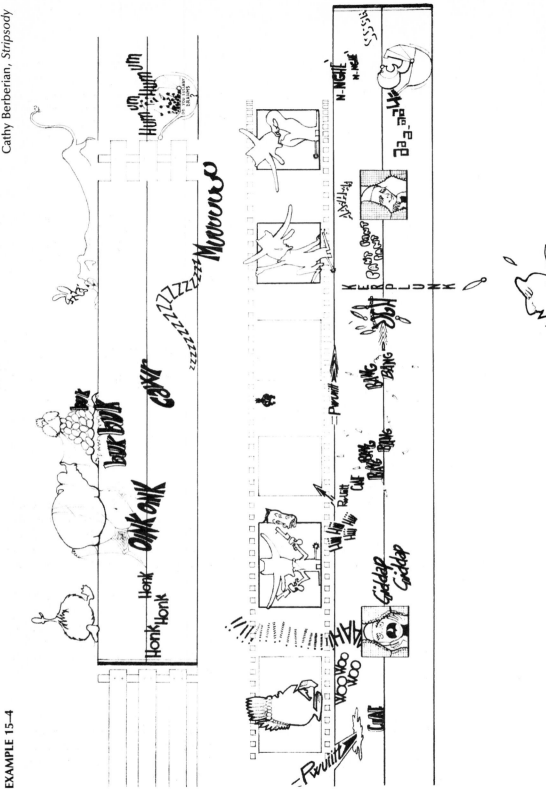

EXAMPLE 15–5   Morton Feldman, *King of Denmark*

THE KING OF DENMARK

MORTON FELDMAN

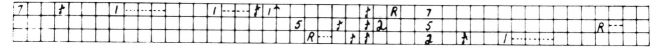

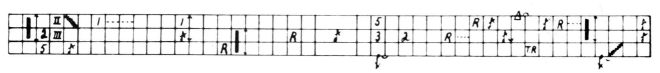

Mobile Structures

MOBILE STRUCTURES represent a type of indeterminacy in which the composer provides the performer with a number of determined events and the performer must decide on the arrangement of those events. A given work will always be unified by the design of the events; the various possibilities for their arrangement, however, usually assure that no two performances will be exactly alike.

The entire score of *Interplay* by Robert Chamberlin is shown in Example 15–6. The musical events are arranged within two basic shapes: interlocking circles and a more angular movement around the perimeter of the page (dotted lines). The performer is free to move around the circles or follow the dotted lines in any direction, making connections between both whenever possible. The duration of the composition is indeterminate.

Frame Notation

FRAME NOTATION refers to scores that include either circles or rectangles (frames) containing pitches or rhythms in a random order. The performer is instructed to *improvise* around the pitches and/or rhythms shown in the frame. Frame notation is shown in Example 15–7.

EXAMPLE 15–6

Robert Chamberlin, *Interplay* (for solo cello)

EXAMPLE 15–7

Luciano Berio, *Circles*

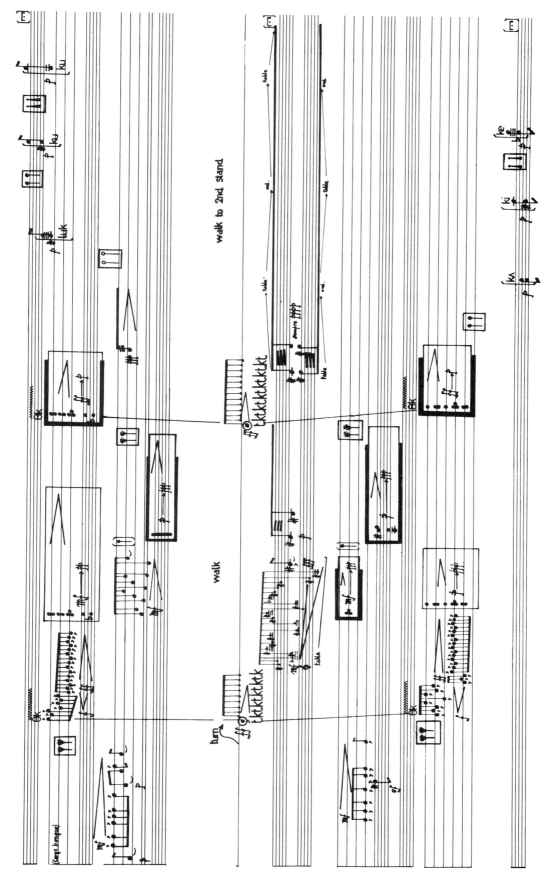

The Analysis of Indeterminate Music

Indeterminate music presents some interesting analytical problems. If scores are traditionally notated (the Chamberlin and Berio examples, for instance), the music can be analyzed as one might study any score. When performer indeterminacy is involved, however, analysis is not so simple. As with electronic music, indeterminate compositions are best analyzed by *listening*. Naturally, scores can be analyzed according to the degree of randomness, but the particular decisions made by different performers (or the same performer in different performances) constitute perhaps the most important consideration.

Because the scores of indeterminate works are often large, involve the use of overlays, color charts, or other complexities, none is included in this chapter for student analysis. The following works, however, represent a wide range of chance procedures; several of them should be available in most college libraries.

Earle Brown, *Available Forms*
Karlheinz Stockhausen, *Klavierstück XI*
John Cage, *4' 33"*
Tom Johnson, *Septapede*
Jan Pfischer MacNeil, *Aureate Earth*

EXTENDED SERIALIZATION

When Schoenberg introduced the concept of serialism, he offered a method of composition which provided systematic control over the parameter of pitch. Almost immediately, other composers experimented with extending this type of control to other parameters as well. One of the most notable early attempts is Webern's *Symphony,* Op. 21 (see pages 383–391). In this work, Webern applied a kind of row structure to both rhythm and timbre. Following Webern's lead were composers like Olivier Messiaen and Milton Babbitt who serialized dynamics and articulations as well as pitch and rhythm.

EXTENDED SERIALISM refers to a systematic method of controlling two or more parameters of a given composition. This term is preferable to "Total Serialization" because in fact, the serialization is not always "total." Composers *extend* the process of serialization to include whichever parameters they choose.

The Serialization of Rhythm

Pitch serialization is based on four row forms: original, retrograde, inversion, and retrograde inversion. These same forms are applicable to the serialization of other parameters as well. For a given set of rhythmic values (the original), the retrograde is simply a statement of them in reverse order.

Inversion.   The inversion of a rhythmic row is a bit more complex than pitch row inversion. Pitch inversion is based on interval size and direction; rhythm has only one parameter: duration. Composers use a number of techniques to arrive at rhythmic inversion. One approach is to assign a duration to each pitch of the pitch row; inversion of the pitch row produces rhythmic "inversion" as well.

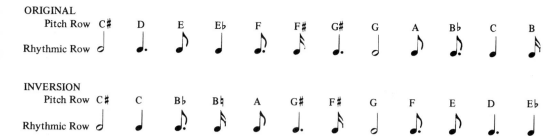

ORIGINAL
Pitch Row C♯   D   E   E♭   F   F♯   G♯   G   A   B♭   C   B

Rhythmic Row

INVERSION
Pitch Row C♯   C   B♭   B♮   A   G♯   F♯   G   F   E   D   E♭

Rhythmic Row

Another system of rhythmic inversion (or the inversion of any other parameter) involves the mathematical manipulation of either individual durations or rhythmic patterns. In the first of his *Three Compositions for Piano* (1947), Milton Babbitt uses a rhythmic row based on sixteenth notes containing the numbers 5, 1, 4, and 2 respectively.

Original   (5)   (1)   (4)   (2)

Babbitt inverts the row by subtracting each number from 6; the inverted row is represented by the numbers 1, 5, 2, 4.

Inversion   (1)   (5)   (2)   (4)

A third approach to "inversion" involves breaking a rhythmic row into segments; the segments are then interwoven so that a new row emerges:[3]

Original   ⌞——1——⌟ ⌞——2——⌟ ⌞——3——⌟ ⌞——4——⌟

"Inversion"   ⌞——2——⌟ ⌞——1——⌟ ⌞——4——⌟ ⌞——3——⌟

Obviously, rhythmic rows cannot be transposed as pitch rows can, but with the retrograde inversion (the reverse statement of the inverted row), there are four forms of any given row. The inversion in the example below was obtained through interweaving segments.

Original

Retrograde

Inversion

Retrograde
Inversion

---

[3]The concept of segmentation presented here is taken from *New Music Composition* by David Cope (New York: Schirmer Books, 1977). This valuable book includes a discussion of most major twentieth-century trends.

The Serialization of Other Parameters

Dynamics, timbres, tempos, and articulations can be serialized in a similar manner. Inverted forms are determined by any one of the methods used for rhythm. Examine the following dynamic and articulation rows (that contain fewer than twelve elements). Inversions were determined through segmentation.

DYNAMIC ROW

Original	*mf*	*f*	*ff*	*mp*	*p*	*pp*
Retrograde	*pp*	*p*	*mp*	*ff*	*f*	*mf*
Inversion	*mp*	*p*	*pp*	*mf*	*f*	*ff*
Retrograde Inversion	*ff*	*f*	*mf*	*pp*	*p*	*mp*

ARTICULATION ROW

Original	–	•	>	±	ʌ	ʌ
Retrograde	ʌ	ʌ	±	>	•	–
Inversion	±	ʌ	ʌ	–	•	>
Retrograde Inversion	>	•	–	ʌ	ʌ	±

Timbres can be serialized either according to terms that indicate a certain "color" or by the arrangement of instrumental groupings. Two possibilities are shown below. The transformations of timbre rows are determined by the same process used for rhythmic, dynamic, and articulation rows.

TIMBRE ROW

Based on Terms	*brilliant*	*dark*	*lightly*	*harsh*	*somber*	*crispy*
Based on Instrument Groupings	*clarinet*	*trumpet*	*piano*	*oboe*	*violin*	*flute*

SUMMARY

Electronic, Indeterminate, and Extended Serial music are major trends, but not the *only* trends in the second half of this century. Microtonal music, for example, although limited largely to voice, strings, and specially designed electronic instruments, has interested a number of reputable composers. In the 1960s and 1970s, a host of obscure individual and regional movements appeared. *Anti-Music,* for example, usually involves "destruction" or music impossible to perform. *Minimalism,* represented by composers such as Steve Reich and Terry Riley, has attracted some recent attention. Some composers, like Harry Partch, have turned to non-Western sources of sound and philosophy. Nor can we ignore the very great influence of jazz and commercial music; a number of composers have adopted styles midway between the "classical" and the "popular." In short, the only "common" element of music after 1945 has been diversity and originality.

SUGGESTED PROJECTS

Electronic Music

1. Choose one or more of the following electronic works and provide an appropriate analysis.

Ilhan Mimaroglu, *Bowery Bum*
Toru Takemitsu, *Vocalism Ai*
Andre Boucourechliev, *Texte I*
Walter Carlos, *Geodesic Dance*
Dean Walraff, *Dance*

2. As an individual or class project, record a variety of acoustic sounds and splice the tape to rearrange and/or alter them. Make a tape loop of the result and discuss the formal structure of the composition. If possible, experiment with placing the speakers in different parts of the room and study the effect of various spacial arrangements.

3. Compose a brief serial work for a solo instrument. Record the composition and make a tape loop of the reverse playback at an altered speed. Perform the original composition with the recorded tape loop as a background ostinato. (Rember, reverse playback is not possible with quarter-track recorders).

4. Record a single sound (a note from a clarinet or violin, for example) and use a variety of techniques to create an electronic composition of at least thirty seconds in length. Vary pitch by changing the speed of the recorder. Use overdubbing, reverse playback, etc. to vary texture and timbre.

Indeterminacy

1. Compose a chance work based on mobile structures. If you wish, use the Chamberlin work as a guide. Engage two different performers to give consecutive performances (preferably without hearing one another).

2. On a number of index cards (twelve or more) like the ones shown below, compose musical fragments using conventional notation, but in any style or combination of styles you choose. Shuffle the cards and perform the composition by playing each card as it appears in the "deck." Reshuffle the cards and study the effect of a new order. To vary the approach, add one or more blank cards to the deck. The blank cards might represent silence, improvisation, or whatever you designate.

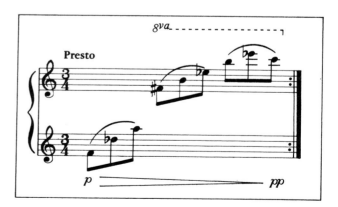

Extended Serialism

1. The following composition is based on the rhythmic, articulation, and dynamic rows given on pages 403–404. The pitches are organized through the following series:

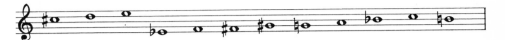

Locate and label each statement of the serialized rows (it may be necessary to make a matrix of the pitch row). Note: the articulation row is incomplete.

After analyzing the various row forms, look for aspects in the work which provide unity and contrast. Notice, for example, that the rhythmic statements of measures 1 and 2 are repeated in different hands in measures 5 and 6.

2. Complete the composition above in a similar style. Supply at least eight more measures and end with a strong cadential effect. (Remember that the articulation row is unfinished).

SUGGESTED LISTENING

Pierre Boulez, *Structures* (1952)

John Cage, *Imaginary Landscape #4* (1951)

Morton Feldman, *Vertical Thought* (1963)

Krzysztof Penderecki, *Threnody for the Victims of Hiroshima* (1961)

Karlheinz Stockhausen, *Electronic Studies* (1953)
        Zeitmasse (1956)

Morton Subotnik, *Silver Apples of the Moon* (1967)

Postlude:
The Future

In attacking Machaut and other innovative composers of the *Ars Nova*, Jacob of Liège proclaimed the "old art" more perfect, rational, and simple than the new. "Music was originally discreet," he wrote in *Speculum musicae*, "have not the moderns rendered it lascivious beyond measure?"[1]

For Jacob, the work of composers like Leonin and Perotin was *music;* the striking new ideas of younger composers were apparently impossible for him to accept. Yet with or without his approval, music changed. In later centuries, the concept of meter (to which Jacob objected) was an essential element of the art.

Familiar as we are today with the elegance of a Mozart sonata or the lush sonorities of a Brahms symphony, it is easy to forget that at the beginning of the Common Practice Period, the composers who conceived of the "new music" were attacked just as bitterly as were Machaut and his contemporaries three hundred years earlier. In his treatise *Delle imperfezioni della moderna musica* (1600), Giovanni Artusi complains about the new concepts of dissonance fostered by Monteverdi and others:

> . . . tell me first why you wish to employ these dissonances as they employ them . . . why you do not use them in the ordinary way, conformable to reason, in accordance with what . . . Palestrina . . . and so many, many others in this Academy have written? . . . even if you wish dissonance to become consonant, it remains necessary that it be contrary to consonance; by nature it is always dissonant and can hence become consonant only when consonance becomes dissonant; this brings us to impossibilities. . . .[2]

History repeats itself. From the chaos of the fourteenth century emerged the High Renaissance style of Palestrina—a style which at the time was illustrative of *music* in its highest order. From the chromatic experimentation and contrapuntal complexities of the late sixteenth century came eventually the concept of tonality underlying the works of Haydn and Schumann—the very models of what was *music* in the eighteenth and nineteenth centuries respectively.

[1]Oliver Strunk, *Source Readings in Music History* (New York: W.W. Norton and Company, 1950), p. 189.

[2]Strunk, p. 400.

Today, what Artusi considered "impossible" (dissonance as a form of consonance) is a regular feature of music. Listening to a work by Morton Subotnik or Karlheinz Stockhausen, one can speak of density, of tension and release, but not really of "consonance" or "dissonance." Can we even imagine how Artusi would have reacted to a composition in which a performer sits in silence at the keyboard for four and a half minutes? Surely this cannot be *music*!

Those of us who practice the art of music are fortunate indeed to live and work at a time when music is changing. Despite what we might think personally about one or another style or particular composition, we have the opportunity and the *responsibility* to create a climate of openness and reflection so that those with new ideas can be heard. From the bold experiments of this century may come a new common practice. What our descendants in the year 2300 will call *music* we cannot know, but it is just possible that the first work in yet another *new music* has already been written.

APPENDIX A
The Materials of Jazz

The distinctively American musical art form known as JAZZ is based on a system of harmonic usage quite different from that of the Common Practice Period. This appendix will survey that system as used by jazz musicians.

JAZZ CHORDS

Jazz musicians base much of their playing on the interpretation of chord symbols. The musician sees the symbol and relates it to a scale or another melodic pattern. While an exhaustive study of chord symbols is outside the scope of this appendix, an examination of the three basic chord families and their corresponding symbols will serve as an introduction. Jazz chords generally fall into three groups: *Major, Minor,* or *Dominant.*

Major Chords

The family of MAJOR CHORDS is based on a major triad with one or more added elements. Upper case letters designate the root of the major triad; the added elements are indicated by numerals, accidentals, and other symbols. The major chord group and their symbols are shown in Example A–1.

EXAMPLE A–1   Major Chords and Symbols

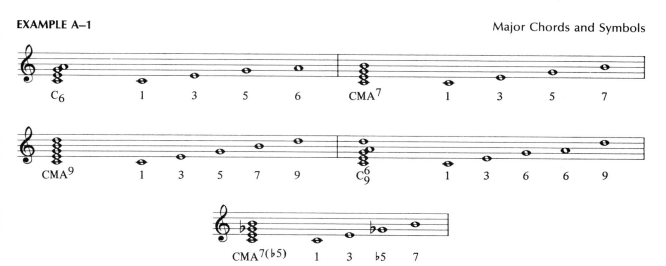

Major chords in jazz tend to take on stable, tonic-oriented functions just as they do in common practice music. When improvising on these chords, a jazz musician would use either the major scale or the Lydian mode. With its raised fourth (lowered fifth) degree, the Lydian mode is particularly suited to use with the major seven flat five chord.

Minor Chords

The family of MINOR CHORDS is based on a minor triad with additions or alterations similar to those found with major chords. In Example A–2 below, the first five chords are all stable and therefore assume tonic functions. The minor seven flat five chord is less stable and is usually heard in a subdominant role, especially at a cadence.

EXAMPLE A–2   Minor Chords and Chord Symbols

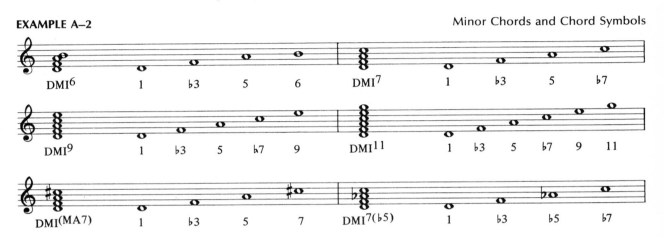

For melodic improvisation, the minor six chord with its major sixth above the bass calls for the Dorian mode. The minor seven, minor nine, and minor eleven chords could use either the natural minor or the Dorian mode. The minor chord with major seven requires the harmonic or melodic minor; the minor seven flat five chord coincides with the Locrian mode which features both the lowered fifth and lowered seventh.

Dominant Chords

The consistent element in the family of DOMINANT CHORDS is a dominant seventh chord; other pitches are added or altered. In jazz, a dominant chord can function both as an unstable, active chord, or one of tonic function. Many jazz tunes end on a highly altered dominant seventh chord. Notice the variety of dominant chords shown in Example A–3.

EXAMPLE A–3   Dominant Chords and Chord Symbols

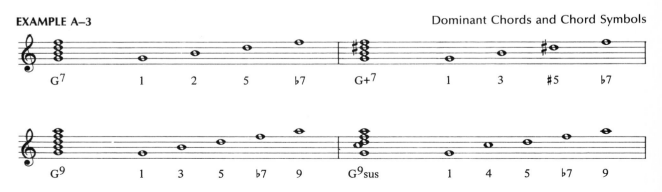

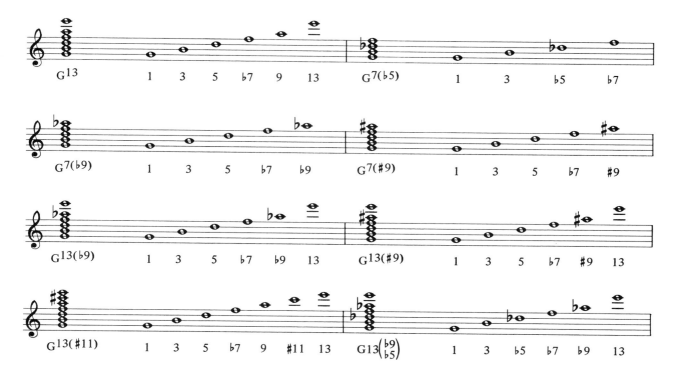

Improvisation based on the unaltered dominant chords (seven, nine, nine suspended, and thirteen) involves the pitches of the Mixolydian mode (which jazz musicians call the *Dominant Seventh Scale*). The augmented seventh chord uses the whole tone scale which includes both the raised fifth and lowered seventh. Dominant chords containing any combination of ♭9, ♯9, ♯11, and 13 require the *Half-Whole Scale* shown below.

G Half-Whole Scale

Chords containing a combination of altered fifths and ninths utilize the *Super Locrian Scale*.

G Super Locrian Scale

JAZZ CHORD PROGRESSIONS

As it is in "classical" music, the single most important chord progression in jazz is ii–V–I—chords of subdominant, dominant, and tonic function respectively.

Many jazz standards, in fact, are comprised almost entirely of ii–V–I progressions and their variants. (*Satin Doll* by Duke Ellington is one well known example). Several possible progressions in the key of C major are shown in Example A–4.

EXAMPLE A–4 Jazz Chord Progressions

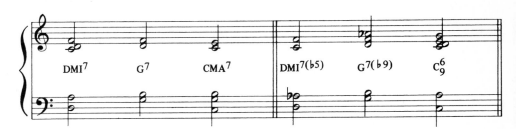

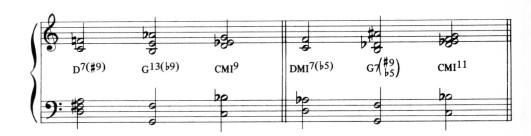

The Twelve Bar Blues

One of the oldest and most widely used song forms in jazz is the TWELVE BAR BLUES—a repeated pattern of chord progressions which is twelve measures in length. Harmonically, the Twelve Bar Blues is structured as follows:

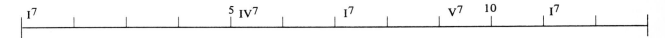

In the key of B♭, for example, the harmonic structure of a Twelve Bar Blues would look quite familiar to any trained musician:

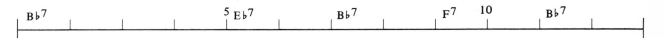

In actual practice, however, jazz musicians usually play a highly complex version of the basic progression; the use of altered chords and harmonic substitutions impart a unique flavor to each twelve measure pattern. One possible harmonization of "B♭ Blues" is shown in Example A–5.

EXAMPLE A–5 B♭ Blues

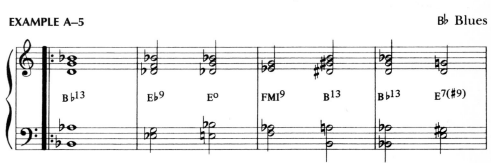

IMPROVISATION

One of the most important elements of Jazz is IMPROVISATION—the creation of new melodies based on a given harmonic formula. Jazz musicians must develop the ability to choose notes from scales that coincide with each chord in the progression.

Jazz musicians often play in a rhythmic style called "swing" in which written eighth notes are played with unequal emphasis. Simple eighth notes ♫ ♫ are performed as triplet figures ♩ ♪ ♩ ♪.[1]

Example A–6 shows a written "improvisation" based on the complex Twelve Bar Blues discussed earlier. Notice the rhythmic variety including the frequent use of syncopation. Remember that in performance, the eighth notes would be played unequally.

EXAMPLE A–6

"Improvisation" on Twelve Bar Blues

[1]The idea of playing equally written notes unequally is not unique to jazz. A similar practice, known as *Inégales*, emerged in seventeenth-century France and was popular for over a hundred years.

The Materials of Jazz **413**

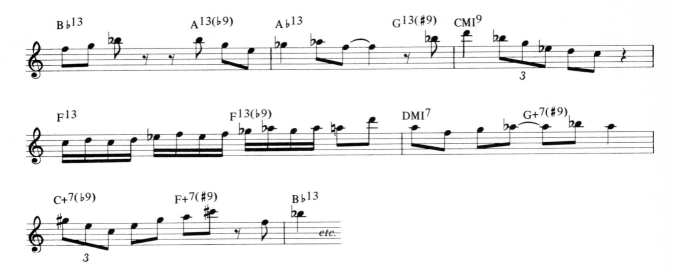

SUGGESTED LISTENING

Armstrong, Louis. *The Louis Armstrong Story,* Vol. 1, 2, and 3. Columbia CL 851–53.

Bechet, Sidney. *Master Musician,* RCA Bluebird AXM2-5516.

Blakey, Art. *Buhaina,* Prestige 10067.

Bley, Carla. *Dinner Music,* Watt 6.

Braxton, Anthony. *Five Pieces,* Artista AL 4064.

Brown, Clifford. *Clifford Brown Memorial Album,* Bluenote BST 81526.

Burton, Gary. *Times Square,* ECM 1-1111.

Christian, Charlie. *Solo Flight,* Columbia CG 30779.

Coltrane, John. *A Love Supreme,* Impulse S-77.

Davis, Miles. *Kind of Blue,* Columbia PC 8163.

_____ . *Bitches Brew,* Columbia PG-26.

Dolphy, Eric. *Out to Lunch,* Bluenote 84163.

Ellington, Duke. *The Ellington Era,* Vol. 1, 2, and 3, Columbia C3L-27 and C3L-39.

Evans, Bill. *The Tokyo Concert,* Fantasy F-9457.

Getz, Stan. *Stan Getz Gold,* Inner City 1040.

Hancock, Herbie. *Speak Like a Child,* Bluenote 84279.

Hines, Earl. *Quintessential Recording Session,* Chiaroscuro 101.

Jarrett, Keith. *The Koln Concert,* ECM 1064/1065.

McLaughlin, John. *Birds of Fire,* Columbia KC 31996.

Mingus, Charles. *Changes 1 and 2,* Atlantic 1667–78.

Monk, Thelonious. *At the Fivespot,* Milestone 47043.

Parker, Charlie. *Bird/The Savoy Recordings* Savoy SJL 2201.

Powell, Bud. *The Genius of Bud Powell,* Verve VE-2-2506.

Rollins, Sonny. *The Bridge,* RCA AFL-1-0859.

Silver, Horace. *Blowin' the Blues Away,* Bluenote 84017.

Tatum, Art. *The Tatum Solo Masterpieces,* Pablo 2525693.

Weather Report. *Heavy Weather,* Columbia PC-34418.

The Smithsonian Collection of Classic Jazz, available from the Division of Performing Arts of the Smithsonian Institution, is recommended as the most comprehensive single purchase.

Index

Date Due

BJJH